A MOSQUE IN MUNICH

BOOKS BY IAN JOHNSON

*Wild Grass: Three Portraits of
Change in Modern China*

*A Mosque in Munich: Nazis, the CIA, and
the Muslim Brotherhood in the West*

A MOSQUE
///// IN /////
MUNICH

NAZIS, THE CIA, AND
THE MUSLIM BROTHERHOOD
IN THE WEST

IAN JOHNSON

HOUGHTON MIFFLIN HARCOURT
BOSTON NEW YORK
2010

For information about permission to reproduce selections from this book,
write to Permissions, Houghton Mifflin Harcourt Publishing Company,
215 Park Avenue South, New York, New York 10003.

www.hmhbooks.com

Library of Congress Cataloging-in-Publication Data
Johnson, Ian, date.
A mosque in Munich : Nazis, the CIA, and the Muslim
brotherhood in the West / Ian Johnson.
p. cm.
Includes bibliographical references and index.
ISBN 978-0-15-101418-7
1. Islam and politics — Germany — Munich — History — 20th century.
2. Mosques — Germany — Munich — History — 20th century. 3. Jam'iyat al-Ikhwan
al-Muslimin (Egypt) — History — 20th century. 4. Islamic fundamentalism —
Germany — Munich — History — 20th century. 5. World War, 1939–1945 —
Participation, Muslim. 6. Ex-Nazis — Germany — Munich — History — 20th century. 7. Mende, Gerhard von, 1904- 8. Cold War. 9. United States. Central
Intelligence Agency — History — 20th century. 10. Anti-communist movements — Germany — Munich — History — 20th century. I. Title.
BP65.G3J64 2010
297.30943'36409045 — dc22   2009035285

Book design by Brian Moore

Printed in the United States of America

DOC 10 9 8 7 6 5 4 3 2 1

"Ginkgo Biloba" from *West-Eastern Divan* by Johann Wolfgang von Goethe.
Translated by Jacques-E. Fortin in "The Armored Key" by Monique Gaudry
and published online at http://archange.tripod.com/thearmoredkey123.html.
Used by permission from Pierre Fortin.

And there are those who built a mosque from mischievous motives, to spread unbelief and disunite the faithful.

— Koran 9:107

N 1947, MARGARET DOLLINGER went for a swim in the Isar, the Alps-fed river that runs through Munich. There she saw a bronzed, vaguely Asian-looking man. He was Hassan Kassajep, a thirty-year-old Soviet refugee hoping to start a new life. The two looked at each other shyly. "I knew he was the man," she said. They parted only at his death, one year shy of their golden wedding anniversary.

This book is dedicated to the Kassajeps and other Muslim émigrés who fought this obscure war. Many of them faced impossible moral choices and ended up thousands of miles away from home, living in countries they didn't really understand, hoping that their work would change history. It did, but in ways that they couldn't have expected.

This is a common refrain in history—the story of unintended consequences. But in this case I felt a special poignancy. I came to know these people intimately through their letters, photos, and, in some lucky cases, through meeting people like Margaret Kassajep in person—aged survivors of another era. I was also struck by the sadness of a life lived in secret. These people could rarely talk openly about what they had done. Sometimes it was because they were embarrassed by their actions—collaborating with an odious regime, for example, or betraying friends. At other times they felt bound by a code of silence, either directly imposed or implicitly understood in covert operations. Most had constructed an alternate reality: that of the scholar or the freedom fighter, the religious activist or the businessman. I wondered what remains of a life when it is stripped of a public identity.

In the case of the people in this book, the answer is, a lot. Though most of them are dead and their life stories obscure until now, their actions reverberate today as we confront similar issues. Like light refracted from a distant planet, they illuminate our own lives.

Berlin
April 2009

CONTENTS

MODERN WARS

CAST OF CHARACTERS

The Main Actors

ROBERT H. DREHER: CIA agent working in Munich for a front organization, the American Committee for Liberation (Amcomlib). Backed the Muslim Brotherhood.

GERHARD VON MENDE: Turkic studies expert who pioneered the use of Muslims against the Soviets in the Nazi era; ran a similar intelligence bureau after the war in West Germany.

SAID RAMADAN: Exiled senior leader of the Muslim Brotherhood, with close ties to Western intelligence. Led Islamists in the battle to seize control of the Munich mosque project.

Other major players, grouped by their primary allegiance:

The Americans

IBRAHIM GACAOGLU: Feisty Muslim leader; served the Germans during World War II but later accepted U.S. aid.

AHMAD KAMAL: California author and Muslim activist who cooperated with U.S. intelligence but ran a rogue operation in Munich.

ROBERT F. KELLEY: Head of Amcomlib's Munich operations.

B. ERIC KUNIHOLM: Amcomlib's political director in New York headquarters; strong backer of using Muslims against the Soviet Union.

RUSI NASAR: Uzbek activist supported by Amcomlib and other agencies in anti-Soviet activities.

SAID SHAMIL: North Caucasian leader close to U.S. intelligence; worked closely with Dreher.

GARIP SULTAN: Worked for von Mende during World War II and immediately afterward; later worked for Amcomlib.

The Germans

BAYMIRZA HAYIT: Uzbek historian and von Mende's right-hand man.

ALI KANTEMIR: Dagestani leader, loyal to von Mende.

HASSAN KASSAJEP: Secretary of Mosque Construction Commission; tried to mediate between ex-soldiers and students.

VELI KAYUM: Self-styled "Khan" of the Uzbeks; mercurial and unreliable.

NURREDIN NAMANGANI: Uzbek imam of an SS division; later employed by von Mende to take control of Munich's Muslims.

The Muslim Brotherhood*

MAHDI AKEF: Current "supreme guide" of the Muslim Brotherhood; headed the Munich mosque for three years.

GHALEB HIMMAT: Syrian businessman and head of the Munich mosque for thirty years; lives near Nada in the Italian Alps.

HAJ AMIN AL-HUSSAINI: Former Grand Mufti of Jerusalem; worked with von Mende and the Nazis during the war and with Ramadan afterward.

YOUSSEF NADA: Egyptian businessman who helped arrange financing for the Munich mosque; helped set up the Brotherhood in the United States.

YOUSSEF QARADAWI: One of the most influential spiritual figures in the Muslim Brotherhood today; helped rebuild the Brotherhood in the 1970s by focusing on the West.

IBRAHIM EL-ZAYAT: Took control of the Munich mosque association from Himmat after the 9/11 attacks.

---

*People considered close to the group or its ideology; not necessarily formal members of the Egyptian political party.

PROLOGUE
On the Edge of Town

IN THE WINTER OF 2003, I was browsing in a London bookstore that sold radical Islamic literature. It was the sort of store that had earned London the nickname "Londonistan": stacked with screeds calling for the downfall of free societies, it tested the limits of free speech — and unwittingly catalogued the troubles plaguing Europe's Muslim communities. I was a regular customer.

Wandering the aisles, I noticed a peculiar map of the world. Countries were color-coded according to percentage of Muslim population. Dark green countries had a Muslim majority; light green, yellow, and beige represented decreasing proportions of Muslims — a typical example of political Islam, which divides the world into *us* and *them,* the only criterion being religion. Famous mosques decorated the edge of the map—the Grand Mosque in Mecca (the yearly destination of millions of pilgrims), the Dome of the Rock in Jerusalem (where Muhammad ascended to heaven), the wondrous Blue Mosque of Istanbul — and the Islamic Center of Munich.

The Islamic Center of Munich? That seemed odd. I had been writing on religion in Europe and other parts of the world for half a dozen years, and had lived in Germany even longer. I had heard of the mosque as the headquarters of one of Germany's smaller Islamic organizations. But the mosque hardly belonged in such august company. Munich was no center of Islam, and the mosque wasn't the biggest in Germany, let alone Europe. Still, it was immortalized in someone's pantheon. I was planning a visit to Munich and decided to find out why.

A few weeks later, I drove along the old main road north from downtown Munich, at first paralleling the sleek autobahn that led to the new airport and the city's futuristic sports stadium. Skirting these exemplars of Germany's vaunted infrastructure, I wove through neglected neighborhoods of the Bavarian capital. The city gave way to suburbs, then to patches of countryside. Finally, the mosque appeared, first just a slender minaret jutting above the pines, a finger pointing toward heaven. Then the rest came into view. It was an egg-shaped house, like a weather balloon held down by a tarp — an ebullient, futuristic design straight out of the 1950s.

I spied a janitor, thin and short, a man of about sixty in a traditional white gown and sandals. I asked why the mosque was so famous. He shrugged without a glimmer of curiosity and said it surely wasn't. I asked when it had been built. He said he didn't know. I asked who had founded it, but he could only apologize.

His answers surprised me. I had visited dozens of mosques around Europe. At each, proud worshipers had regaled me with the story of its founding, often by immigrants who had scraped together construction money. But this ignorance — or was it amnesia? — was odd.

I looked more closely, and the mosque seemed to age. Built of concrete and tile, it had faded and cracked. The trees seemed to swallow the buildings. One of the world's great mosques? I wondered what had happened here.

That question launched a research project that has taken me to unexpected places and consumed a great deal more time than I ever imagined it would. I had supposed I would find the answer quickly by talking to a few members of Germany's Muslim community who had immigrated to Europe in the 1960s, part of a great population shift that has altered Europe's demographics. I guessed that the Islamic Center of Munich had emerged during this era.

Instead, I found the answer much further back in time — the 1930s. I did interview many German Muslims but spent most of my time in U.S. and European archives. There, among boxes of long-neglected and newly declassified documents, I pieced together the stories of the remarkable people who laid the ideological foundations for the mosque and then battled for control of the building itself.

Contrary to expectations, these founders had little to do with the wider population of immigrants. Instead, I found that three groups supported the mosque in order to attain certain goals. Some were Nazi thinkers who planned to use Islam as a political weapon during World War II and then extended this strategy into the Cold War. Others, primarily members of the Central Intelligence Agency, built on the Nazis' work, hoping to use Islam to fight communism. A third group was made up of radical Muslims — Islamists — who saw the mosque as a toehold in the West. All had one thing in common: their goal was to create not a place of worship but rather a center for political — and even violent — activity.

At first, the story had a familiar ring. The United States had tried to enlist Muslims to counter the Soviets in Afghanistan in the 1970s and '80s, famously contributing to the birth of Al Qaeda. But the Munich mosque was built thirty years earlier, during the opening phases of the Cold War, not near its conclusion, and the goals that informed its foundation were also different. In places like Afghanistan, Islam was mobilized to fight a war with guns and soldiers. But here in Germany Muslims were drawn into a psychological war — a battle of ideas. I began to realize that the events in Munich were a precursor to developments, both ideological and military, ranging from Afghanistan to Iraq.

Then, as now, such tactics backfired. The battle for Munich's Muslims helped introduce a virulent ideology to the West: Islam-ism — not the ancient religion of Islam but a highly politicized and violent system of ideas that creates the milieu for terrorism. In the attacks on New York and Washington in 2001 the West experienced this violence firsthand, but it has a long history, having plagued countries around the world for decades. Islamism's most prominent group is the Muslim Brotherhood, and it was the Brotherhood that turned the mosque into a political cell for its partisan goals. Almost all the Brotherhood's activities in the West originated among the small group of people who ran the mosque. Munich was the beachhead from which the Brotherhood spread into Western society.

The parallels between the 1950s and today are striking. While our societies remain consumed with on-the-ground events on battlefields like Iraq, it is the ideological war that will determine success or failure. Now, like half a century ago in Munich, Western societies are seeking Muslim allies, hoping to find people who share our values in the struggle against a persistent enemy. Munich shows the danger of doing so without careful reflection and scrutiny.

Western governments have made this scrutiny a difficult task. By and large, intelligence agencies' files on Islam are still closed; it was only through some extraordinary luck that I was able to obtain the documents describing this story. In the United States, it took an act of Congress to pry open the CIA's files on Nazis who survived the war or were suspected of war crimes; perhaps it will take a similar law to get a complete view of U.S. dealings with Islamist groups.

In the meantime, this book fills some of the gaps. One reason for writing it now is that eyewitnesses from this era are passing away. Many collected remarkable personal archives, which are becoming scattered. As it is, most of the people I talked to were in their eighties and nineties. Several have died since. To wait another few years would have meant forfeiting their insight and advice.

These people and the archives tell a story that takes us from Hollywood to Jakarta, Washington to Mecca. But as so often seems to be the case in Germany, the story begins on a World War II battlefield.

HOT WARS

——

This leaf from an Oriental tree,

Transplanted to my garden's soil,

The secret sense does decree,

For the knowing man to uncoil.

—from "Gingko Biloba,"
GOETHE

THE EASTERN FRONT

ARIP SULTAN LAY FLAT in a machine-gun nest, his stomach pressed to the ground. He craned his neck forward, looking out into the grasslands for the enemy. His superiors had ordered him to hold one of the Red Army's forward positions outside the Ukrainian city of Kharkov. It was May 1942, and the Germans were launching a giant counteroffensive. All around him he heard shells roar and panzers rumble. The nineteen-year-old swept his binoculars left and right across the Ukrainian steppes but saw nothing. He felt doomed.*

He thought back unhappily to how he had ended up here. Sultan was a minority in Stalin's Soviet Union, a Tatar from the district of Bashkir. Turkic peoples had settled this region when the last great wave of nomadic invaders swept out of Central Asia in the thirteenth century, under Genghis Khan. As Russia expanded, the Tatars had lost their independence, becoming one of the many non-Russian peoples who made up nearly half the vast country's population.

Under Soviet rule, oppression of these peoples had increased, especially for those like Sultan's parents who had run small busi-

---

* This book is a work of history, based on interviews and documents. Unless explicitly noted in the text, sources are listed in the notes at the back of the book.

nesses. Soviet cadres called them capitalists and took everything. They nationalized his father's transport business and confiscated the family home. Even their horse was taken. The family, once rich, was able to keep just two pieces of furniture bought during a trip to England: a mirror, now cracked, and a clock, now broken. Before Sultan's father died, he encouraged his son to join the Young Pioneers, then later the young people's organization Komsomol, and eventually the party. This was the only way to survive in Stalin's Soviet Union, the older man had said. Sultan followed his father's advice. He joined Komsomol, attended high school, and had planned to study metallurgy. He tried his best to become a new Soviet man.

Then came June 1941 and the German invasion. The Red Army wasn't yet the formidable fighting machine that would eventually destroy the bulk of Hitler's armies. In the first year of the war it suffered enormous casualties and surrendered huge territories. Every available man was called up and thrown straight into action. Sultan was conscripted and quickly assigned to a ragtag group of non-Russians like himself, miserably equipped and poorly led. They were set to disintegrate upon contact with the enemy.

As his unit took up position outside Kharkov, Sultan keenly felt his status as a minority. When the troops lined up for inspection, the commanding officer, a Russian, asked minorities to step forward. The officer gave four of them, including Sultan, the suicidal task of creeping across the no man's land between the two armies and throwing German-language propaganda toward the enemy lines. According to this quixotic plan, the German soldiers would read the pamphlets, revolt against their officers, and surrender. No one anticipated that the Germans had set up tripwires. Sultan's group was cut to pieces by the ensuing machine-gun fire; Sultan was the only survivor. He hid for two days in the high grasses of the steppe before creeping back to his lines. For his bravery, his commanding officer promised him a medal. But Sultan felt the honor was hollow. His loyalty to the Soviet system, which he had honestly tried to cultivate, was evaporating.

Then his unit was ordered to make ready for the German offensive. Again, Sultan observed the brutality of Stalin's regime. Soviet officers forced prisoners from the gulag labor camps to work in the open, digging anti-tank trenches while facing German fire. One old prisoner, also a Tatar, talked to Sultan during a break. Gaunt and weak, he told Sultan how he had fought in World War I and been captured by the Germans. Life in the German camps had been better than in the czar's army. The prisoners had even fought for the Germans against the Russians. Sultan listened carefully and went back to work. The officers finally selected soldiers to man various positions on the front. Sultan felt that the minorities were selected for the most hopeless placements, but he trudged to his post.

He was lying in a shallow foxhole with another minority soldier, who manned the machine gun. Sultan had nominal command — he had served in Komsomol. But he had no idea how to stop the tanks with machine guns or what the point was of holding one piece of land at all costs in a fluid, mobile front. Sultan put his binoculars down for a moment and listened carefully. He could hear gunfire getting closer but couldn't see any movement.

Suddenly, a squad of Germans burst through the grass from one side. The gunner swung partway around, but at the same time another group of Germans rushed from the opposite flank. The young Soviets had been surprised; if they fired at one group of Germans, they would be cut down immediately by the other. A hero's death: Sultan's officers expected soldiers to attain it. He had a split second to choose his fate.

"No, don't do it," the German squad leader yelled as his men flung themselves to the ground and took aim. "Don't fire. Surrender!" Sultan hesitated. In his mind flashed images of the gulag slaves and his own family forced from their home; this didn't feel like his war. He raised his hands and the gunner did too. They became prisoners.

"Shoot them," several of the Germans shouted. This often happened; the eastern front was brutal and both sides ignored international protocols for the conduct of war.

As the soldiers debated, an officer walked up, and Sultan sensed an opening. He could speak a bit of German — he'd learned it in high school — and decided to give it a try.

"Sir, you are an educated man," Sultan said, addressing the officer. "What did you study?"

Surprised that a Soviet soldier could speak German, the officer smiled and answered: "Law."

"Judges are supposed to show mercy," Sultan said. "Don't kill us."

The officer laughed. He was wearing the Nazi swastika, but he was old-school Prussian. The men were his prisoners, his responsibility. Duty bound, he sent them to the back lines to be processed.

Sultan's surrender formed a small part of the Red Army's colossal collapse. Already, a staggering three million Soviet troops had surrendered to the Germans. Demoralized by Stalin's reign of terror, Soviet soldiers were capitulating wholesale. Many supposed the Nazis couldn't be worse than the communists. Soviet minorities were especially unenthusiastic about the Russian cause. To them, the Soviet Union was nothing more than a more brutal version of the old Russian Empire. In the eighteenth and nineteenth centuries, Russia had expanded south and east. By the time the czar was deposed in 1917, almost half the country's population was made up of non-Russians.

The Soviet Union inherited from the czar two large regions where Russians were in the minority: Central Asia and the Caucasus. The former is made up of present-day Kazakhstan, Kyrgyzstan, Tajikistan, Turkmenistan, and Uzbekistan. Back then the region was simply known as Turkestan, a Muslim part of the world whose various peoples spoke Turkic dialects. It encompassed nomadic peoples and great cities like Samarkand and Tashkent. Located far from the fighting, the region held little appeal for the Nazis.

The Caucasus lay closer to Nazi interests. It was the mythic home of the Caucasian people, important in Nazi lore, and a region of impenetrable hills and mysterious legends. Noah, it was supposed, landed here after the Flood. The Greeks saw it as one of the pillars of the world, its mountains holding up the sky and marking the edge of civilization. In geographic terms, the Caucasus Mountains were traditionally seen as a dividing line between Europe and the Middle East.

It was also a region Moscow had never subjugated. The area was demographically complex. The southern Caucasus had three clearly defined sectors: Georgia and Armenia, both Christian, and Muslim Azerbaijan. The north was a different story. It was mostly Muslim and dotted with small but fiercely independent peoples, such as the Dagestanis, Kalmyks, Chechens, and Ossetians.

Nazi ambitions were simple. The cities of Baku, in Azerbaijan, and Grozny, in Chechnya, were then key centers of oil production. Germany had plans to take over the oil fields and use them to fuel the Reich. But unlike many parts of the Soviet Union, the Caucasus was not slated for German colonization. That let the Germans play the role of liberators — and many locals greeted them as such. Even if the people were skeptical about the intentions of the Nazis, they were glad to see someone stand up to their oppressors.

This local reaction provided a glimpse of the Soviet system's fragility — something that would become apparent several decades later as the Soviet Union collapsed. In the early 1990s, these largely Muslim regions would shatter into more than a dozen countries. During the war, a similar splintering happened among individuals who felt loyal to their homeland and religion rather than to the Soviet Empire. There were hundreds of thousands of men like Sultan: Tatars, Georgians, Chechens, Kazakhs, Uzbeks. Most of them were Muslims, and many were happy to fight against the Soviet Union.

In time, they would congregate in Munich, a group of bitter anticommunists who would prove valuable to the West. Trained and organized by the Nazis during the war, they would eventually be discovered after the war as potential ammunition in the fight against communism. Islamists too had designs on them: these co-religionists now located in Germany could provide a beachhead to the West. But at this moment, they were a group of men—boys, really—unformed and untrained. Sultan was sent to a prisoner-of-war camp designated for educated Soviet prisoners. The Germans were beginning to realize that they possessed a potent weapon.

In October 1941, an Uzbek named Veli Kayum visited a Muslim prisoner-of-war camp in the German province of East Prussia. Conditions there were appalling. Typhus was rampant and most prisoners were near death; all were slowly starving. The men were also in shock because thousands of their comrades had been shot by Nazi liquidation squads. A young Uzbek soldier remembered thinking: "How long does it take to die?"

Kayum appeared with a German major, who shocked the captives by speaking in Uzbek and promising to improve conditions. Then Kayum addressed them.

"I am Uzbek. My name is Veli Kayum-Khan. I was born in Tashkent and came to Germany in 1922 when the Soviet government wanted helpers that could control Turkestan and were sending people to Germany to school. I decided to stay in Germany where we have a political organization formed to liberate Turkestan from Russia. You will hear very soon from me some good news."

Kayum kept his word. Within two weeks, conditions in the camp improved dramatically. Food was suddenly plentiful, and medical care became available. Then the Germans culled the educated prisoners and sent them to a German army camp south of Berlin. There they learned to handle German weapons, breaking down and cleaning rifles, machine guns, and mortars. Most important, émigrés like Kayum gave them political training, including history lessons—a topic about which many of the young Soviets were ignorant. They learned that their homelands had a long, proud history and could rise again if liberated from Soviet rule.

By November 1941, these trainees were reunited with the twelve hundred Soviet Muslims who had stayed behind in the prisoner-of-war camp. Jubilant celebrations followed, tempered with fear: the

men began to realize that they were being groomed to fight the Soviets. All of them hated the Soviets, but it was a shock to make such
a dramatic change in direction: they now must serve their former
enemies, the Germans, and become traitors to Moscow. It was a
point of no return.

Another Uzbek spoke to the prisoners, a schoolteacher named
Baymirza Hayit. He had also been captured by the Germans and
would be their chief officer, a direct liaison with the German high
command in Berlin and East Prussia. The soldiers, he said, should
think of themselves as an army of liberation.

"You are the foundation of the Eastern Legions," Hayit said. "One
day, when the eastern countries are free, you will be the backbone
of the homeland."

The men's fear swung back to jubilation. The next month, the
Germans gave the soldiers uniforms of the German army, or Wehrmacht. They were identical to standard uniforms except that they
lacked epaulettes. Instead, the men got something more powerful
than a measure of rank: an arm patch with a stitched outline of the
famous Chāh-I-Zindeh mosque in Samarkand and the phrase *Biz
Alla Bilen* — "God with us."

The training was part of a little-known plan called Operation
Tiger B. Kayum had put it together in close cooperation with the
Wehrmacht's intelligence division, the Abwehr. While believers in
Nazi racial theories held every "Asian" or "Slav" to be racially in-
ferior, many Germans were eager to make allies out of the prisoners. The German army had already set up formations of Cossacks,
feared horsemen with little love for the Soviets. Tiger B was part of
this experiment.

In early 1942, the soldiers were sent to the front west of Stalingrad. They acquitted themselves with distinction, following German tanks into battle and attacking Soviet troops in a pincer movement that garnered hundreds of Soviet prisoners. Tiger B was
deemed a success and the idea of predominantly Muslim units was
pushed forward.

Other Soviet minorities would also fight for the Germans, but the Muslims were special: their identification with the Soviet Union seemed especially weak. When the first Muslim Soviet prisoners began arriving, the Germans surveyed them. Many didn't identify themselves as Kazakhs, Dagestanis, or members of other ethnic groups, let alone as Soviets. Instead, they simply said, "I am a Muslim." That made them especially interesting to the Germans; here were men fighting for a religion that was diametrically opposed to communism.

Two Turkish generals had put forward the idea of Muslim units. Although Turkey was neutral in the war, the generals had traveled to Berlin and lobbied senior German military leaders for better treatment of ethnic Turkish soldiers. The Wehrmacht quickly expanded Tiger B into a regular unit, the 450th Infantry Battalion. It was staffed almost exclusively with Turkic soldiers and officers. Three other legions were soon added.

These were not elite units. Their morale fluctuated wildly; initially high, it fell as the Germans were pushed back from Muslim areas. The troops were also lightly armed. One unit of ninety thousand men had just over four thousand machine guns, three thousand grenade launchers, and three hundred artillery pieces; it entirely lacked tanks and self-propelled guns. Its main tasks were fighting partisans and guarding supply lines.

But the numbers were significant. By the end of 1942, roughly 150,000 Turks, Caucasians, and Cossacks were fighting. Throughout the course of the war, roughly one million Soviet citizens of several faiths and ethnicities served the Germans in the war, most in nonmilitary roles. The best estimate for the Muslim participation is 250,000, with most in military roles.

The preference for Muslims was clear from the start. In March 1942, the Wehrmacht issued an order allowing Soviet minorities to serve in armed units for police and anti-partisan actions. These units were explicitly not allowed to serve at the front or possess heavy weapons. An exception was made for "Turkic peoples," who were trusted enough to fight the Soviets.

Hitler himself backed these policies. He seemed to have a soft spot for Muslims, perhaps because the Austrian-born dictator had dealt with Muslims in the Austro-Hungarian Empire or because Turkey had been one of the Central Powers during World War I, in which he had fought. It was also true that the Muslims occupied few territories that the Germans wanted to colonize. In any case, Hitler explicitly blessed the use of Muslims.

"I consider only the Mohammedans to be safe. All the others I consider unsafe," Hitler said during a talk at military headquarters in 1942. He warned the military leadership to be careful in setting up military units of subjected peoples but allowed for an exception: "I don't see any risk if one actually sets up pure Mohammedan units."

Soon, the SS wanted non-German troops, too. When the 450th and other units were grouped into a division in 1943, the SS took it over, renaming it the East Turkestani Armed Formation. The unit fought partisans in Ukraine, Greece, and Italy. It won infamy for helping put down the Warsaw city uprising in 1944.

Soon after Sultan was sent from the front to a prisoner-of-war camp, an inspection team from Berlin paid a visit. It was headed by Heinz Unglaube, a German lawyer with a love of Tatar language and culture. Unglaube had been recruited into the army, but officials recognized that his knowledge was more valuable elsewhere. He was sent to a new bureau, the Ministry for the Occupied Eastern Territories, or Ostministerium, and put in charge of the Tatar liaison office.

Sultan immediately impressed Unglaube. Here was a youngster, not even twenty-one years old, who spoke German and hated the Soviets. He would make a good ally. Unglaube pulled Sultan out of the line for a chat. He asked the usual questions: how he had learned German and what he thought of the Russians. Sultan decided to showcase his German by telling a bit of family history.

"I learned German because a distant relative is related to a German."

"Interesting," Unglaube said.

Sultan sensed the German's indifference but plunged on.

"One of my mother's distant relatives married a German woman who had served as a nurse in World War I. She had tended to my relative. They fell in love and got married."

"Interesting."

"The German nurse had an unusual name."

"Which was?" Unglaube said, his ears perking up.

"Von Mende."

It was the name of Unglaube's boss. Sultan was now slated for something better than a low-level position in a Muslim unit. He was quickly put on a train to Berlin. His destination: the Ostminis-terium and an appointment with Gerhard von Mende, the architect of Nazi Germany's use of Muslims.

2

THE TURKOLOGIST

I N THE NINETEENTH and early twentieth centuries, German thinkers helped define the modern world. The country had only united in 1871 and never had much of a colonial empire. But its intellectuals made up for that, their minds ranging from one end of the globe to the other. Theories and ideas conquered countries, rewriting local histories and putting a German imprimatur on parts of the globe where few Germans had traveled. For example, in the nineteenth century, Alexander von Humboldt led expeditions to Latin America, describing that region scientifically for the first time and laying the foundation for the disciplines of physical geography and meteorology.

German scholars were especially fascinated by the Orient — the huge swath of the world that stretched from Turkey to Japan. Today few use the word *Orient* because it lumps together places and peoples with little in common other than being located east of Europe. But back then, the word fired the imagination. When a German geographer coined the term Silk Road to describe the ancient trade route through Central Asia, German explorers launched expeditions to prove its existence. Archaeologists joined in, plundering Buddhist pilgrimage sites to stock Berlin's Museum of Mankind. Eventually, political ambitions followed. In the early twentieth century, Kaiser Wilhelm II tried to extend German influence into the region, dressing up like a sultan for a widely publicized visit to Constantinople and Damascus. During World War I, a German diplomat convinced the Ottoman caliph — nominally the supreme religious leader of the Muslim world — to declare holy war against the Allied powers. Some historians consider this the first modern use of jihad.

Underpinning it all was German scholarship, then a model for the rest of the world. The country's great minds probed many aspects of the East; Ignaz Goldziher wrote one of the first histories of Islamic traditions, and Theodor Nöldeke penned a history of the Koran that posited theses about its secular origins, which today are still considered cutting-edge (and taboo in many parts of the Muslim world). In the 1930s, a new scholar was poised to enter this pantheon: Gerhard von Mende.

Von Mende was physically unremarkable, even slightly odd-looking. At five foot eight, he was of average height for the time, but in photos he appears gaunt, at just 140 pounds. His hair was light blond and his eyes blue — desirable traits during an era that highly valued "Aryan purity." Yet his teeth were crooked and his face round and puffy. Most striking was a minor genetic defect. His right eye wasn't able to track and his left eye sometimes overcompensated, so he seemed to look in two directions at once. Like a sphinx, he appeared to be fixed on his subject yet staring off into the distance.

Von Mende was born on Christmas Day, 1904, into the influential German minority in Riga, Latvia, descendants of the German knights and merchants who had settled along the Baltic coast in the Middle Ages, controlling trade and intellectual life there until the twentieth century. Like many ethnic minorities, he had the old-fashioned graces of someone cut off from the home country. He was fastidiously polite, listened carefully to what people said, and dressed conservatively — in three-piece suits that seemed more English than German. Military brush cuts or rakish Führer-style parts were not to his liking. He kept his hair short but combed straight back from his hairline, a habit that remained as constant as his manners. People inevitably described him as *gut geflegt* — well kempt.

"He was a tall man, thin and stood upright," recalls Ehrenfried Schütte, a former colleague in the Ostministerium. "He was a real gentleman, quietly spoken but very effective."

Von Mende was incredibly driven, a diligent worker, but part of his success came from energetic socializing. He was always willing to go out and, in good Baltic style, knock back a few vodkas with his colleagues. He was an intense networker, equally at ease in the highest intellectual circles and with the staff driver. His early life experiences had made him comfortable with people from all walks of life, and a series of traumas had toughened him, making him determined to succeed.

When von Mende was fourteen, just after Germany's collapse in World War I, Russian Bolsheviks shot his father, a local businessman. Along with many other Baltic Germans, his family fled to Germany. But the old country turned out to be hardly better than Latvia; the kaiser's empire had disintegrated into chaos and hyperinflation, and von Mende's family fell many social rungs. His mother supported them by working as a secretary and a private tutor to children of the nobility, while von Mende attended trade schools, thanks to the aid of Baltic-German solidarity groups that helped ethnic Germans fleeing that region.

As a young man he toiled as a sailor, a coal miner, and an assembly-line worker. He later worked for four years as an apprentice in a Hanseatic trading firm. In 1927, with enough money in his pocket to afford an education, he quit his job and entered Berlin University. He was already twenty-three, four years older than most first-year students. But that would not prevent his startling rise to the top of German academia.

At the time, Berlin was the world center of Russian studies. The historian Otto Hoetzsch turned the University of Berlin into a magnet for gifted academics, including the young American diplomat

George F. Kennan — the future author of the theory of containment. Bolsheviks traveled regularly to the city, mixing with émigrés
and immigrants and adding an edge of controversy to the world
of academics. Von Mende concentrated on contemporary Russian
studies and economics. In just six years he obtained his doctorate,
summa cum laude. Already fluent in Russian, Swedish, and Lat-
vian, he dazzled with his almost intuitive ability to pick up new languages. During his studies he mastered Turkish, including the different Turkic dialects spoken in the Soviet Union, as well as Arabic,
French, and English. A few years later, when he met his future wife,
a Norwegian, he learned her language too, tricking passengers on
the ferry to Oslo into thinking he was a native.

Marrying Karo Espeseth was something of a risk for the up-
wardly mobile von Mende. She was well educated and could be
charming, but she wasn't a safe choice. She had an independent,
emotional streak and thought of herself as an artist. Espeseth had
come to Germany in the late 1920s on a cultural pilgrimage, where
she had been inspired by the postwar outburst of creativity in art
and thought. Bauhaus architecture, expressionist painting, and new
interpretations of history seemed to offer a way out of the dead-end
path of nationalism. After she returned to Oslo, psychoanalysis,
another invention of the German-speaking world, inspired her to
write an avant-garde novel about the damage caused by war. *Sores
That Still Bleed* concerns a German World War I veteran who pours
out his soul to a young Norwegian exchange student. He beats her
and, at her insistence, has sex with her. The book caused a scandal
in Norway, where Espeseth was accused of sullying the young nation's honor.

Stung, she fled back to Germany. She landed a job accompanying a group of French students and academics as they toured the
Rhineland. Their German guide was von Mende, who was making money on the side while writing his dissertation. The couple
fell in love, and Espeseth followed von Mende back to Berlin and
eventually Breslau, where he continued his studies. After a some-

what stormy courtship—her moodiness sometimes drove him away—they eventually married, with Espeseth serving first as his conscience and later his unconditional supporter, scribe, and adviser.

While Espeseth's writing career languished, von Mende's flourished. He got his Ph.D. in 1933, writing a book that explained the Soviet Union's intricate ethnic makeup. Three years later, he published his most influential work: *The National Struggle of the Turkic Peoples of Russia: A Contribution to the Nationalities' Question in Soviet Russia.*

The book's thesis was explosive: that the Soviet Union's non-Russian minorities formed a bloc of disgruntled, unassimilated citizens. It was the first non–Russian language book to describe the growing political consciousness of these peoples. Von Mende saw the main conflict as between the "Turks" (modern-day Uzbeks, Kazakhs, Kyrgyz, and Tatars) and the Bolshevik state. But he warned that without outside help the Turkic peoples would not achieve independence: "Because of the strict political unity of the Soviet Union, the concentration of its power, and the economic links of all its parts, a change in the position of the Turkic ethnic groups can only be expected when the Soviet Union is confronted with a severe shock. Then it will become clear if the Soviet policy of separation has achieved its goal—the splintering of the Turkic peoples into several unviable tiny nations."

His conclusion was prophetic—both for the coming war and the decades after. As he surmised, these groups would gain independence only after a "severe shock"—the Soviet Union's collapse—and not by their own efforts. Also farsighted was von Mende's questioning of these potential states' viability—think of the region's current dysfunctional dictatorships, which are kept afloat by oil and gas revenues.

Had he continued as a scholar in this field, this achievement could have helped von Mende become one of the world's authorities on Soviet and Central Asian politics. But instead, he followed another path. By the time the Nazis took power in 1933, von Mende had begun to dabble in politics. That same year, he had joined the SA, Hitler's storm troopers. Espeseth wrote in her memoirs that he did this because he wanted political backing in Germany in case the Soviets attacked him for studying a sensitive topic. They had already turned down his request for a visa on the grounds that he was a spy, not a real academic.

On the other hand, perhaps he acted out of opportunism. Despite his courtly manners, von Mende had suffered hardship and seen his family destroyed by the Soviets. The Nazis were eager to build a new German empire in lands occupied by the Soviets. Von Mende was one of the world's few experts on the Soviets' Achilles' heel. He may have seen the Nazi movement as a potentially powerful patron and wanted to join.

At that time, joining the Nazis wasn't all that easy; by 1933 the party had put a stop on new members — an effort to keep out people who just wanted to climb onto the bandwagon. People interested in joining the movement often chose the SA (the Sturmabteilung, or Storm Division). Although it was famous for its storm troopers — working-class bully boys who led pogroms and attacks on enemies — many others signed up too. As the Nazis rose to power, membership in the SA mushroomed, from 60,000 in 1930 to 200,000 in 1933.

Three years later, von Mende quit the SA. Family lore has it that Espeseth made him quit before she would marry him. Indeed they married in 1936, after he had done so. In his résumés, von Mende writes that he left the SA because new teaching duties left no time for political activity. But the SA's star was soon to fall, and von Mende may simply have realized that he had chosen the wrong fascist club. Shortly after von Mende joined, Hitler got rid of the SA leader Ernst Röhm in a bloody coup — the Night of the Long Knives. The SA quickly lost influence.

In any case, this experience left von Mende politically vulnerable. Soon after his second book was published he was offered a job as an

adjunct professor at Berlin University. This appointment was immediately opposed by a colorful but dangerous man, Oskar Ritter
von Niedermayer, a soldier and adventurer who had tried to foment
jihad against the British in World War I. He now headed the university's Institute of Military Geography and Politics and was seen
as loyal to the government.

Von Niedermayer bitterly objected to von Mende on two
grounds. One was standard for academic battles in any era: that von
Mende was a poor scholar. The other was dangerous in Nazi Germany: that von Mende had the wrong political outlook. Von Mende
had a "group" of strange supporters and was unreliable, von Niedermayer wrote in 1937, in a letter opposing the appointment. "Out
of this there should, according to my view, be an according judgment of his ideology." The "group" von Niedermayer referred to
could have been the SA. More damaging was questioning his ideology. To get ahead at a university in Nazi Germany you had to follow
the party line.

Whether as a result of this attack or simply out of opportunism,
von Mende now completely embraced Nazi ideology. His letters
show that he was constantly writing to anticommunist groups or
Nazi party organizations engaged in anticommunist propaganda.
He began to write book reviews for Nazi publications and advised
an elite Nazi school, the Adolf-Hitler-Schule in Sonthofen, on hiring decisions. Important for his later work, he kept in regular contact with Georg Leibbrandt, the head of the Nazis' external affairs
office.

Espeseth wrote in her autobiography that she didn't like the Nazis and asked von Mende if they could oppose them. Von Mende
said no; he knew from his work studying the Soviet regime that
the individual stood no chance against a totalitarian system. They
would have to conform.

Not surprisingly, anti-Semitism began to play an increasing role
in his works. In 1938, he was asked to edit a brochure published by
the Anti-Komintern that described "the exceptional Jewification of

the communist apparatus in the Soviet Union." He also dutifully replied to queries from the education ministry about a Jewish colleague, suggesting where the officials could look to find more documentation on him.

This political work was reflected in his third book, *The Peoples of the Soviet Union*. It contained no new ideas and seemed more of a cheat sheet for Nazi ideologues. The title page featured a series of slogans highlighting his main points: "The Great Non-Russian Peoples in the USSR Seek Their Own Statehood!" and "Since 1917 the National Consciousness of the Great Non-Russian Peoples in the USSR Has Awakened!"

The book was rife with anti-Semitism. In a series of crude character sketches depicting the Soviet Union's ethnic groups, the book included one chapter entitled "The Jews." In it, von Mende surveyed their wide-ranging geographic distribution. Then, in turgid, inflammatory prose, he wrote: "Bolshevism has given a push to the expansion of those Jewish circles, which reject all alliances except for a blood-defined cliquish confederacy. Through an unparalleled desire for and exercise of power, it destroys and damages in its sphere of influence any organic cohesion, especially any unity of peoples.

"It seems that the main danger of Judaism for other peoples lies in the fact that it is a unit not comparable to a nation, but in its unity it surpasses the unity of some nations . . . The Jew cannot be put back in the circle of his people, because it doesn't exist, so he has all the possibilities of an opportunist: he is a Jew and at the same time demands recognition as a Russian, Englishman, or something else."

Unexplored in this torrent of prose was a point von Mende probably would not want to acknowledge: his reason for hating Jews was exactly his reason for embracing Soviet Muslims. He rejected Jews because of their extra-national links, yet he advocated the use of Soviet Muslims precisely because of their lack of allegiance to the Soviet state. But von Mende's book was not a work of analysis: it was meant to lay to rest any questions about his political reliability. It did so, but it also helped destroy his postwar academic career, setting the course of his life for the next twenty-five years.

When World War II began later in 1939, von Mende ratcheted up his political work. After France fell in 1940 and the Nazis prepared to invade the Soviet Union, he helped the Nazis by organizing émigrés in Berlin to write reports on the Soviet Union. The reports went straight to von Mende's old contact in the Nazis' Foreign Office, Georg Leibbrandt.

In November 1941, von Mende obtained the coveted rank of full professor. But by then he was no longer an academic. Four months earlier, on June 22, Hitler had invaded the Soviet Union. That same day, von Mende had begun working for the Ostministerium, where he developed plans for harnessing Islam, a strategy that would last long after the Nazi defeat.

3

THE NAZI PROTOTYPE

EVER SINCE THE mid-eighteenth century, Berlin's Tiergarten has been the city's green center, an elegant swath of lakes, fields, and woods connecting its western suburbs with its political and cultural heart in the east. Even the Nazi architect Albert Speer, whose megalomaniacal plan to turn Berlin into "Germania" — the new capital for the thousand-year Reich — planned only minor changes. He envisioned transforming its southern border into a lush diplomatic district.

The land near the Tiergarten was expensive, but Speer could rely on the Nazis' Aryanization policies for cheap real estate. In 1938, for example, one of Berlin's most famous Jewish families, the Mendelssohn-Bartholdys (the family of Felix Mendelssohn, counted among the great German composers) fled and sold their property for the fire-sale price of 170,000 reichsmarks. Speer had a new piece of land. The plot was small, so the government awarded it to a minor European power, the kingdom of Yugoslavia.

The city tore down the Mendelssohn-Bartholdy house and commissioned the architect Werner March to build the Yugoslavian embassy. March's most famous work is Berlin's Olympic Stadium complex in Berlin's western suburbs. The stadium's rough-hewn stone, severe lines, and imposing entrance make it a landmark of the Nazi era. March put similar touches on the new embassy. Its gray travertine walls invoked severe solidity, and its small windows and black grilles were reminiscent of an Italian palazzo. The new embassy opened in 1939, but two years later, Hitler invaded Yugoslavia and the Nazis confiscated the embassy. They handed it over to a new government agency: the Ministry for the Occupied Eastern Territories, or the Ostministerium.

The Ostministerium's mission was crucial to Hitler's vision. Everything in the war until then — the conquest of western Europe, the pummeling of Britain, and the battles in North Africa — had been means to an end. Hitler's dream was to create a giant land empire for Germany, one that would expand eastward into Poland, Belarus, Ukraine, and Russia. Hitler liked to call Russia "Germany's India" — a vast continent of a country with seemingly inexhaustible resources. Everything up to the Urals would be under German control. Germany would reorganize political boundaries and the conquered territories' ethnic groups. The rest of Russia would be left for later. The Ostministerium was to oversee this massive transformation. It was conceived of in April 1941, when Germany was drawing up invasion plans. In theory, the German army was to have little to do with the conquered lands. As quickly as possible, it was to turn their administration over to the Ostministerium.

Control of the Ostministerium was given to an old friend of Hitler's, Alfred Rosenberg. Rosenberg was a Baltic German who went to Germany after World War I and quickly joined the fledgling National Socialists. He even led the movement when Hitler was briefly sent to prison after a failed coup in 1923. But Rosenberg was ill-suited to bureaucratic infighting. He was slowly shunted aside, referred to derisively as "the philosopher." He edited the Nazi party newspaper and wrote an apology for racism, *The Myth of the Twentieth Century*. Tellingly, when the Nazis took power in 1933, he was given no ministry to run. Instead, he continued to lead the Nazis' foreign policy office.

Rosenberg, however, had definite ideas about the new territories. As a Baltic German, he sympathized with the non-Russians in the

Soviet Union. As early as 1927 he wrote that dealings with the Soviets must take "into account the strong separatist movement in the Ukraine and the Caucasus." He planned to use his ministry to create a buffer of countries around the remainder of the Soviet Union. That would mean at least nominal independence for Ukraine, Belarus, the Baltic states, the Caucasus, and Turkestan.

He began to staff his new ministry. It included a political section to oversee various geographic areas, such as Ukraine, the Caucasus, and the Baltic states. A panoply of other departments were to look after culture, the press, youth, women, health, law, finance, agriculture, lumber — every aspect of the new empire.

Rosenberg scoured the Nazi party apparatus and other ministries for promising staff. He commanded a seemingly powerful organization and should have attracted top talent. But few were interested. Power rested in Nazi institutions like the SS and not in government ministries. In addition, Rosenberg's plans ran counter to many of Hitler's own ideas. Hitler wanted to enslave many of the peoples with whom Rosenberg wanted to create alliances. What talent he did attract would soon be sidelined, victims of political infighting and their master's impotence. Von Mende was an exception.

Von Mende now lived in the well-to-do district near Charlottenburg Palace, the Prussian kings' old summer residence. The commute to the ministry took about half an hour by streetcar, much easier than crossing to eastern Berlin where the university was located. The von Mende family had grown to four, with the birth of a daughter and a son.

Von Mende was given control of the ministry's Caucasus division, reporting to his old contact in the Nazi party, Georg Leibbrandt. Von Mende recruited a group of men who had been in exile for years. Most were part of an anti-Soviet movement called Prometheus — named for the mythological hero who championed humanity by defying the god Zeus. It was founded in 1925 by men who had hoped the destruction of the czarist empire would free their peoples from Russian rule. When that didn't happen, the Prometheans published and agitated against Moscow from Warsaw and then Paris. By the 1930s, the group was being backed by French, Polish, British, and German intelligence. The German conquest of France brought the group completely under German control.

Von Mende had known and cultivated some of these men even before he worked for the Ostministerium. After the war, Prometheans such as Mikhail Kedia of Georgia and Ali Kantemir of Turkestan would play major roles in von Mende's entanglement with the United States. Kantemir would also become a key player in the Munich mosque.

One man would top them all in importance during and after the war: Veli Kayum, the political activist who had addressed the Muslim soldiers, including Sultan, in the camp. Kayum was initially unimportant in the Promethean movement but soon emerged as the most prominent Central Asian exile following the death of Mustafa Chokay, who had headed a short-lived rebel government in Tashkent. To further consolidate his position, Kayum added the honorific suffix *Khan* to his name. The Germans were delighted with Kayum's rise in influence because he had been helping the Nazis since the 1930s. They considered him loyal and trustworthy. They embraced the same vision: to build Turkic-Muslim armies that would fight the Soviets.

Von Mende was a civilian, but as the war progressed he was seen as essential to the Nazis' military success. In 1943, the SS chief Heinrich Himmler engineered the ouster of Leibbrandt, von Mende's boss in the Ostministerium. Himmler installed one of his loyalists, hoping to gain control of the rival ministry. But von Mende emerged from the shakeup unscathed. Indeed, he got a promotion — advancing from head of the Ostministerium's Caucasus division to head of the "Foreign Peoples" division — essentially overseeing the Ostministerium's entire policy toward Soviet minorities. The reason? Von Mende had hit upon an ingenious way of motivating the Soviet minorities, one that would echo into the postwar years.

Sultan arrived in Berlin just as von Mende's plans were taking shape. In 1942, von Mende set up "liaison offices" to give the soldiers some representation in the Nazi hierarchy. The liaison offices were soon heavily engaged in political work. In early 1942, the Ostministerium and the Wehrmacht launched an ad campaign in the Crimea, asking for Tatar recruits. The results were sensational. About 200,000 Tatars lived in the Crimea, and about 10,000 of them had been drafted into the Red Army. But a stunning 20,000 volunteered — basically the entire male population of ages eighteen through thirty-five who weren't already fighting for the Soviets. The Germans could not have enlisted more if they had used conscription.

Such success depended on convincing soldiers in the field that these liaison offices were indeed quasi governments in exile. The offices held out the hope of independence to the various non-Russian ethnic groups, even if the Nazis had little intent of actually ceding it to them. The West Germans and the CIA would duplicate the structure and staffing of the liaison offices after the war in their attempts to organize Muslims.

Sultan joined the Tatar liaison office as a propagandist. The office ran a radio station, a dance troupe, and a theater, as well as newspapers crucial to the effort. Except for one aimed at Georgians and another at Armenians, the rest of the papers, including *New Word*, *The Volunteer*, and *The Holy War*, were published with Muslim soldiers in mind. Many, such as *National Turkestan*, *New Turkestan*, and Sultan's newspaper, *Idel'-Ural* (or *Volga-Ural*), were aimed specifically at the Turkic soldiers. Sultan later ran the *German-Tatar Newspaper*.

Sultan's newspaper was overseen by the Wehrmacht's propaganda office, which supplied most of the information. Many of the articles were taken directly from Nazi newspapers, such as the *People's Observer* and *The Attack*. Often, they included anti-Semitic statements. *Idel'-Ural,* for example, claimed in one issue that Jewish labor bosses had exploited honest, hardworking union members in Western societies — a standard anti-Semitic stereotype.

A few years later, when the war was over, Sultan set down his thoughts in a lengthy memoir. The high percentage of "German" topics in the papers, Sultan wrote, was a mistake. Not because repeating Nazi propaganda was morally dubious, but on practical grounds: the Tatar legionnaires saw little difference between Nazi and Soviet propaganda. The publications would have been more effective, he wrote, if they had been more objective.

Not all the Soviet minorities were worried about such tactical issues. Some saw a deeper ethical problem in fighting for the Nazis. The most famous was Musa Ğälil, a prominent poet. He served in a performance troupe but used the freedom of movement it allowed to build anti-Nazi cells among the Tatars. He was betrayed and hanged at the notorious Moabit prison in Berlin.

The Germans had a hard time finding qualified men to run the liaison offices. The head of the Tatar group was widely seen as an incompetent drunk. Sultan was considered for the top post, but he was still legally a minor (at the time, that meant under twenty-one years of age) and therefore rejected. The committees lurched along, without real power yet demonstrating how religion and even the faint hope of realizing a national identity could motivate people — a valuable lesson that others would apply years later.

At a 1942 conference held at a villa on Lake Wannsee in a Berlin suburb, plans for the Holocaust took shape. Although the murder of Jews began earlier, the meeting brought the full might of the bureaucratic, totalitarian state into alignment against them. Key ministers and Nazi officials attended. The meeting lasted just ninety minutes, but its message was clear: the state would now coordinate efforts in a single, awful focus.

The Ostministerium was represented at the conference; von Mende's boss and pre-war contact in the Nazi party, Leibbrandt, at-

tended on behalf of the ministry. Its officials had called for a definition of who counted as a Jew, so the Germans could properly prepare the eastern territory for German settlers by eliminating Jews
and other undesirables.

Nine days later, the Ostministerium held the first of a series of
meetings to iron out legal details stemming from the Wannsee conference. Although the Nuremberg race laws precisely specified who
was to be considered a Jew, the situation in the east presented complications: poor record keeping made tracing a person's origins
more difficult, but the Nazis desired to kill quickly without careful
deliberation. Many wanted a flexible guideline that would allow officials on the ground to kill as they saw fit. Von Mende was one of a
dozen midlevel bureaucrats who participated in the meeting. The
minutes do not set down any of his comments. Surviving Ostministerium records show no effort on von Mende's part to use his power
to slow down the process or raise objections. And he certainly knew
of the genocide against the Jews by January 1942.

This behavior doesn't fit von Mende's postwar image. He liked
to portray himself then as having been the Soviet minorities' best
friend. He was one of the key sources of information for the Harvard historian Alexander Dallin, whose work *German Rule in Russia* (1956) is one of the classic accounts of the Nazis' occupation.
Dallin variously dubs von Mende the "lord protector" and "master
protector" of the minorities — a sort of benevolent figure looking
out for these groups' best interests. He never mentions von Mende's
pre-war anti-Semitic writings or his participation in the Holocaust-
related meetings — perhaps Dallin wasn't aware of the documents
or was protecting a source.

One of the stories von Mende and the Muslims around him liked
to tell after the war concerned the Karainen. Known as the "Tats"
or "Mountain Jews" ("Bergjuden"), they were a tribe that had converted to Judaism. Recent scholarship backs von Mende's claims
that the Karainen were protected, but his private papers show the
extent of his involvement in the Holocaust. After the war, he wrote,

"I still think back with some horror at an Orientalist conference in Berlin during the war. I had back then the unpleasant task to send a request to our Orientalists to help out with current questions. I brought a long list of requests that stemmed from practical policy, for example, the history of the Crimea and what were the Karainen (they were supposed to be handled as Jews)." In other words, von Mende had treated the Nazis' request seriously, helping define who would live and die.

That after the war von Mende thought back with "horror" might be seen as a sign of remorse. Or it could have been a recognition that his public participation in the Holocaust helped ruin his academic career, making permanent his turn from academics toward politics and espionage.

As the German army pressed forward in 1942, it reached more densely populated Muslim areas. The Wehrmacht took the North Caucasus in August 1942. When a German general announced that the mosques there would be reopened, the elated citizens hoisted him on their shoulders, tossing him in the air and shouting hurrahs. The German advance was in fact running out of steam — the Stalingrad debacle was looming — but for now everything seemed to be working smoothly.

The military victories increased Berlin's interest in the minorities. The Foreign Office tried to take control of the minorities' émigré leaders — especially those in the Promethean movement. But the Ostministerium ended up victorious. Von Mende was the main winner, officially gaining responsibility for all Turkic peoples, including those in Central Asia. That meant he was in charge of all the émigrés from this region as well as responsible for solving important problems, such as how to use Islam to motivate them to do the Germans' bidding.

Von Mende moved to strengthen the liaison offices. They were mostly staffed with émigrés — in contrast to the new recruits in the Wehrmacht and SS fighting units, who were former Red Army sol-

diers. He put the émigrés on the Ostministerium's payroll and renamed the liaison offices "guiding offices" and then "national committees"—a semantic move that implied that the émigrés would
guide the soldiers in the field and the people back home, as if they
were nascent governments in exile.

Von Mende then allowed the guiding offices to place staff nominally in charge of the military units, further strengthening the impression that the minorities were running their own show. By 1943
he allowed Azerbaijanis, Volga Tatars, and Turkestanis to stage congresses in order to establish "representative" committees, small par-
liaments that would give voice to these peoples. The most important among them was the National Turkestani Unity Committee,
headed by Kayum.

Kayum was von Mende's personal protégé—and the Muslim
leader who most neatly parroted Nazi slogans. He repeatedly expressed his "faith in Germany," criticizing enemies of Germany as
enemies of Turkestan. His committee had its own Turkic-language
newspaper, *Millî Türkistān,* in which he blasted "imperialist, democratic, and liberal states" as enemies of Turkestan.

But Kayum's political style alienated people, and it would haunt
him in the postwar era. In 1944, a group of Kyrgyz and Kazakhs in
the Turkestani Unity Committee clashed with Kayum, appealing to
the Ostministerium for its own representation and legions. Kayum
retaliated brutally, denouncing the dissidents to the Gestapo. That
could have meant the gallows for his opponents, but the Gestapo
dropped the case, viewing it as a spat among émigrés. As he would
so often in the future, von Mende came to the rescue of his protégé,
organizing a Turkestani congress in Vienna that chose Kayum as its
head.

These events took on an aura of unreality: as German armies were
pushed back, they lost control of the very territory the Ostministerium was supposed to oversee. Even von Mende's own home was
under siege; in 1944 he evacuated his family to the countryside just
before their apartment was destroyed in an air raid.

And yet it was exactly at this point that von Mende's work reached a fever pitch. Perhaps it was desperation, or simply the iron logic of von Mende's case: these Muslim men want to fight for us and all we have to do is make some promises. Never mind that the Nazis likely had no intention of fulfilling them; they were happy to let von Mende organize congresses and draw up fanciful plans if it meant that the soldiers would fight just a bit harder to keep the Soviets at bay.

After the war, von Mende would claim that the Soviet Muslims were not particularly religious — perhaps to allay fears that they were religious fanatics. But during the war, von Mende and others did their best to foster an Islamic identity among the soldiers. They did this by getting an endorsement from a top Muslim leader and by setting up Islamic seminaries.

The endorsement came from the Grand Mufti of Jerusalem, Amin al-Hussaini. Son of a prominent family of clerics, Hussaini inherited the position of Grand Mufti and set about building his power. He saw in the Nazis an ally against the British, who controlled his homeland, Palestine. During the war he escaped from Palestine and made his way to Europe, where he met Hitler, created bitterly anti-Semitic propaganda for the Nazis, and reviewed Muslim troops. After the war he was a staunch opponent of Israel and would come into contact with almost all the groups striving to control Islam in Munich. In 1943, von Mende decided he wanted a religious head for the Crimean Tatars — to cloak German rule in religious garb. Von Mende sought Hussaini.

"The Islamic world is a whole," von Mende later wrote, explaining his actions. "German action toward the Moslems in the East must be such as not to prejudice Germany's standing among all Islamic peoples."

In other words, Germany could score points in the Muslim world by appointing a mufti for the Crimea. Von Mende and the Grand Mufti met again in July 1944. By then, the Red Army had regained control of the Crimea. Hussaini said that given the situation on the ground, appointing a mufti was pointless. But von Mende pushed forward on other fronts. In June 1944, he and the Islamic scholar Benno Spuler set up mullah schools in Göttingen and Dresden. Spuler was especially ambitious — he intended to heal the thirteen-hundred-year split between Shia and Sunni Muslims and therefore trained only bi-denominational mullahs for the German army.

None of this saved the Germans. By early 1945, the Ostministerium had been bombed out of its building, and most of its files had been destroyed. Von Mende had one last card to play. Over the previous months, he may have arranged for the Muslim units to be transferred to the western front so that U.S. and British troops would capture them — falling into Soviet hands would have meant certain death.

Many of the units simply fell apart. Most of the SS division defected to partisans in Czechoslovakia. A Georgian battalion rebelled against the Germans. In February 1945, Turkey declared war on Germany, dealing the Muslims' morale an even more devastating blow. Rosenberg said he would "recognize" the national committees as governments — even though his ministry was now officially abolished. Even Sultan got his promotion. In early 1945, the Tatars set up a provisional government with Sultan as head of the military department.

But von Mende's efforts did serve an important function, especially for the political use of Islam after the war. Muslim minorities could claim they had been fighting for a quasi government in exile, not for the Nazis. Instead of a messy mixture of motives — from wanting to escape dreadful prisoner-of-war camps to sheer opportunism — they could claim the purest of reasons for their actions: national liberation. Forget that the Muslim organizations were essentially German creations meant to keep the troops in the field. The rationale of freeing a people from the Soviet oppressors to govern themselves and freely practice their faith would legitimize the entire effort and provide a blueprint for the Muslims' new friends, the Americans.

COLD WARS

———

Is it but one living soul,

That in itself has split to two?

Or is it the two do form one whole,

Each chosen part to the other true?

4

REVIVING THE OSTMINISTERIUM

I N THE EARLY 1950S, Munich was a ruined city. During the war it had been far enough from the bomber bases in Britain to escape the worst damage. But it had still been hit hard and the scars were readily visible: the great Odeonsplatz was cratered and the Bavarian royal palaces gutted. Churches and theaters were shells. Survivors lived in camps. More than six thousand people died and fifteen thousand were wounded in the air raids. Bombers dropped more than three million firebombs, destroying half of the city's buildings and almost all of the old city. By the war's end, almost half the pre-war population of 900,000 had fled, while 300,000 of the remaining half million were homeless. For years, housing was at such a premium that three, four, or five families shared one apartment. Doorbells sometimes had signs directing visitors to ring once for the Schmidt family, twice for the Braun family, three times for the Muellers, and so on.

But reconstruction was the demon that possessed the city. By day, women hauled rubble from the bombed-out buildings, while others used small chisels to break apart the bricks for reuse. Construction crews strung light bulbs on wires to light up the wrecks at night. Workers cast bizarre shadows as they scurried among jagged walls, carting debris out and hauling new bricks in. In other areas, the wrecked buildings were simply clear-cut, leaving a blank slate for architects. Rubble was the only constant. Mountains of it ringed the city like druidic monuments. Even into the 1950s, the city sponsored "reconstruction days," when employees were given the day off to clear war wreckage. In one action, seven thousand people hauled away fifteen thousand cubic meters of rubble, supported by the U.S. Army, which lent 264 trucks and 4,000 liters of fuel to the effort. At the end of the day everyone got two sausages, one roll, and one liter of beer.

Almost faster than any other city in Germany, Munich recovered. As early as 1946, the great Jewish-Hungarian conductor Georg Solti was running the Bavarian State Orchestra there. Berlin had been the nation's industrial, scientific, and entrepreneurial capital up until the war, but its businesses deserted the city after the division of Germany left Berlin isolated in the middle of communist East Germany. Huge engineering and industrial conglomerates such as Siemens and financial houses such as Allianz fled to Munich. As reconstruction picked up, local companies began to gain traction. In 1951, the city celebrated as a Munich factory exported a locomotive to India — an early sign of West Germany's startling economic ascent. The English language even borrowed a word to describe it, *Wirtschaftswunder,* "economic miracle."

West Germany had been formed in 1949, and its capital was Bonn. But Bonn, as the spy novelist John le Carré put it, was little more than "a small town in Germany." Because of its location and size, Munich was the country's secret capital. The city was just 120 miles from the iron curtain, which ran through the heart of Europe. The U.S. consulate in Munich was reputedly the second largest in the world, behind only China's listening post in Hong Kong. For about twenty years after the end of the war, Munich was a front-line city in one of history's great ideological struggles.

Hundreds of thousands of eastern European refugees flooded Munich. Most were ethnic Germans driven off lands annexed by Poland or the Soviet Union, but the city was also a magnet for people representing almost every ethnic group or cause. Most hoped to stay for as little time as possible and immigrate to more stable, prosperous countries. But many lingered. Munich had scores of émigré groups, a swarm that was constantly forming, merging, splitting, and feuding. Murders were as common as the grandiose plans hatched in cafés to retake homelands. Soviet propaganda hated the city, referring to it as *diversionnyi tsentr,* "center of subversion."

All this made Munich an ideal home for Radio Liberty, which was formed in early 1951 when a group of concerned U.S. citizens got together to do something about the biggest problem of their day — communism. The United States and Soviet Union were locked in a military stalemate. What was needed was a way to subvert communism from within. The United States was the media center of the world. If a group of media people joined forces, couldn't they use new technologies and advertising-age strategies to beam a message of freedom through the iron curtain? The war could be won without a bomb being dropped. These Americans set up a nongovernmental organization called the American Committee for Liberation. Led by the former *Reader's Digest* editor Eugene Lyons and a group of prominent journalists, the committee founded Radio Liberation, which later would be renamed Radio Liberty. The goal, in their own words, was to make a radio station available to "democratic elements among the emigration from the Soviet Union so that they could talk to their fellow countrymen in the homeland."

Radio Liberty was based at the Oberwiesenfeld Airport on the outskirts of town. It occupied a gray, oblong building that was itself an infamous landmark; there, in 1938, Hitler had greeted the British and French prime ministers when they arrived for the conference that carved up Czechoslovakia, making Munich a synonym for weak diplomatic will. The building had been damaged during the war and then hastily fixed up for the radio staff, which would swell to more than a thousand writers, producers, technicians, accountants, and advisers. In the winter, wind rattled the windows and whistled through the cracked walls. Rubble was piled at one end of the airfield, but German aviation buffs were able to use the remainder of the runway.

"I would look out the window of my corner office to see a plane headed right for me, piloted by some frustrated ex-Luftwaffe ace who would peel off and just miss the corner at the last second," recalled the ex–Radio Liberty official Jim Critchlow.

Most of the expats were, like Critchlow, housed at the Regina-Palast Hotel, which was still in partial ruins. At the end of each hallway was a tightly locked door — opening it and stepping in would mean falling headlong into a bomb crater. From the street, pedestrians could see a bathtub still hanging from the fourth floor by its pipes. Many of the Americans who worked at Radio Liberty had fought in the war; others had followed it at home as teenagers. For them, the city was rife with reminders of that dark age, as Critchlow remembered it: "We sometimes ate in the American officers' club in the Haus der Deutschen Kunst, a mammoth columned building that Hitler had turned into a shrine of 'non-decadent,' purely Aryan German art. Down the street was a house where the Führer himself had lived. One of the best restaurants in town was the Osteria Italiana on Schellingstrasse, which had been Hitler's favorite and where the waitresses told stories of his visits."

Many U.S. employees at Radio Liberty were young, idealistic people like Critchlow. A radar technician in World War II, Critchlow was working for General Electric in 1950 when he heard that the U.S. government was desperate for Russian speakers. He took advantage of the GI Bill to enroll at Georgetown University, immersing himself in the Russian language. After graduating he took a job with the Atomic Energy Commission, but when a friend said he was going to help found a radio station in Munich, Critchlow jumped. He went to Munich on a one-year contract and stayed for twenty. About a year after joining, Critchlow was taken aside and told something that he had already figured out. Radio Liberty was not run by Soviet émigrés. It was not financed by well-meaning Americans. It was a CIA front organization, dedicated to overthrowing the Soviet Union. And it was doing so by recruiting key members of von Mende's Ostministerium team.

When most people think of U.S. Cold War policy toward communism, one word often comes to mind: *containment*. First defined in 1946 by the diplomat George Kennan, containment was designed to keep communism from spreading by isolating it and taking a stand whenever it threatened to envelop another country. It was seen as a tough policy, contrasting favorably with the appeasement of Hitler in the 1930s. Outright confrontation with the Soviet Union was nearly impossible, but democracies could take a stand to limit its reach. But by the 1950s, however, many Americans were fed up with this cautious policy. Containment, they felt, ran counter to Americans' idealism; communism should be overturned entirely. Other terms began to gain favor, such as *liberation* and *rollback*.

The Truman administration began to reflect the new mood. In 1948, Kennan himself wrote an internal position paper backing the idea of covert operations and propaganda. This led the National Security Council to adopt a formal policy that authorized a vast array of covert operations, including "propaganda, economic warfare; preventive direct action, including sabotage, anti-sabotage." Covert action was limited only by the need to ensure plausible deniability and the capacity to conceal U.S. sponsorship. Not all of these actions were meant to be violent. Many fell into the realm of psychological warfare, aimed at the enemy's civilian population.

Communications technology would become a significant means of confronting the communist threat. Just a few years earlier, the Nazis had tried to terrorize the British into surrender by bombing London. But the West had turned the London Blitz to its advantage, in part thanks to radio. The chimes of Big Ben, followed by the defiant words "This Is London Calling," on the BBC, and the rooftop dispatches of Edward R. Murrow on CBS remained inspiring memories to most Americans. Similar media tactics might help lead to victory in the Cold War.

How to get the message across? After the war, Truman had dismantled the main U.S. intelligence agency, the Office of Strategic Services, and closed U.S. propaganda bureaus. After World War I similar steps were taken because then, just as in 1945, many Americans felt that the United States shouldn't be engaged in underhanded actions. But the Cold War changed that. In 1947, in a sharp policy U-turn, the National Security Act created two new institutions: the Central Intelligence Agency and the National Security Council. The CIA was to collect and analyze secret intelligence, while the NSC was to advise the president on matters relating to national security. Cold War propaganda developed along two tracks: overt and covert. Programs such as the State Department's support of film, radio, art, and exchange programs, and the Voice of America broadcasts were considered overt propaganda because they could be clearly identified as government efforts. Covert operations ranged from secretly funded magazines to anonymous smear campaigns.

As Truman's second term in office was drawing to a close, efforts at psychological warfare were scattered among many agencies, causing confusion. So in 1951, Truman created the Psychological Strategy Board to unify planning and cut through red tape. Its aim was nothing less than the breakup of the Soviet bloc through psychological operations. Covert operations weren't to be limited to the communist world but would include the "free world" as well. Put less euphemistically, the U.S. government would secretly manipulate public opinion at home and in scores of other noncommunist countries.

Truman's efforts were strongly supported by his successor, Dwight D. Eisenhower. As a World War II general, Eisenhower had been a big fan of psychological warfare, routinely ordering that leaflets be dropped from planes before an attack, in hopes of misleading the enemy. While running for president in October 1952, he gave a speech in San Francisco supporting psychological warfare. "Don't be afraid of that term just because it's a five-dollar, five-

syllable word," Eisenhower said. "Psychological warfare is the struggle for the minds and wills of men." He invoked the "basic truth"
that "humans are spiritual beings; they respond to sentiment and
emotions as well as to statistics and logic . . . The minds of all men
are susceptible to outside influences."

The new administration ramped up psychological warfare. Eisenhower appointed C. D. Jackson, a World War II psychological
operations specialist, to a post in the White House, designating him
special assistant for psychological warfare. Jackson had worked at
the *Time* magazine empire, where he was the right-hand man to the
magazine's founder, Henry Luce, and well known for his staunch
anticommunism. Jackson headed the Psychological Strategy Board,
which was later renamed the Operations Coordinating Board. This
body headed most of the covert propaganda activities in Munich
and the Muslim world during the 1950s.

Another boost to psychological warfare came from Eisenhower's
National Security Council, which approved an order giving the CIA
even more power to manipulate popular opinion. Later, the CIA director William Colby would estimate that up to half the CIA budget
at this time went to propaganda, political action, and paramilitary
operations. Recently declassified documents show that the U.S. Information Agency alone spent about $50 million per year on cov-
ert operations during the 1950s. Overall, the United States spent
roughly half a billion dollars per year trying to influence world
opinion — in 1950s dollars — a vast and unprecedented undertak-
ing. One of the least-understood creations of this era was Radio
Liberty's parent organization, Amcomlib.

On January 21, 1951, the American Committee for Freedom for the
Peoples of the USSR was incorporated in the state of Delaware. It
sounded like the name of a nongovernmental organization — after
all, it was incorporated, with a board of directors and staff — and
giving that impression of course was the idea. But from the start it
was a product of U.S. intelligence.

In 1948 Truman's National Security Council passed a memorandum outlining the need for political warfare. The document surveyed recent history, saying the British Empire had survived so long because it understood that very thing. The Kremlin had the "most refined and effective" strategies in history. But the United States, it claimed, had historically been handicapped by a sentimental attachment to fair play. The paper suggested creating "Liberation Committees" and said an "American Committee" should be formed to keep émigré leaders in the public eye.

The group's name would change repeatedly as it struggled to find a title that would define its mission. Later in 1951 it became the American Committee for the Liberation of the Peoples of Russia — it was bad form to mention the USSR, which some of the group's members considered illegitimate. But the word *Russia* itself became a problem. It seemed too narrow because it excluded non-Russians, who made up nearly half the country's population. So in 1953 the group changed its name again, to the American Committee for Liberation from Bolshevism. That in turn seemed a bit quaint — even in the 1950s no one but the hardest-core anticommunist spoke of Bolshevism, a term out of the 1920s and '30s. So the last two words were dropped in 1956, leaving the group with a bizarrely generic name: the American Committee for Liberation. Outsiders often knew it simply as the American Committee — which gave it a wholesome, patriotic ring. Internally, it was known by the acronym Amcomlib. The term has a delicious jargony mystique, perfect for an era that coined obscure and clipped nomenclature for military and espionage missions. Amcomlib could have been a code word for a parachute operation behind enemy lines.

Over time, Amcomlib would command a large budget and a staff of thousands. Its main duty was to run Radio Liberty. But it had two other important tasks. It operated a supposedly independent think tank, the Institute for the Study of the USSR, which published papers by Amcomlib employees and people close to intelligence agencies. It also had an émigré relations department that recruited agents, mostly in Munich, and sent them around the world on covert propaganda missions. U.S. government involvement was carefully masked. Amcomlib's board misled listeners and supporters in the United States into thinking it was run by émigrés and prominent journalists, instead of the CIA. When leaflets were printed, listing radio broadcast times and frequencies, the American role in the endeavor was purposely obfuscated, according to minutes of Amcomlib board meetings.

Perhaps for this reason Radio Liberty never entered the popular imagination as did its better-known sibling, Radio Free Europe. Although both were front operations based in Munich, the two were quite different. Radio Free Europe focused on eastern Europe — Poland, Hungary, Czechoslovakia, and other countries dominated by the Soviet Union — while Radio Liberty beamed into the Soviet Union itself. Radio Free Europe's parent organization, the National Committee for a Free Europe, solicited funds from ordinary Americans, and high-profile public figures sponsored it. It penetrated public consciousness to such an extent that, decades later, it inspired a hit song of the same name by the rock group R.E.M.

Amcomlib might have been relatively unknown, but it never lacked money. Its exact budget is hard to reconstruct, although some information has escaped the CIA's information blockade. Records show that in 1955 its budget was $2.8 million (roughly $23 million in 2010 terms). It grew to $7.7 million in 1960.

People working for Radio Liberty quickly realized that such funding had to come from somewhere significant. "I doubt that there was a single stoker or sweeper in our building out at Oberwiesenfeld who did not have some inkling of the true state of affairs," said Critchlow, who worked in the radio's programming department.

Critchlow has strongly defended Radio Liberty. In 1995, he wrote a charming memoir called *Radio Hole-in-the-Head/Radio Liberty* that took its name from the station's bumbling ways — at least as it was seen by those who doubted its value. He notes that the CIA largely stayed out of the broadcasting side: "If you stop to think about the massive volume of material that goes into a daily broadcast, and the speed with which it must be handled, the instant decisions that must be made, it should be obvious that no agency outside our building could exercise effective control. They had to trust us."

And of course the CIA was clever to do so. Propaganda doesn't have to be false; it is most effective when it is true or as close to the truth as possible. So most employees on the radio side of the operation felt quite comfortable with what they were doing — spreading information about an awful regime.

It is a tribute to Radio Liberty that it attracted capable people like Critchlow. From the start, the radio station's roster included legitimate journalists such as Edmund Stevens, a Pulitzer Prize winner who was hired to train the staff. The heart of the operation was Boris Schub, a son of Russian émigrés. Intellectually brilliant, he inspired his colleagues with his vision of a democratic, free Russia. It was Schub's idea — and it became a classic CIA strategy — to use disillusioned leftists to attack the Soviet Union. Schub called it his "left hook."

Radio Liberty developed a strong esprit de corps. Many employees still remember their years working there as some of the best of their lives, a time when they got to travel overseas and work with a fascinating group of émigrés. Several former Radio Liberty employees have written accounts of life at the station. Like Critchlow, most play down the CIA connection, or skirt it. Critchlow wrote somewhat defensively that "I would demean the many devoted men and women who conscientiously put out the broadcasts if I tried to link them with the shadowy world of intelligence."

This is undoubtedly true. Critchlow and others who worked at Radio Liberty were no stooges. Critchlow became a classic news journalist during his two decades at the broadcasting station. To him the CIA was unimportant — he contemptuously called the CIA "the boys in the back room."

Yet others saw the experience in a different light. The senior Radio Liberty manager Gene Sosin said he found it odd to lie in the name of broadcasting the truth. In his memoirs, Sosin wrote of going to Cornell University to talk with a professor who was an expert on Soviet education. The professor had traveled to the Soviet Union on a grant from the Human Ecology Fund; later on he learned that the CIA covertly supported the fund. Sosin worried that the professor would think that Radio Liberty too was a CIA project and therefore he might not grant an interview with the station to report on what he had seen — when, in fact, his giving an interview about the USSR was the whole idea behind the trip. Sosin was there on damage control, to keep the professor in line and to reassure him of the station's independence.

"I could not help seeing the anomaly of working for a medium that was communicating 'THE TRUTH' to the Soviet peoples while we were lying to our own people," Sosin wrote. But Amcomlib had another secret, one that most Americans would have found more unpleasant. That was the issue of its émigré employees.

When the war ended, most of the Soviet soldiers who had served Germany landed in Western prisoner-of-war camps. Many credited von Mende for this, stating that he engineered their deployment west in the waning months of the war. That is impossible to prove from the historical record, but in any case winding up in the camps helped few of them. At the Yalta Conference in 1945, Britain, the Soviet Union, and the United States agreed that all citizens should be repatriated after the war. That seemed harmless then, even a good idea — most people would naturally want to go home. For the hundreds of thousands of Soviet citizens fighting for the Germans, however, it meant disaster. Most correctly assumed they would be shot immediately or, if lucky, face a long stay in the gulag for their treason.

When the war ended, soldiers in uniform were sent to holding camps, and most were repatriated. But Europe was in a state of near chaos, and Germany was awash with "displaced persons," or DPs.

They consisted of the Nazis' slave laborers, concentration camp prisoners, Germans who had fled the Soviet onslaught, and thousands of Soviet citizens who had fought for the Nazis but avoided a prisoner-of-war camp. The Red Cross and German officials estimated that eight million DPs were in Germany by war's end, and most would have to be repatriated. Within a short while, British and U.S. authorities would deliver two million of these people to the Soviet Union in accordance with the Yalta agreement.

But the occupying forces were overwhelmed. For the quick-witted and lucky, the anarchy of the situation meant a chance to start a new life. Muslim soldiers were especially fortunate. For most of the war, Turkey had remained neutral and maintained normal diplomatic and academic exchanges with Germany. A Turkish student union had been formed to represent Turks studying in Germany during the war. Nationalistic and pan-Turkic in their thinking, the students hit upon a simple solution to save their fellow ethnic Turks: declare the soldiers Turkish and issue them student identity papers.

The idea wasn't as far-fetched as it sounds. Most of the soldiers were in their late teens or early twenties. If they had had the presence of mind to ditch their Wehrmacht or SS uniforms and papers before entering the DP camps, no proof existed of their nationality or profession. Their mother tongues were Turkic dialects. With a bit of polish they could pass as Turkish students.

The Turkish student union had been based in Berlin, but when the bombing got too fierce, it moved to the medieval university town of Tübingen in southern Germany. That put the students in close range of the refugee camps, especially in the U.S. sector. Within months, they were issuing Turkish identity papers wholesale. To vary the story and thus throw suspicious officials off their trail, they also claimed that some of the young men were from Xinjiang, China, a western province with a large Turkic minority.

That became Garip Sultan's new homeland. After the war ended, he was sent to a DP camp. There, the students gave him a new first name, Garip, in place of the Russified name he had previously used, Garif. "We became ethnic Turks," Sultan said. "They gave me an identity from Kashgar in Xinjiang. So that's why I survived."

It was a ruse used by many of von Mende's top deputies, including two who would play a key role after the war: the political activist Veli Kayum and the military liaison Baymirza Hayit. They made their way to Czechoslovakia and surrendered to the U.S. Army. They were immediately sent to be debriefed by the army's Counter Intelligence Corps, or CIC, and then to a DP camp. The Turkish student group in Munich vouched for Hayit and Kayum, and the UN did not repatriate them.

Hayit, who later became a historian of the liberation struggles of Central Asians, estimates that eight hundred Muslims from Central Asia avoided capture this way. Other estimates are higher. In the 1950s, one German author wrote that seven hundred Kalmyks lived in West Germany. The Kalmyks were small compared to the other ethnic groups; if one extrapolates proportionally from their numbers, then around ten thousand Soviets of various backgrounds stayed after the war in West Germany. This number is certainly too high, but it's safe to say that several thousand remained.

The ploys of the Turkish students might not have succeeded indefinitely, but it was unnecessary to keep up the subterfuge for long. By late 1945 the repatriations had stopped. General Dwight D. Eisenhower ended the practice after criticisms arose that the men were being sent back home to certain death. Even if they had fought for the Nazis, that made them no worse than millions of Germans, who were not being condemned wholesale to death. Why should the Soviet ethnic minorities be singled out for such punishment? Their desperate situation became impossible to ignore when 230 Turkestani officers, held in a camp outside Munich, committed suicide the night before they were to be returned to the Soviet Union. They doused themselves with benzene and set themselves alight. Only one of the group survived; he was taken to Ankara and died in 1950.

Within months, efforts to repatriate the minorities had reversed into a free-for-all to keep and recruit them. One of von Mende's main leaders in the Ostministerium, the Georgian prince Mikhael Alshibaya, was saved by the CIC. He had already been meeting with CIC officers when one pulled him aside to say that Alshibaya should expect a visit the next day from a Soviet repatriation squad, adding significantly, "You don't have to be there." Alshibaya took the hint and fled to the hills of northern Bavaria for a few days until the Soviet search team had left the area.

Such help became increasingly common. Even in 1945 Western intelligence agencies were suspicious of the Soviets' postwar intentions. They began to pick up agents who could operate in the Soviet Union, coming up with novel ways to find and recruit them.

Charity organizations also got into the act. The Tolstoy Foundation was set up as a cultural group for Russian exiles by the granddaughter of the famous novelist. In postwar Munich, the organization tried to aid refugees, sending employees to the DP camps to sort out their identities and help them immigrate to the United States or start afresh in Germany. But the foundation also appears to have been closely linked to intelligence work, and perhaps was even directly funded by the CIA. Alshibaya's wife worked for the foundation. She says U.S. intelligence subcontracted work out to the foundation. "We did interviews for them," Mrs. Alshibaya said. "We asked people about their background, what they did, and so on." The goal was to recruit the men for covert operations.

In 1952, Garip Sultan was looking for work. He was married and had a permanent West German residency permit. But what would he do for the rest of his life? Now twenty-nine years old, Sultan had matured into a strikingly handsome man, with black hair, an elegant aquiline nose, and a strong chin. He and his wife were thinking of starting a family. He had survived Stalin and Hitler and was ready for a new phase in life. He latched onto anticommunism with a vengeance.

In the 1940s, Sultan had joined the Scottish League for European Freedom. Backed by Britain's foreign intelligence agency, MI6, the league tried to line up members of Soviet minority groups such as the Tatars to combat the Soviet Union. It led to a more durable organization, which Sultan also joined, called the Anti-Bolshevik Bloc of Nations. Both were largely the creation of British intelligence services and rife with von Mende's ex-Ostministerium collaborators. Now Sultan was looking for something that paid a real salary but would allow him to keep fighting communism. He found what looked like a perfect fit: Radio Liberty.

One reason Sultan found it easy to choose Radio Liberty is that he already knew most of its employees. The station was organized into "desks," each with a specific nationality — Russian and non-Russian. Programming concepts and guidelines were developed in New York, but the desks in Munich had autonomy to pick topics to cover and people to interview. This is not in itself unusual for broadcasters. The non-Russian desks, however, duplicated the Ostministerium's nationality committees in many ways, hiring similar personnel and even using Nazi ethnic terms such as Idel-Ural to refer to Tatars from the Volga River region.

The people on the desks had almost all worked for von Mende in the Ostministerium. Besides Sultan, other top-level Ostministerium employees included Aman Berdimurat and Veli Zunnun on the radio's Turkestani desk, Hussein Ikhran on the Uzbek desk, and Edige Kirimal on the Tatar desk. The Ostministerium stalwart Abdul Fatalibey ran the Azerbaijani desk. A year after Radio Liberty went on the air, Fatalibey didn't show up for work one day. Police eventually found his body, bound with wire and mutilated, in the apartment of another Azerbaijani, who had fled to East Germany. Next to Fatalibey was a sign inscribed with the warning TRAITORS TO THE MOTHERLAND. (Not long after, the body of an employee of the Belarussian desk was found in the Isar River. Police never established a motive, but radio employees assumed the Soviets were responsible for both deaths.)

Intelligence hires usually are vetted to ensure their personal histories contain nothing compromising, but that requirement was apparently waived for the émigrés. Radio Liberty relied so heavily on Nazi collaborators that the station would have closed without them. One estimate put the proportion of Radio Liberty employees who had worked for the Nazis at 75 to 80 percent.

"At RL we had a special problem: the tendency of many in the audience to view our émigré staffs as traitors to their homelands," Critchlow wrote in his memoirs, adding that "for Americans of my generation, many of us World War II veterans, there was initially something distasteful about having to associate with people who had worn German uniforms, whether or not they had committed war crimes. Yet there were scores of such people in our building in Oberwiesenfeld."

There was a way of dealing with this discomfort. Typically, the American would have a proper sit-down talk with his ex-Nazi colleague, who would give assurances that he had had no choice but to serve the Reich, or — perhaps in a fit of candor — that he had been young and foolish. These former Nazis never claimed to believe the anti-Semitic propaganda they had produced or been fed. Everyone had been a victim. Then the two coworkers would go out for a drink, their friendship reestablished.

But from the vantage point of history, the parallels between Amcomlib and the Ostministerium appear striking and belie this distancing from the Nazi past. The ex-Soviets working for Radio Liberty were not ordinary soldiers or even officers who had joined the Wehrmacht or the SS out of desperation. Most of the foot soldiers who had served the Nazis had been repatriated. Those who remained had been cultivated by the Nazis to work in the Ostministerium and had thus become a political elite. Many, like Sultan, had been in charge of propaganda — which in the Nazi era meant heavy doses of anti-Semitic and racist language.

Employing such people was more than a moral problem. The Soviets were aware of their backgrounds and had an easy time discrediting Radio Liberty staffers with the charge of being not only CIA employees but also former Nazi collaborators. The government regularly lured Radio Liberty employees back to Moscow — by holding family members hostage, for example. In exchange for amnesty, these ex-employees had to name which of their former colleagues had worked for the Nazis.

Thus the Muslims at Radio Liberty were ultimately ineffective. When they were sent on covert propaganda missions abroad, the Soviets could easily discredit them as Nazi stooges. They also lacked credibility as religiously observant Muslims, since they'd had almost no religious education in the Soviet Union or Nazi Germany. When the United States tried to use them to communicate propaganda, critics would say their Nazi past had disqualified them. Their failure had significant repercussions for the future of Islam in Europe; the United States would eventually look for more credible Muslims among radical groups.

Before the radio station started to broadcast, Amcomlib officers decided it would be credible only if backed by émigrés. This would create the impression that a broad coalition had formed against the Soviet Union and was broadcasting news back home. As one Amcomlib employee put it, "Our goal was to provide the myth that Amcomlib was made up of émigré groups and not the CIA. That's why the émigré groups were so important."

But the émigrés were not united. They were divided along ethnic lines — roughly, the Russians on one side and on the other the non-Russians: Ukrainians, Georgians, Armenians, Turkestanis, and many others. To force a marriage, Amcomlib set up a "Coordinating Center" in Munich in January 1951 and put the émigrés on its payroll. But for two years the U.S. efforts went nowhere. Amcomlib was trying to broker the kind of deal that had eluded the Nazis. They too had tried to force émigré Russians and non-Russians to work together, but had failed. The Americans controlled the groups' purse strings but couldn't make any headway. One Amcomlib report put it this way: "Whether this analogy is justified or not, we seem to be wrestling today with the same problems and émigré personalities which shaped up within the German Government between 1941 and 1945 in its war with the Soviet Union."

When Eisenhower took office, one of his top aides received a scathing letter from an official at Radio Free Europe, saying Amcomlib had been "an almost complete failure," bogged down in arcane disputes. It hadn't even started broadcasting and instead spent lavishly on the émigrés, trying to iron out their differences. Amcomlib officials defended themselves, saying they needed a united front in order to give the radio station credibility.

In desperation, Amcomlib brought in a veteran State Department officer, Isaac "Ike" Patch. Patch had served in Moscow and Prague until the communist government expelled him. One contemporary described him as "a tall, shrewd string bean with a deceptively mild appearance and manner." But Patch's task was hopeless.

"It was the Muslims against the Slavs, the Russians," Patch recalled. The Muslims, Patch said, felt the Russians were chauvinists. "They [the Muslims] were so interested in independence. That was their emphasis. Not the big picture" — meaning the fight against communism that so interested the Americans.

Amcomlib made a last-ditch effort to forge a consensus at the Tegernsee, a lake resort south of Munich. It was a disaster. Then someone had a new idea: if the Americans were having the same problems the Germans had faced ten years earlier, it might make sense to ask Germans from that era for help. So Patch and other Amcomlib officials turned to an old friend of U.S. intelligence, Gerhard von Mende.

On November 2, 1944, the CIA's forerunner, the Office of Strategic Services, sent an agent code-named "Ruppert" across the front lines near the French town of Gérardmer. Ruppert had an unusual mission and was equipped accordingly. His job wasn't to ferret out intelligence, such as discovering any last-gasp offensive the Germans might have in store. Instead, he was there to plan for the postwar era. A key goal was to induce top-ranking Nazis to defect. So instead of carrying a wireless transmitter or another device to send back urgent messages, Ruppert traveled light, armed only with $10,000 in bribes, including *louis d'or* coins slipped into his shoes.

Ruppert made straight for Berlin. He spent five and a half months there, posing as a Nazi security service officer and talking to Nazi party members. Then, his mission accomplished, he left for Switzerland. He hadn't discovered any postwar Nazi resistance plots, nor had he enticed any top Nazis to defect. But he had recruited a group of people who would at once repulse and fascinate his American employers: Nazis eager to fight the Soviet Union. Ruppert's top recruit was von Mende, who was especially prized because U.S. intelligence believed he had tight ties with the German army's Abwehr intelligence unit.

After Ruppert left, von Mende made his way to Switzerland too. In her memoirs, von Mende's wife stated that he was hoping to meet Carl Burckhardt, president of the International Committee of the Red Cross, and get his help to save the Soviet soldiers involved with the Ostministerium. According to Red Cross files, one of von Mende's men indeed arrived in Geneva in late 1944, which meshes with Ruppert's activities in Berlin. But Red Cross files show that no meeting took place. By the time von Mende arrived at the Swiss border in May, the war was basically over and he was turned back. He and three Georgians from the Ostministerium were sent to a U.S. prisoner camp in the Austrian town of Höchst.

It was there that U.S. troops found them. The Germans immediately asked to be put in touch with the OSS, and in fact, they were talking to an OSS man — this may have been arranged in advance by Ruppert. "I am sure that in spite of everything, the group knows that it is OSS who is interested in them," the OSS officer wrote in his report. "They are very clever, highly cultured . . . They are only too willing to talk and too willing to work."

It was the start of several courtships between von Mende and U.S. intelligence that would take place over the next fifteen years. At this point, the U.S. goal was to capture intact von Mende's émigré network. From the Americans' point of view, they could constitute a turnkey operation to penetrate the Soviet Union. Von Mende and his men were sent to a suburb of Frankfurt, where a special OSS counter-intelligence unit, X-2, handled his case. Von Mende wrote for days on end. He and the three Georgians authored twenty-three reports, including opinions on conditions in Soviet Russia, the role of minorities in the Soviet Union, Nazi indoctrination methods, and descriptions of the various ministries in Berlin.

The X-2 officers were impressed but had some doubts. Von Mende seemed too pushy, too much a man with his own agenda — virulent anticommunism that bordered on fanaticism. The Americans shared the anticommunist perspective but also recognized that the Nazis had failed miserably in the East. Von Mende claimed to be different — he criticized his superiors in the Ostministerium — but his American handlers weren't sure. In detailed sketches, the OSS men described him as a moody prima donna: "Personal description: 5 ft 8; about 140 lbs, slender, light blond hair, light blue eyes, light complexion, one tooth in lower jaw protruding noticeably, courteous, moody, gives impression of fairly young, relatively insignificant person; obviously very clever and seems to lead."

And in another description Mende is depicted as "without doubt a man of exceptional intelligence and an outstanding linguist, it is hard to speak of him as a person who 'kept his personal integrity and cleanliness to the last.' While there is little doubt that Mende would work for the Americans . . . there is also little doubt that he would be an untrustworthy contact unless the Americans would agree to swallow fully his ideology and approach to the handling of the USSR problem."

Still, his interrogators bought — or at least were willing to tolerate — his story that he hadn't been a real Nazi. He never admitted to membership in the SA so was released with a document certifying that he hadn't joined a Nazi-affiliated party or political organization and had opposed the Nazis' foreign policy. Von Mende went home and began his new life as a freelance intelligence operative.

"My husband has a group of gentlemen, who has worked with him during the war and these gentlemen are also experts for different east-European questions. This group consists of some German gentlemen, chiefly 'Baltic-deutsche.'" So began a long letter by Karo Espeseth in November 1945, written on behalf of her husband. Her English might have been imperfect, but her meaning was clear: von Mende had assembled the old Baltic-German leadership from the Ostministerium and was looking for work. Later in the typewritten letter, she wrote that many other émigrés could help out too. The group could constitute a sort of academic research service. "This cooperation could take place in a scientific institute and this institute should be at the disposal of the British Empire."

The letter was one of several that von Mende and Espeseth wrote after he returned from the U.S. interrogation camp. He was fortunate to find his family safe in the western zone of occupation. As the war ended, they had been living north of Berlin in the hometown of Heinz Unglaube, von Mende's employee at the Ostministerium who handled the Tatars. But as the Red Army surged through Germany, von Mende arranged for the family to travel west toward British lines.

Reunited with his family, von Mende had to figure out what to do for a living. Berlin University was under Soviet control and the Ostministerium was no more. But he was fascinated by education. In his letters, he warned Allied officials that with Nazism discredited, German youth was susceptible to the new all-embracing ideology of communism. He proposed some sort of youth education project that he and his men could run. He even wrote to the famous British historian Arnold Toynbee asking for help. But to no avail.

Academia did not seem an option. He did work briefly at a university right after the war but was not offered a full-time position.

It's impossible to know precisely why: clearly he had published groundbreaking work and still had the position of a full, tenured professorship. And at this time many people with Nazi backgrounds were being rehired. But whatever impression he may have given to the OSS, von Mende's career had indeed been tied to the Nazis. Even before working in the Ostministerium he had been an enthusiastic Nazi — not in the narrow sense of being a formal party member, but in his efforts to fit into the party program and embrace its ideology. He had written nasty anti-Semitic tracts. He also participated in the academic quackery of defining who was a Jew. His family said he had taken a liking to politics; it might be more accurate to say that his politics had destroyed his academic career.

In any case, he was soon in direct contact with the British. In October 1945, he wrote to a "Major Morrison," complaining that employees of the Ostministerium were facing discrimination. At the end of the six-page letter, in which he lauded his former colleagues as "European, thinking people," he attached a treasure-trove: a who's who of von Mende's Ostministerium network. The names included Kayum, Alshibaya, and two dozen more, many of whom were still stuck in Allied interrogation camps.

The information must have interested the British intensely. Many of the men von Mende listed had been Prometheans— the early group of émigrés who opposed the Soviets. Back then, the British had worried that the Soviets and Nazis would form an alliance and had contemplated parachuting Prometheans into the Caucasus to blow up Soviet petroleum installations in order to deprive the Germans of oil. That region was still strategically important, and von Mende knew the émigrés better than anyone else.

By 1946 von Mende was living a privileged existence. When many Germans were literally starving, he had an automobile. His family also had a horse, a maid, and a house — all of this, of course, with no official source of income. As early as 1946, von Mende had spread his operations to the U.S. zone of occupation. According to a U.S. counter-intelligence report of 1947, von Mende drove down to Munich to visit his old Georgian colleague from the Ostministe-rium, Prince Alshibaya, presumably to recruit him for the British. Later that year, Alshibaya drove up to Hamburg and came back with four hundred imported cigarettes, three bottles of cognac, packages of chocolate, and three boxes of cigars. He could sell these goods on the black market to support his lavish lifestyle, which in-cluded a car and a mistress.

In the late 1940s, the newly formed CIA decided to take another look at von Mende. He was given a code name — a cruel one, really: "Capriform," "having a goat's shape." Then he was brought down to Munich for extensive interviews. The CIA got the university in Mu-nich to agree to give him a job, and von Mende expressed an eager-ness to work for the more prosperous U.S. side.

Around this time, the United States and Great Britain were keen to use the émigrés for covert operations inside the USSR. It was still the era of rollback — the more muscular counterpoint to contain-ment that valued adventures like the famous Nazi Operation Zep-pelin, of 1942, when some of von Mende's émigrés were parachuted into the Soviet Union with radios and maps. They were to scout out the land and assess the potential for sabotage or political organi-zation. These forays were sometimes successful but often ended in disaster, as the secret agents were caught soon after landing. But to Allied intelligence agencies at the start of the Cold War, they seemed like an instant solution to the West's almost complete lack of agents in the Soviet Union.

Von Mende, however, knew that these projects typically failed. He favored another approach: collecting information and engaging in covert propaganda. The Americans weren't interested. The proj-ect was shelved — temporarily.

In 1949, West Germany was created out of the three zones that the United States, Britain, and France had occupied after the war ended. West Germany was not fully sovereign — the three powers still stationed large numbers of troops on its soil, and its foreign policy was circumscribed, mainly by U.S. objectives. With the slow emergence of West Germany as a country in its own right, however, von Mende could slowly extract himself from working for foreigners. He began to line up agencies and offices in the West German government that might pay him to bring his vision to fruition: to re-create as much of the Ostministerium as possible — to hire back onto a German payroll those of his former colleagues whom the Americans hadn't already taken. Over time, he became directly employed by Bonn.

Von Mende may have been motivated by a humanitarian drive — giving work to some down-at-the-heel foreigners exiled far from home. But as always with von Mende, his charity was hard to separate from his ambition. He liked the Soviet minorities and they liked him. He needed them and they needed him. As in the Ostministerium, he became — depending on how charitably you choose to view von Mende — either their advocate or their puppet master. Von Mende's Ostministerium colleagues credited him with generously using his power to help. He wrote a series of what the Germans called "Persil certificates." Persil is Germany's best-known laundry detergent; a letter from the right person could wash away Nazi stains. He also helped Soviet minorities receive an education. Von Mende mentored Sultan, who studied law at Hamburg University. "He helped a lot of the people from the national committees," Sultan said. "We were grateful."

After Sultan went to Amcomlib, von Mende relied heavily on two émigrés: Hayit and Kayum. Hayit had been the bridge between the Ostministerium's national committees and the Wehrmacht, with a reputation for being a straight and true military man. After the war, he would be von Mende's most important colleague. Von Mende hired Hayit to gather intelligence on émigrés and write pamphlets. Later, von Mende would send him overseas on covert missions. The two also shared a touching friendship.

"Without you I would be in Germany an island in a dead sea," Hayit wrote in one letter to von Mende while on a trip to London. Hayit's letters, usually in cramped handwriting that flowed in wavy lines along the page, were always full of solicitous questions about von Mende's health, his wife, and his children. Although von Mende was never as openly affectionate, his tireless efforts on Hayit's part are clearly evident. Despite his long years in Germany, Hayit's German was always poor and it was von Mende who ghostwrote his papers and even his memos, turning Hayit's rocky prose into the smoothest bureaucratese or formal academic prose.

Hayit had always been interested in history, and after the war von Mende helped him obtain a Ph.D. from the University of Münster and write books on Turkestani history. In 1956, Hayit published *Turkestan in the Twentieth Century,* which was reviewed in academic journals and judged as an important, if subjective, view of the region's struggles against Russia. Throughout his life, Hayit continued to publish prolifically on Turkestan.

During the war and after, Veli Kayum cut a less appealing figure. After the war, he rebuilt his Ostministerium national committee, naming it the National Turkestani Unity Committee. Most of the prominent Central Asians who had worked for von Mende joined. But Kayum's Nazi service had tainted him. In 1951, the influential left-wing U.S. magazine *New Leader* carried a two-part series called "Allies We Don't Need," which nicely laid out how émigrés who had once worked for the Nazis were now heading groups backed by the former Allies. The first installment criticized the National Alliance of Russian Solidarists, known by its Russian acronym, NTS, for having allied itself with the Ostministerium and promoted anti-Semitism. The second was a direct challenge to Western intelligence agencies' machinations in West Germany. It featured a picture of the Ostministerium boss Alfred Rosenberg, with the caption "His memory lingers." It dissected the ABN, or Anti-Bolshevik Bloc of Nations. The article took the ABN to task for its racist, anti-Russian statements (one ABN paper had said Russians had never been able to form "an order of society worthy of human beings") and then ticked off the ABN's ex-Ostministerium "minions," including

Kayum. After the article appeared, von Mende immediately sent a letter to an ABN official, asking if he thought Kayum should reply. He also chided the group for using such inflammatory language and mused that the *New Leader* must have been informed "by a man who worked for U.S. intelligence." The allegation isn't implausible because Amcomlib and von Mende were competing for the same men to staff their versions of a revived Ostministerium.

Von Mende would often get angry at Kayum for his indiscretions and bottomless appetite for money, but he remained a loyal employer. Von Mende paid Kayum 3,600 deutsche marks as an annual salary. The only activity that Kayum engaged in was sending bits of gossip about the émigrés to von Mende; judging from the extant records of von Mende's offices, Kayum never wrote serious reports or analyses. Von Mende also tried to subsidize Kayum's newspaper, *Millî Turkistān*, "in recognition of his earlier services for Germany" — one can only suppose this refers to his work in the Ostministerium.

Rounding out von Mende's team was a German, Walter Schenk, who functioned as von Mende's deputy. Schenk had not worked in the Ostministerium, but von Mende knew him from the war, when he headed the Lemberg office of the Nazis' Sicherheitsdienst, or Security Service, where one of his responsibilities was Desk IIIB, which oversaw Poles, Ukrainians, and Jews. Lemberg (known between the wars by its Polish name, Lvov, and today by its Ukrainian name, Lviv) was at the time in eastern Poland, meaning Schenk was at the epicenter of the Holocaust. Schenk had quit university to join the Nazis, making him even less employable than von Mende after the war. He put in long hours helping von Mende design his evolving organization.

Like his counterparts in Amcomlib, von Mende was constantly changing his office's name until he found something suitable. He finally settled on a dual name: Research Service Eastern Europe and Bureau for Homeland-less Foreigners. The latter was ostensibly to help foreigners facing various problems, and the former was

a quasi-academic research office for government agencies in need
of information. As von Mende tried to get established, he moved
around the countryside, working in small towns in the British sector: Detmold, Uelzen, and Brackwede. He settled in Düsseldorf,
which became the center of West Germany's efforts to harness the
Soviet minorities and, in time, Islam.

An elegant city on the Rhine, Düsseldorf was the capital of West
Germany's economic powerhouse, the state of North Rhine–
Westphalia. Just a tram ride from Cologne, this ancient city had
grown in importance as the neighboring Ruhr Valley became, in
the nineteenth century, Europe's industrial sector: a string of grimy
mining and steel towns. Düsseldorf was its parlor: the region's banking and fashion capital, as well as its center of commerce.

Von Mende took a grand office facing the Rhine. In this region,
the Rhine does not resemble the tourist destination farther up-
stream, where the river is lined with faux-medieval castles and pic-
turesque small towns. Here it is flat and deep, a commercial water-
way filled with big barges and low-slung river craft plying the route
to the Ruhr and back. A broad waterfront park with a double row of
chestnut trees shielded von Mende from this scene. From his window he could look out onto trees and a horse path. Behind it, a vast
field dotted with bushes and linden trees ran down to the river's
edge.

His offices were financed by various West German agencies.
The government's interest was to keep tabs on the roughly 220,000
stateless foreigners left in West Germany as a result of the war.
Money initially came from the Federal Office for Protection of
the Constitution — West Germany's domestic intelligence agency
aimed at keeping track of extremists. Later, the bureau's Bavarian
branch paid von Mende an extra five thousand marks per month
to keep an eye on the émigrés in Munich and dubbed his offices
its "Northern Office." It was tasked with evaluating Munich's émigré population. He eventually added money from the Foreign Of-

fice and would collaborate closely with West Germany's refugee
ministry. Von Mende's intelligence enterprise was located on the
ground floor. His family took a spacious apartment upstairs. That
allowed him time to see his family, and for his wife, Karo, to help
out with office affairs.

As before, Karo helped her husband write letters in English. For
all his facility in languages, von Mende never felt confident in the
new international language and relied on his wife to correspond
with the outside world. It was an odd turn of events for the lin-
guistically gifted von Mende, as if his intellectual development had
stopped once he joined the Nazis. For many of his visitors, his language limitations were no problem. Amcomlib officials, many of
whom were fluent in German, visited him regularly. One such
meeting took place in 1954 when Amcomlib's political coordinator,
Ike Patch, was desperate to solve the problem of his feuding minorities. Also at the meeting was Robert F. Kelley, a retired diplomat who had taken over Amcomlib's Munich operations as his final
posting, and Professor Ballis of another major Amcomlib front organization in Munich, the Institute for the Study of the USSR.

Kelley and Patch told von Mende how disappointed they were at
their inability to build a united front of Russians and non-Russians.
In an account of the meeting von Mende wrote for his files, he slyly
noted that he knew of these troubles already, thanks to a "V-man" in
Munich. In German *V-Mann* is short for *Vertrauungsmann*, "confidence man" — in this case a person inside the U.S. organization
sending reports to von Mende.

Patch asked von Mende for advice. Von Mende said Amcomlib's
political organization had to be stronger. Radio Liberty, he noted,
had "desks" representing each of the major nationalities. They were
in charge of broadcasting in that language but also played a political role. Like the Ostministerium's national committees, Radio Liberty's broadcast services were quasi governments in exile — after all,
the personnel structure was almost identical to the Ostministerium's. This was good, he said, but they had to be more effective

— not in how they ran the radio but in their political work. Kelley agreed, according to von Mende's account. Kelley, he wrote, "considers it necessary to create a political background for Radio Liberation as for the Institute."

The key, von Mende said, was to improve the staffing of these desks and give the employees a higher profile. They had to link up better with other émigré groups around the world. Von Mende pointed to the Azerbaijani section, headed by Ismail Akber, Mecid Musazade, and Fatalibey (who would soon be murdered). That section, he said approvingly, "had a certain political authority" but could be strengthened. He knew that Akber was planning a trip to Turkey and suggested that Amcomlib pay for it so he could beef up the department by bringing in more Azerbaijani émigrés living there. Patch agreed.

Von Mende was able to give a tip to Professor Ballis of the institute. Ballis had hired one of von Mende's old protégés, Edige Kirimal, to write a report on the Crimean Tatars during the war. Von Mende noted dryly that Kirimal had already written a similar report for "the British"; the Americans, he advised Ballis, could save money if they ran such projects by von Mende — implicitly acknowledging that he knew what British intelligence had commissioned and could get copies to Ballis, saving him the expense of ordering new reports. It was, of course, a convenient way for von Mende to learn what the CIA was up to.

A year later, in 1955, Ike Patch organized a big dinner at his home in Munich. He was still getting nowhere in his efforts to unite the non-Russians and Russians. Patch made it a social occasion. He invited von Mende and his wife, Karo, down to Munich for dinner with him and his wife, who would also be joined by the U.S. consul general, E. Alan Lightner Jr., and another married couple from the consulate. Von Mende, though, was not in the mood for socializing. He wanted to talk about a common problem: how to use the émigrés more effectively.

The basic conundrum, von Mende said, is that if the émigrés

couldn't assimilate, they wouldn't find jobs and would end up as permanent outsiders in West German society. But if they became truly integrated into the local culture, they would lose their usefulness to Western countries, whose anticommunist propaganda had to depict suffering émigrés rather than well-adjusted immigrants. Von Mende was worried that mishandling the refugees would "do damage to émigré morale and western psychological warfare efforts," as Lightner wrote in his account of the meeting. The key point, von Mende urged, was to support the Soviet minorities — and forget about the Russians. Patch, who had spent two years trying to unite the two factions, could not conceive of alienating the Russians. Von Mende, though, took the old Ostministerium view: the minorities were the Soviets' Achilles' heel. If it really wanted to damage the Soviet Union, the United States should use them more forcefully.

Von Mende had a problem convincing the Americans to take his advice: he was dealing with Russophiles. Kelley and his men came at the problem as Russian speakers with long experience and fascination with that country. Intellectually, they knew of course that the Soviet Union was made up of many minorities. But in their hearts they didn't want to abandon the Russians. Others in Amcomlib, however, were embracing von Mende's position. They saw the Soviet minorities — especially the Muslims — as key tools in attacking the Soviet Union. The idea wasn't just to use them to influence Muslims in the Soviet Union, but throughout the vast Muslim world.

5

THE KEY TO THE THIRD WORLD

O NE OF THE FIVE pillars of Islam is the Hajj, the once-in-a-lifetime pilgrimage to Mecca that every Muslim is encouraged to undertake, financial means and health permitting. Devotees make their way to the holy city to see where their religion was founded and ritually relive the prophet Muhammad's struggle to bring the word of God to humanity. Reinforced in faith, the pious traveler returns home, inspiring others in the community to follow God's word.

For some pilgrims, the 1954 Hajj was a bit different. Armed with ripe tomatoes and strong lungs, two CIA-sponsored Muslims turned Mecca into the site of a Cold War showdown. Two eager young men, Rusi Nasar and Hamid Raschid, had followed the now-familiar path to the West: born in the Soviet Union and captured by the Germans, they collaborated with the Nazis and finally were recruited by U.S. intelligence. Their target: Soviet *hajjis,* who, they claimed, were engaged in spreading propaganda. Sponsored by Amcomlib, Nasar and Raschid flew to Jeddah, the Saudi Arabian city closest to Mecca. They claimed to be Turks, got seats on a bus carrying twenty-one Soviet pilgrims to Mecca, and began their work, talking to the Soviet Muslims and trying to sow seeds of doubt about their homeland. When that didn't work, they tailed their prey in Mecca, heckling them.

"You're no pilgrims; you're communist propagandists!" the American propagandists shouted. "You serve the Moscow atheists!"

Nasar and Raschid recruited local Muslims to help out. They pasted anti-Soviet posters on the walls and harassed the Soviet pilgrims at every turn. Once, they threw tomatoes at them on the streets of the holy city. Perhaps due to the Americans' work, Saudi Arabia's King Saud turned down the Soviets' request for an audience. The Soviets did get one chance to talk about the situation of Islam in the Soviet Union to a gathering of pilgrims. But as they spoke in Mecca's Grand Mosque, Raschid challenged them, asking how they could condone the Soviet Union's persecution of Muslims. One Soviet replied that the persecuted had been punished by God. Standing not far from the Kaaba, a small stone building that contains the Black Stone, said to have been given by the angel Gabriel to Abraham, Raschid bitterly criticized him.

"Haven't you a drop of shame left that you can say such things in front of the holy Kaaba itself, old as you are, with one foot in the grave, soon to stand in the presence of God?"

Nasar and Raschid's foray was portrayed in the West as part of a spontaneous uprising of disgust at the Soviet Union — two Muslim refugees poking their finger in the Soviet Goliath's eye. That was the story that ran in *Time* magazine and the *New York Times*. However, their fake Hajj was part of an aggressive U.S. policy to counter the Soviet Union in a new battleground: the third world.

By the mid-1950s, the Cold War had reached a stalemate in Europe. As the East German uprising of 1953 and the Hungarian uprising of 1956 showed, the Soviets were determined to keep control of their satellites, and the West was unable to do more than protest. Both sides had tried aggressive policies — the Soviets had squeezed West Berlin by cutting ground transport, while the United States had encouraged the Hungarian uprising. Europe, which would be the site of communism's collapse in 1989, remained the fault line during the Cold War. But for many of the intervening years the real action took place elsewhere.

In fact, the third world was arguably the Cold War's most important battleground. Incredibly bloody wars were fought there, not in Europe, and propagandists on both sides aimed their messages there. While both the U.S. allies and the Soviets continued to beam programs into each other's airspace, only in the third world did Cold War propagandists actually stand a chance of scoring meaningful points.

This part of the world has been referred to by different names: the developing world, the third world, or simply the South — because most of its countries lay in the Southern Hemisphere. Some would later consider the term "third world" pejorative, as if third-world countries had finished third in some sort of global competition. But its original meaning is simpler and more useful. As coined by the French demographer Alfred Sauvy, the name was meant to distinguish certain sectors of the globe from those directly caught up in the duel between the "first world" — the United States and its allies — and the "second world" — the Soviet Union and its satellites. Sauvy defined the third world as a vast area, encompassing most of Asia, Latin America, and Africa. The common denominator: in the 1950s most were in the early stages of industrialization and, excluding Latin America, most were emerging from colonialism. A handful of European powers — especially the British and French — had controlled these regions. Now these ancient European empires were collapsing and their territories acquiring independence. Every year, a few new countries were added to the family of nations.

The superpowers were eager to win over these countries as allies. Both the West and the Soviet Union wanted new trading partners and sources of raw materials. Although at the time many of these countries were poor, their strategic importance wasn't overlooked; think of how different the modern world would be if economic powerhouses such as South Korea, Taiwan, Singapore, Malaysia, and Thailand had become communist instead of pillars of the global trading system. And even those that remained poor could vote in the United Nations. The United States and the USSR (along with

Britain, China, and France) had veto power in the Security Council, but the two superpowers needed votes to pass resolutions. Although many Americans today disparage the UN, it was a fresher, more idealistic institution during the early Cold War. Effective or not, it was the only global forum for the showdown between Moscow and Washington.

The United States was badly handicapped in this new battle. During World War II, it had shown contempt for European colonialism. Most American thinkers assumed that Europe's colonies would gain independence after the war and that the United States would benefit — after all, it was founded by rebels fighting British colonialism. Who could sympathize more with newly independent countries than the United States?

What actually happened was different. Worried that the newly independent countries were going communist, the United States began to aid the colonial powers. After the French setback in 1954 at Dien Bien Phu, the United States sent France weapons to rebuild its colonial army. And in the Middle East, U.S. oil firms seemed to be picking up where the old colonial powers had left off. Egged on by critics in the Soviet Union, many new countries began to call the United States the new colonizer.

Both superpowers decided to strengthen their position by using Islam as a weapon. In the United States, Cold War interest in Islam predated the Eisenhower administration. Under Truman, U.S. intelligence reportedly was on the lookout for a charismatic figure who could rally Muslims in an anticommunist crusade. Truman's Psychological Strategy Board drew up a program for the Middle East that was adopted in February 1953, shortly after Eisenhower's inauguration. "No consideration of the traditional Arab mind is possible without taking into consideration the all-pervading influence of the Muslim faith on Arab thinking," the report stated. It went on to warn that — contrary to received wisdom in the West — Islam was not a natural barrier to communism. Many reformers who took power in these countries put economics before religion; that weakened the role of faith and made the region vulnerable to communism. Von Mende and his group also figured prominently in early U.S. analyses of Islam's potential. In April 1951, the CIA received a report from an informant at a major U.S. university stating that von Mende had collected key Muslims and was setting up a think tank of sorts. His efforts to rebuild the Ostministerium team were being noticed. The tightly spaced three-page report was a sign that Americans were starting to think about how to make use of Islam.

The Eisenhower administration boosted these efforts. Its overall view was that the Truman administration hadn't been aggressive or focused enough. Even as the Psychological Strategy Board was adopting the new program on the Middle East in early 1953, one of Eisenhower's chief psychological warfare strategists, Edward P. Lilly, drew up a memorandum called "The Religious Factor." It called for the United States to harness its spiritual advantage and use religion more explicitly. Lilly described the great religious revival going on in the Muslim world. For the past few decades, Muslim thinkers had been trying to figure out how to harness their religion to save their countries from colonialism and subservience to the West. Groups like the Muslim Brotherhood promised national salvation by hewing tightly to the Koran. Lilly compared it to the great Wesleyan Christian revival in eighteenth-century England. Later in 1953, he asked his staff to evaluate the feasibility of helping out with Saudi Arabia's annual Hajj; because of logistical problems, that year thousands of Muslims were left stranded and couldn't reach Mecca. In the future, could the U.S. Air Force fly them in? Lilly's adviser shot down the idea. "While the desirability of uniting the Christian world and Islam to maintain freedom of worship, etc., etc., is obvious, I do not feel that this project would help very much," the official wrote. It would be seen as "a deliberate coldblooded attempt by the infidel to organize Islam [that] would, I think, fall flat on its face and would be recognized as a bald psychological gimmick."

Yet officials remained fascinated with the idea of using religion as a weapon. In 1954, "The Religious Factor" was sent to the National Security Council. The NSC had just passed a landmark document, widely known as Paper 162/2, that called for massive retaliation against the Soviet Union. This document is often seen solely in terms of its implications for nuclear war, justifying obliteration of the enemy. But it also called for "mobilizing the spiritual and moral resources necessary to meet the Soviet threat."

The State Department, the CIA, and the U.S. Information Agency were called to action. But how ought they to proceed? The Soviet Union had upwards of thirty million Muslim citizens. For years the Soviets had worked at rooting out religion, closing mosques and persecuting those who practiced their faith; this was one reason why the Germans had an easy time recruiting Muslims to the Wehrmacht and the SS during World War II. But by the 1950s, the Soviets had reversed course, at least superficially. Mosques were reopened and imams trained. As Nasar discovered when he was in Saudi Arabia, Soviet officials had been sending Muslims on the Hajj to score points with the Muslim world. As home to ancient and important Muslim communities in Central Asia, the Soviet Union wanted to show that its Muslims were well treated and enjoyed religious freedom.

The United States had no such reservoir of Muslims. Its only such population of significant size was the Nation of Islam, but this group was at odds with the government, and its members were unlikely to find much common ground with Eisenhower and U.S. intelligence officials. And even if an alliance could be struck, involving the Nation of Islam would probably have been counterproductive; many mainstream Muslims blanched at what they saw as its heretical teachings (for example, that God manifested himself in 1930 to the group's founder; traditional Islam holds that God's final revelation was through the prophet Muhammad). The United States would have to look elsewhere for help.

For decades, Bandung had been known simply as an Indonesian resort town, a cool mountain retreat where Dutch plantation owners had built luxurious clubhouses and hotels as an escape from the tropical heat. But after a seven-day conference in 1955, it became a symbol for the third world's central role in the global Cold War.

The conference was held in the former Concordia Society, the most exclusive club that Dutch settlers had built in the wealthy colony. A grand art deco building in the center of town, it featured Italian marble floors, a great oaken bar, and crystal chandeliers. It had restaurants, meeting rooms, and a vast common area where the colony's European bosses met to socialize and discuss business. Now the two-acre complex was given over to colonialism's subject peoples. The Afro-Asian Conference — which became known as the Bandung Conference — gave third-world leaders a chance to get to know one another and find common ground. Organized and hosted by Indonesia, along with several major decolonized countries, including India, Ceylon, Egypt, Burma, and Pakistan, it was the birthplace of the Non-Aligned Movement, a group of countries that did not want to be subsumed into the Soviet or the U.S. camp. Washington saw the movement differently: a group of countries soft on communism that could be used by Moscow. China (at that point still a close Soviet ally) sent its suave premier, Zhou Enlai. In Washington, developments at the Bandung Conference were characterized as a Manichaean battle, and some of the most populous nations in the world were at stake.

Even before the conference started, the National Security Council jumped into action. In January 1955, its Operations Coordinating Board set up a Bandung working group made up of the CIA, the U.S. Information Agency, the State Department, and other offices "to place the Communist Bloc countries represented at the conference psychologically on the defensive." A few days later, the board issued a report, presenting the conference in the starkest of terms: "The Afro-Asian Conference, with Chinese Communist participation, will present the grimly amusing aspect of a spectacle of world communism holding itself up as the protagonist of local nationalist movements and anti-colonialism. Unless this plan is exposed and turned against them, the Communists will succeed in moving another step toward their goal of world domination."

Officially, President Eisenhower would send his best wishes to the delegates. Behind the scenes, however, the United States, which was not invited, would use proxies to distribute covert propaganda. The Soviet weak point was identified: Islam. As one Eisenhower administration official put it, the United States would use it to engage in "some 'Machiavellian'" engineering at Bandung: "I wonder if some of our friends at Bandung might not also have prepared in their briefcases an exposé of the East's [Russia's] 'colonial' practices in its governing of the Moslem peoples of the fictitious states of Uzbek and Turkestan. I am given to understand . . . that we have some devastating literature on how the Russians punished these 'uncooperative' peoples during and immediately after the war by removing thousands of persons from their homes to new lands and by exterminations en masse."

Indeed, "devastating literature" had been prepared. And once again it was Amcomlib's Rusi Nasar who saved the day. A year after playing the role of pilgrim, Nasar traded in his robes for a journalist's press card, landing an accreditation with the *New York Herald Tribune* in Bandung. During the conference, the U.S. embassy in Jakarta cabled back information on Nasar, saying he was working for the newspaper "this week" — implying that the job was short-term, perhaps a cover — and also claimed to be representing the National Turkestani Unity Committee, which was the most influential of the émigré groups speaking on behalf of Soviet Muslims. It was also funded and closely monitored by von Mende, one of whose paid agents, Veli Kayum, headed it. In the cable, the State Department officer said he wouldn't bother sending the material that Nasar was distributing at the conference because he assumed Washington already had seen it — implying at least familiarity with, if not a prior vetting of, Nasar's work.

The Soviets weren't fooled. The Soviet newspaper *Trud* (*Labor*) attacked Nasar "as a U.S. agent sent from West Germany to demand independent Turkestan and attack Soviet nationality policy, thus providing US 'representatives' at conference basis for 'slanderous anti-Soviet fabrications.'"

But the Munich Muslims landed some punches. In addition to Nasar's attacks, Kayum also sent an appeal on behalf of the National Turkestani Unity Committee. Kayum grandly called the committee the "supreme organ for the liberation of the Turkestanian [*sic*] people," which had been "authorized" by Turkestanis back home to speak for them. The three-page appeal made numerous factual statements about the conquest of Turkestan by the Russians/Soviets and the Chinese. The communists had carved up this region into pseudo-nation-states — in an attempt to divide and rule. Nasar's paper called for a commission to investigate the area's lack of religious freedom.

Nasar's role in the Muslim propaganda war was at times opaque. Although he appeared in the media during the Hajj and the Bandung episode, he disappeared from public view afterward. He would reappear only after the fall of the Soviet Union as an Aksakal, or community leader, of Uzbeks living in the United States. When I interviewed him in 2006, he was eighty-nine years old but spry, intelligent, and lively. He easily recalled events from half a century earlier, his nimble mind sorting through people and places.

Born in 1916 in the Uzbek district of Namangan, Nasar had direct experience of Soviet brutality. His family had been deported to Ukraine in an effort to remove the region's intelligentsia. When the war started, he avoided service and hid with a Ukrainian family. After the Germans overran the region, he heard that the great Turkic leader Mustafa Chokay was trying to unite Turkic peoples and form a government in exile. He found out that Chokay had died of typhus while inspecting a German prisoner-of-war camp. Still, Nasar joined a Turkic unit and fought for the Germans. He was wounded twice and sent to officer training school in the German province of Lothringen (now the French province of Lorraine). Nasar was later attached to the Oberkommando der Wehrmacht, the German army's supreme command, and during the last days of the war managed to escape to Austria and then Bavaria. He was sheltered by a farmer for a couple of months until the Yalta repatriations subsided. In 1946, he served as a representative to the Anti-

Bolshevik Bloc of Nations but declined an offer from his old friend
Baymirza Hayit to leave the U.S. sector for the British sector and
work for the National Turkestani Unity Committee. In the early
1950s he was recruited by the legendary CIA spymaster Archibald
Roosevelt Jr. to go to the United States. When I suggested that he
had worked — even just indirectly — for the CIA, he bristled. He
said he had engaged in "strategic studies" for the Pentagon but
never worked in covert propaganda. In fact, he was derisive of Amcomlib.

"I had no respect for them," Nasar told me. "They were pro-
Russian. They didn't care about the minorities."

Many people I talked to in the course of researching this book
have come to think of themselves as nationalist leaders who kept
the flame of independence burning during the dark days of Soviet
rule. Nasar, for example, was now a respected Uzbek leader, an el-
der. The fact that some of his work was done in the service of another nation, for its goals, doesn't fit this image. Nasar said Amcomlib tried to recruit him several times; the Amcomlib trustee
Isaac Don Levine promised him a "big villa and a car" in Munich
if he joined. But he says he scorned the group. Once when visiting
Munich he discovered that an Uzbek he knew from the war, Amin
Burdimurat, worked for Radio Liberty. Burdimurat said he couldn't
broadcast what he wanted because of Amcomlib's pro-Russian
slant. Nasar lambasted Burdimurat. "I said, You idiots, why are you
working for this organization?"

Nasar might have looked down on Amcomlib, but evidence sug-
gests he worked for it. In their articles about Nasar's Hajj in 1954,
both the *New York Times* and *Time* magazine reported he had been
sent by Amcomlib (which was depicted as a private organization).
Minutes of Amcomlib board meetings show that group members
viewed Nasar as a key to their covert propaganda strategy, calling
him a "damn good man, useful in several operations of the American Committee." They also tried to get him a full-time job.

Whatever Nasar's allegiances or fate, at the Bandung Conference,
the use of Soviet Muslim exiles who had congregated in Munich

constituted a U.S. coup. Even the White House was ecstatic. During the April 29 cabinet meeting Secretary of State John Foster Dulles said everyone had initially assumed the communists would dominate Bandung. In the end, U.S. efforts had paid off, and the tables had turned. "Secretary Dulles considered it quite significant that [the Chinese premier] Chou [Enlai] made no attempt to defend the USSR at the conference — even though the Soviet Union came under intense criticism on 'colonialism' charges."

Washington wasn't alone in recognizing Bandung's importance. Most of the major players from Munich appeared there, from leaders of the Muslim Brotherhood to freelance intelligence operators like the U.S. novelist Ahmad Kamal. Of the Munich cast, only von Mende wasn't present. But his people were, and they sent him detailed analyses of the conference and its participants. Even though Bandung went better than expected for the West, von Mende was growing worried. The United States seemed to be trying to poach his organizations. Nasar, for example, had showed up at Bandung claiming to represent the National Turkestani Unity Committee. Von Mende had sent Kayum to the U.S. consulate in Munich to find out why Nasar had claimed to represent Kayum's group. Kayum told the Americans that he knew that Nasar was on their payroll. The Americans were shocked that von Mende knew their financial arrangement with Nasar and brought it up a few weeks later during a meeting with von Mende.

"Prof. von Mende said that last year Nasar had also been at Mecca and had indicated there that he was sent by the Americans, that he was known to have received 600 dollars from the CIA representative in the U.S. Embassy at Jeddah. Prof. von Mende said that he was telling us this because he felt that it was against U.S. interests to have this kind of an operation bungled."

Von Mende probably didn't care if the operations were bungled. It was who the Americans were recruiting that rankled him. The two Western allies were headed for a clash that would open the door to a third force.

6

LEARNING THEIR LESSON

B Y THE MID-1950S, most of the displaced persons in Germany had found homes. Foreign prisoners had been sent home, Jewish survivors had emigrated, many to the United States or Israel, while millions of ethnic Germans had been resettled, mostly in West Germany. Only one major group remained living in camps: stateless foreigners with no place to go. A German newspaper dubbed them "homo barrackensis," people consigned to live in camps. And they were, by and large, Muslims. One social worker visiting a group of two hundred Albanians in the southern Munich suburb of Ottobrunn said they lived eight to a room, without electricity and with the only source of water a six-hundred-meter walk away. Tuberculosis had infected several of the children. A sign outside the building said DILAPIDATED: ENTER AT OWN RISK.

Not all Muslims in Munich lived in such conditions. Many had found homes, started businesses, or begun working with the American Committee. But many others needed help. To their rescue came Ibrahim Gacaoglu, a gruff, poorly spoken, but honest imam. During the war, Gacaoglu had been a trusted Muslim headman. Born in the North Caucasus in 1903, he was fiercely loyal to the Germans. Most of the Germans' Muslim soldiers had been young, many of them teenagers. But Gacaoglu was old enough to be their father. Simple and poorly educated, he relied on friends to write letters for him. Yet he was pious and his age commanded respect.

In 1953, he founded a religious group called Islam: The Moslem Religious Society in Western Europe. Its goal was to keep the religion alive among the estimated three thousand Muslims still living in German camps for displaced persons. When Gacaoglu formed the group Islam, he said his goal was to prevent the soldiers from losing their loyalty to Germany; the camps, he thought, were so squalid that they were causing many to give up and return to the Soviets.

Von Mende initially supported Gacaoglu's new group, but for reasons that are not clear he distanced himself relatively quickly. It could be that Gacaoglu seemed too crude and unsophisticated to lead Munich's Muslims or simply that von Mende didn't yet see the importance of cultivating Islam as a force to use in the Cold War — although he had helped many Muslims, he had done so as part of a broad effort to help all émigrés. Or perhaps U.S. officials offered Gacaoglu more money and lived closer at hand — von Mende was up in Düsseldorf, while Amcomlib was right there in Munich. Within a couple of years, Gacaoglu was handing out food packages from the U.S. humanitarian organization CARE. Some Muslims said he had received the packets from the U.S. consulate in Munich. He was also distributing goods from the Tolstoy Foundation, a charity aimed at helping Soviet refugees that also had links to the intelligence community. By 1955, Amcomlib was funding Gacaoglu directly. It paid for the community's Bairam, a major event on the Muslim calendar. Gacaoglu held the festival in the Deutsches Museum, a cavernous building of exhibits that trumpeted German industrial and scientific prowess. He invited scores of Muslims and attracted local media attention.

Gacaoglu seemed like a good catch. A Chechen who taught at the CIA school in Bavaria strongly backed his fellow Caucasian. Gacaoglu also commanded a wide following because of his charitable work. Alex Melbardis, who was Amcomlib's deputy head of émigré relations at the time, said Gacaoglu once called him at 4 A.M. to ask for a lift to visit a dying man outside Munich. Melbardis was impressed by his dedication and hopped in his car to pick up Gacaoglu for a two-hour drive to the village where the man lived. "Gacaoglu administered the last rites," he said. "He was a decent man."

Soon, Gacaoglu was firmly in the U.S. camp. "We helped him and he helped us," Melbardis said. "He did propaganda for us." The United States now had a man who could lead Munich's Muslims — a counterbalance to the Muslims used by the Soviets. There was an inherent absurdity to this effort: Moscow controlled millions of Kazakhs, Kyrgyz, Tatars, and Azerbaijanis; at best, Bonn and Washington might claim a few hundred or thousand in Munich as under their sway. But in the media age all that mattered was to have a spokesperson who could attend the Hajj or a conference, declare himself a Muslim leader from the West, talk up the freedoms back home, and criticize Soviet repression. Gacaoglu was at least credible and clearly had a following in Munich, where hundreds had signed up as members of his group.

But dissatisfaction lingered. Gacaoglu might have been a decent man and able to connect with the Muslims in the camps, but did he have the authority to credibly represent Western Muslims on the world stage? Could he stand up as their leader and attack the Soviets? The staff at Amcomlib's headquarters in New York were skeptical. They began casting about for other options — looking for a quick-witted, charismatic figure who could work in the fast-paced propaganda wars.

At first, Robert H. Dreher had little use for Muslims, but by the late 1950s, he would become the man most closely identified with cultivating them in Munich. Early in the decade he was a confirmed Russophile, reveling in aspects of that culture that matched his own interests. Tall and good-looking, he had joined Amcomlib as a way to get back to Germany and the good times he had known there as a CIA man. He spoke Russian, liked vodka, and could keep up with the best of his Russian friends at dancing. But Islam? Like most Amcomlib officials, Dreher had no idea what to make of it.

That would soon change, thanks to the influence of one of his colleagues, B. Eric Kuniholm. Kuniholm was senior to Dreher and, initially at least, more influential. He headed Amcomlib's political wing, one of its three main branches of operations, along with the radio station and the institute. The political operations oversaw Amcomlib's covert propaganda efforts, which were increasingly directed toward Muslims around the world.

Kuniholm had been born to Swedish and Finnish parents and was fluent in both those languages as well as German and Russian. His cosmopolitan background — both his facility with languages and his outlook — made him special among Amcomlib's U.S. staff. Kuniholm was skeptical of Russians and doubted they would overthrow the Soviet Union. He thought the minorities were the key. He often spent time with non-Russians, inviting Tatars, Uzbeks, and others back home for dinner, drinks, and stories about the homeland. West German intelligence pegged Kuniholm as a "splittist" — eager to split the Soviet Union by pitting the non-Russians against the Russians.

Kuniholm had long experience in intelligence work overseas. While working for the U.S. government, he had observed and reported on the Nazis' anti-Jewish pogrom in 1938, called Kristallnacht, and witnessed antimonarchy riots in Tehran, where he had supervised Lend-Lease shipments to the Soviet Union during the war. Later he had observed protests in Palestine as the state of Israel was being born. At Amcomlib his work was more strategic, and he rarely went abroad. Staffers recall him as involved in setting policy and parameters.

Dreher was Kuniholm's opposite, an odd combination of glad-handing charm and ideological fervor. Born in 1916, Dreher had grown up in a Pennsylvania family of German descent. The Great

Depression shaped him: he was thirteen when it started, and he remembered counting every penny. He put himself through Lafayette College, working forty hours per week. He graduated with honors in 1938. Like many Americans who faced hardship during this era, he was attracted to the Soviet Union's promise of justice and welfare. He took a job with Standard Oil in New Jersey. The next year, he was awed by the World's Fair in New York. His favorite pavilion was the Soviets'. "From that time on, I followed things Soviet with an extremely 'educated' interest," he later wrote, "devouring the current press accounts and books, practically all of which were strongly — even ridiculously, as it later appeared — pro-Soviet in their slant."

Dreher began a graduate degree in engineering at Columbia University but joined the navy when World War II began. His engineering skills landed him a desk job in Jacksonville, Florida, where he worked for the supervisor of shipbuilding. As the war wound down, the navy issued a circular soliciting volunteers to learn Russian. Dreher signed on and went to language school in Boulder, Colorado. He completed the course in 1946. By then, the war was over and he could have been discharged. But just then, the navy's liaison with the Soviet Union in the port of Odessa resigned. Dreher was asked if he'd extend his service.

"Would I?" Dreher replied, and he was off to the Soviet Union — just as the Cold War was gaining momentum.

It was there that Dreher became briefly famous. Odessa was the Black Sea port through which most of the United Nations' humanitarian aid to the Soviet Union was channeled. The country was devastated by the war. U.S. ships delivered most of the supplies — hence the navy's role in supervising its flotilla. But tensions were rising rapidly between the two former allies. While in Moscow, wrapping up some paperwork before returning home, Dreher was detained after a brief scuffle and quickly expelled from the Soviet Union. The incident was front-page news in the *New York Times*. The United States claimed Dreher had been set up. *Pravda* said he was a spy.

The Soviet allegations can't be dismissed as propaganda. Dreher had served in the Office of Naval Intelligence and by his own account had spent much of his time in Odessa driving around the countryside, picking up hitchhikers, and generally befriending anyone he could find. In Moscow he romanced a medical student, getting a tour of her research facility. He gave accounts of his forays to the top naval man in the embassy, Admiral Leslie Stevens.

"I had more direct, intimate contact with more people over a wide range of education, occupational, economic, and political strata in the Soviet Union during these critical post-war years than any other American, or possibly any other foreigners from any country. My dossier with the MGB [forerunner of the KGB] was undoubtedly the fattest of all contemporary foreigners," he wrote in the opening chapter of an unpublished account of his Russian adventures.

Years later, when he wrote of his arrest, he said he was sure the hitchhikers had been later interrogated — in other words, he knew he had been tailed. As for the medical student, he figured she would be arrested for her indiscretion, and in fact she was. She spent eight years in the gulag, fixing roads and eating barley gruel. Dreher blamed the arrests not on his own indiscretions but on the Soviets.

The experience turned him into one of Amcomlib's most hardened cold warriors. After his expulsion, he returned to Washington to head naval intelligence's USSR desk. Three years later, in 1951, he joined the CIA. On his CIA application, his reason for leaving the navy is stated as a wish "to contribute more directly to liberation" — the new U.S. policy of aggressively overturning, not containing, communism. He joined the CIA at a time when it was still the front line of the next great struggle. A Roosevelt Democrat, his political liberalism wasn't at odds with covert operations. He saw it as a means to defeating a totalitarian state.

His résumé seemed tailor-made for a job in covert operations. It wasn't just his Russian and, to a lesser degree, his German language skills or the background in military intelligence. It was his personal life, which on the application seemed a blank slate.

He had only three relatives: father, mother, and sister, all born in the United States. He never married. He had never joined a political party or anything more controversial than Phi Beta Kappa and the American Society of Mechanical Engineers. He had never even taken a loan. Under "credit references" in his CIA application he apologetically explained that he'd plunked down cash for his 1948 Chevy.

CIA background checks, however, apparently weren't too thorough back then. On his CIA application form, Dreher wrote no in answer to the question about anything in his life history that might be potentially compromising. Yet Dreher was an inveterate womanizer, often boasting about his conquests with staff and friends. That in itself wasn't disqualifying, but during an earlier trip to Munich, he had started a special affair: a long-running relationship with an ethnic Chinese woman from Southeast Asia. She bore him a daughter, a secret both kept until Dreher was an old man. Women and liberation were the twin poles of his life.

The CIA sent Dreher back to Munich for a year, but he soon returned to the United States. He had been given a job in New York with the newly formed Amcomlib, which was headed by his old boss from Moscow, Admiral Stevens. He was essentially seconded to Amcomlib as its CIA liaison man — he kept his CIA rank and pay and a few years later would return to the agency. At Amcomlib, Dreher was given a high-ranking job — head of the Radio Programming Support Division — vetting what was produced in Munich and making sure the right message got out. The salary was also generous for that era: $10,000 a year, one of Amcomlib's highest.

Dreher joined Kuniholm, working out of Amcomlib's headquarters in New York. The offices were located on East 45th Street, just off the advertising center of the world, Madison Avenue. Down the street was the Roosevelt Hotel, where staffers sometimes went for a drink after work. The offices themselves were anodyne: outside, a fourteen-story gray brick building; inside, subdued carpets, quiet secretaries, and humming fluorescent lights. Everyone wore a conservative suit. One Jewish staffer remembers it looking like a "WASPish bank," which made him feel uncomfortable.

Although Amcomlib officers in Munich had considerable lee-way, New York — especially Kuniholm and Dreher — set the tone and strategy. That led to an almost inevitable cleft between on-the-ground operations in Munich and headquarters in New York. Staff-ers in Munich thought the New York bureau was out of touch — too hard-line anticommunist and unable to understand the complexi-ties of dealing with people from other cultures. That would become especially pronounced as Amcomlib turned its attention to Islam.

But Dreher chafed at living in 1950s America. He took a flat in a brownstone walkup in Greenwich Village, living a bachelor's life and angling to get back overseas. He also had professional reasons for returning to Europe. The radio, he thought, was doing well, but the covert operations there were weak. They needed beefing up. Ex-actly how he would accomplish this wasn't yet clear. It would be up to his boss, Kuniholm, to chart Amcomlib's strategy.

In the early years of the Cold War, CIA men like Bob Dreher were far from unusual. The agency comprised two factions: the profes-sionals, who had served in the wartime intelligence agencies, and the eccentric newcomers. Of the second group, many had seen ac-tion in World War II but were recruited to the CIA with a specific purpose in mind: to jump-start an agency that was already seen as staid and overly bureaucratic. Dreher was firmly in the latter camp.

This group's founder and inspiration was Frank Wisner, one of the legendary figures in U.S. intelligence. Wisner came from a wealthy family in Mississippi and worked as a Wall Street lawyer before joining the navy in World War II. He quickly switched to the Office of Strategic Services, the wartime intelligence agency, and witnessed firsthand how the Soviets overran southeastern Europe in the waning days of the war. After he was demobilized, he went back to Wall Street, where the former OSS officer Allen Dulles was also working. The two would meet regularly for lunch and bemoan the U.S. government's dismemberment of its intelligence services. A friend who sat in on one lunch remembers them as "pining to get back . . . They were both great romantics who saw themselves as saviors of the world."

In 1947, Secretary of State Dean Acheson recruited Wisner to join the State Department and keep an eye on Soviet activity in eastern Europe. Wisner bought a farm in Maryland and a townhouse in Georgetown. Compact, powerfully built, and uniformly described as brilliant, he became a star of dinner parties among the Washington elite, where he argued vigorously for action against the Soviets. Like many in Washington, he felt that the United States needed a new agency to do this, one beholden to no politician or civil servant, one that could match the Soviets dirty trick for dirty trick.

In fact, the United States had just such an agency — the newly formed CIA had an Office of Special Operations, made up of wartime intelligence veterans. But the CIA reported to the National Security Council, meaning it was held accountable by, and its actions could be traced to, the U.S. government. Even though the OSO had just successfully intervened in Italian elections to prevent that country from going communist, it was seen as engaging in espionage, not political activism. Maybe more important, Wisner despised the OSO, saying its agents were too staid — perhaps because they were accountable for their actions. He called them a "bunch of old washerwomen exchanging gossip while they rinse through the dirty linen." He wanted action.

Wisner began to lobby for his new agency and in 1948 he got it — the innocuously named Office of Policy Coordination. The office was housed in the CIA but reported only to the secretaries of state and defense. Wisner was put in charge, instantly becoming one of the most powerful men in the U.S. government. He raced to recruit émigrés in Europe — an army of disgruntled anticommunists, or so Wisner imagined them, eager to fight in the hot war just around the corner. To run the operation, Wisner sought out unusual men. He recruited many from Wall Street, believing they had the risk-taking mentality needed to get things done. He also recruited extensively from Ivy League schools and paid accordingly. Wisner convinced Washington officials that his team was composed of the elite, and they automatically got higher pay grades. The CIA's parking lot reflected this distinction: the old-school agents drove Chevrolets and Fords; Wisner's men drove Jaguars and MGs.

Improbable plans were hatched and sometimes carried out. At the height of the Korean War, Wisner's OPC men hijacked a Norwegian freighter heading for North Korea. But Wisner was sometimes spectacularly unsuccessful. Once, he spent $400,000 on a Polish officer who pledged to fly the latest-model Soviet fighter over to Munich. Instead, the officer spent the money in a Munich hotel on champagne and prostitutes. Bizarre undertakings were commonplace. For example, just to show that they could do anything, two OPC agents blocked off the intersection of Madison Avenue and 42nd Street, dug a giant hole, and walked off. "It was prankster stuff," one veteran recalled. Wisner boasted that his OPC was like a "mighty Wurlitzer," an organ on which he could play anything, from diplomacy to military action. His Wurlitzer was amplified and blasted through two giant speakers: Radio Liberty and Radio Free Europe, the largest covert operations of their era.

The organization Wisner headed was no secret cabal. The small group of politicians, officials, and journalists who held sway back in 1940s Washington were all in broad agreement that the United States had to fight the Soviets. This was not the age of George Smiley, the fictional spy in John le Carré's novels, a jaded and spent figure working in a milieu of ambiguities. This was a confident and ambitious group of men sure that they could fight Stalin just as U.S. citizen soldiers had defeated Hitler. Now enthusiastic amateurs were ready to go up against the KGB. All they needed were the right allies among the émigrés.

In September 1955, Eric Kuniholm arrived in Istanbul and reserved a berth at Cook Wagon-Lits for the night train to Ankara. Then he set off for the famous Restaurant Abdullah for a quick supper. "And then all hell broke loose," he wrote back to his colleagues in New York. Protests against Greece's presence on the island of Cyprus had morphed into xenophobic, anti-Christian riots. At first only Greek businesses were torched, but by the end of the evening six churches had been gutted. The cathedral next to the Naval Museum burned all night, lighting up the Bosporus. Just as he had many times before when witnessing violence, Kuniholm wrote up a coolly analytical report. The protests, he wrote, had not been as spontaneous as the government claimed. They had been highly organized by rabid anti-Greek nationalist groups. His proposed solution was more police.

It was an attitude much appreciated by Kuniholm's contacts in the Turkish secret police, who likewise thought more law and order was needed. Kuniholm was in Turkey on a sensitive trip. He wanted to line up Muslims to join Amcomlib's covert propaganda battle in the third world. But Turkey was worried that U.S. support could embolden émigrés to demand that the Turkish government help them. The Turks supported the anticommunist goals of Kuniholm's work but wanted to be sure that the émigrés didn't get out of control and start their own riots. Kuniholm assured them that the work would be discreet, covert, and quiet. The Turks were especially concerned about religion. After the overthrow of the Ottoman Empire, Turkey had adopted a militantly secular ideology. When Kuniholm met the interior minister, he was warned against getting involved with the Muslim Congress — one of several bodies being formed at this time, by mostly Arab Muslims. Acceptable, the general said, would be a "research institute" that would mask a CIA-run "Action Committee" to push more vigorous anti-Soviet actions. The Turks also congratulated Kuniholm for having sent Rusi Nasar to Bandung earlier in the year. That Nasar's success was mostly due to his emphasis on Islam was left unspoken.

Kuniholm's six-week trip occurred after Amcomlib had basically given up on the old paradigm of coercing Russian and non-Russian émigrés to work together. The goal had been to set up a front group to run Radio Liberty, making it seem like a grassroots creation rather than an intelligence construct. That had failed spectacularly, despite the efforts of seasoned diplomats such as Ike Patch. Clearly the United States needed to spend more time thinking about how to harness Islam — and this, without a significant Muslim population of its own to be recruited. Kuniholm's trip was a chance to take stock and formulate new ideas. He spent nearly six weeks on the road and apparently met nearly every émigré leader in Paris, Munich, Istanbul, and Ankara. Most were Muslims.

One such key leader was Said Shamil, whose family was one of the most famous Dagestani clans. In the nineteenth century Said Shamil's grandfather, Imam Shamil, had led the resistance to Russian expansion into the Caucasus, fighting a bitter civil war. He eventually surrendered, was placed under house arrest, and was later granted permission to retire to Mecca. The elderly Shamil bought huge tracts of land in Medina, which the family kept after he died. By the twentieth century the land was worth a small fortune, and the family was rich. They moved to Switzerland and had little contact with those back home in the Caucasus.

Said Shamil had also participated in the Nazi efforts to harness Islam. After the war, he returned home to Geneva and was active in efforts to unite Muslims around the world. By 1955, he was close to the Americans. The Amcomlib officer Alex Melbardis summarized how the Americans viewed him: "The family was really famous and wealthy. We wanted him on our side."

U.S. intelligence documents indicate that Shamil provided information on émigré leaders, indicating he was at least cooperating with, if not working directly for, the Americans. Shamil's expat lifestyle, however, led many to question whether he could really help the United States. Kuniholm reported that Shamil had lived in the Caucasus but since the communist takeover hadn't been back home; he'd floated between Medina, Mecca, Beirut, Cairo, and, of course, Geneva. On Kuniholm's last night in Istanbul, Shamil hosted a big dinner for him. It was fun, but hardly a meal one would expect from a serious Muslim leader.

"I do not mind a succession of vodkas," Kuniholm wrote

back home. "But I object to vodka being served in water tumblers, *full.*"

In Munich, Kuniholm again met with Muslims. Almost all the people involved in efforts to harness Islam were present, including Ali Kantemir, whom Kuniholm humorously described as "as astute as ever, with the same nose for intrigue," and Ahmet Nabi Magoma, "an old revolutionary, who was in the British pay for long years." Both also had long-standing contacts with U.S. intelligence. He also met Garip Sultan and other Amcomlib employees with Radio Liberty. They pleaded for more leeway to take "political action" — Amcomlib code for covert propaganda action — like the operations that had succeeded during the Hajj and at Bandung, instead of just broadcasting anti-Soviet propaganda. Kuniholm told them that political action would be coordinated through Istanbul, where Amcomlib was establishing better contacts.

Gacaoglu was next on Kuniholm's list of influential émigrés. Even though Amcomlib had begun to back him, Kuniholm was unimpressed. "Mr. Gacaoglu of the 'Islam' Society then called, along with a couple of his henchmen, to plead for help for his group. I gave him little encouragement. I do not believe that we should have anything to do with this unsavory character, whose past is filled with much that is suspicious, and whose reputation in the Middle East is definitely bad. He is an uncultured 'low-brow' who is trying to capitalize on his religion."

Kuniholm was probably unfairly harsh in this assessment. But clearly, like von Mende, Kuniholm was looking for someone more modern in style, more charismatic. Gacaoglu, poorly educated and simple, didn't present the face the Americans felt could take their case to the Muslim world. Kuniholm also mentioned how Munich's Muslims espoused a particular dream: to build a mosque. It was the first mention of this goal, but Kuniholm considered it a pie-in-the-sky plan and dismissed it.

The clubroom of Munich's Bayerischer Hof hotel was, in the 1950s, wood paneled and lined with beer steins and hunting trophies —

the sort of place guests would frequent for a light meal, a heavy Bavarian beer, and a bit of rustic Germany in the middle of a bustling city. In August 1956 it was set up for another kind of theater. Alex Melbardis and other Amcomlib employees spent the better part of a day hanging Central Asian rugs on the walls and replacing the beer steins with porcelain plates decorated with Islamic motifs. Tables were set with exotic fruit. Even the napkins had been chosen with care: they were green, the color representing Islam.

More than forty-five journalists crowded into the room for the show. The host was Gacaoglu, who greeted the guests and then introduced Garip Sultan as a member of his society. Gacaoglu said, in his barely comprehensible German, that he had just been on the Hajj and had information to report about the sorry state of Soviet Islam. Then he turned the floor over to the smooth-talking Sultan.

Sultan told of his trip to Mecca, accompanied on the Hajj by Gacaoglu and another Radio Liberty employee, Veli Zunnun, of the station's Uzbek desk. Sultan ripped the Soviets for misusing the Hajj for propaganda purposes. He claimed that the Soviet *hajjis* were government employees and that some of them were sent as spies.

Of course none of the journalists in the ballroom could know that Sultan was not really a member of Gacaoglu's group, or that it, in turn, was funded by Amcomlib, which in turn was a CIA front. Instead, they did as expected: they relayed the propaganda to the public. The two most important Munich newspapers printed articles on the Hajj, including a long feature that recounted Sultan's exploits. A few weeks earlier, on their way back to Munich via Istanbul, Sultan and Zunnun had been interviewed by the newspaper *Milliyet*, which also published a long piece on their trip.

Amcomlib was happy with Sultan's performance. Robert F. Kelley, Amcomlib's boss in Germany, gave him a glowing commendation for "an outstanding contribution to the anti-Bolshevik struggle" that "provides us with a much better understanding of the growing communist menace in the Near East."

Behind the scenes, however, Amcomlib was concerned. In an internal account of his trip, Sultan reported that public opinion was firmly in the Soviet camp. "Here one should cite the notion of a simple, old Arab who works at the Hajj Administration as a servant, about the USSR," Sultan wrote. "When I told him from where I had come, he said at once, 'Moscow is good. There are also our Moslems there. The Hajjis from the USSR comes [sic] to Mecca every years [sic]. England, France, America are all unbelievers. They are our enemies.'" More serious was Amcomlib's dearth of "assets." Sultan and Zunnun had almost not made it to the Hajj because they'd started late and had to be bailed out by Said Shamil, who was in Saudi Arabia at his family's home. He had intervened with local authorities to allow the two men to proceed to Mecca. Without his assistance, the propaganda pilgrims would have returned home.

The press conference was another near debacle. Sultan had been recruited to lead it because Gacaoglu's German was too poor. But Sultan didn't look like a religious leader. He came across to everyone who met him as secular. He dressed sharply and was clean-shaven; everyone knew he loved to dance and drink the occasional vodka. Plus, he would soon be sent back to the United States to work in Amcomlib's "Special Projects" department. Amcomlib needed someone new. Men like Ike Patch were supposed to be marshaling the émigrés for covert action, but he didn't seem to get the job done. Back in New York, Kuniholm and Dreher watched him impatiently. Dreher, especially, was eager for another stint in Munich, where he hoped to put rollback theories into practice. The problem was more urgent than ever.

Von Mende, Amcomlib's one-time friend, was developing his own plan to win over Munich's Muslims. Unlike Kuniholm, von Mende wouldn't ignore the Munich Muslims' desire for a mosque. It would be his top priority.

7

"A POLITICALLY SMART ACT": THE MOSQUE IS CONCEIVED

I N 1956, GERHARD VON MENDE received a memo from Theodor Oberländer, head of the West German refugee ministry, outlining an important national goal, one that required help from an unlikely source: Munich's Muslims. West Germany was home to thousands of émigrés, Oberländer wrote, but many had been recruited by foreign intelligence groups such as Amcomlib. This could not be allowed to continue, he said, because West Germany needed these same Muslims. One day soon communism would fall, and they would return home to be future leaders of their homelands. There, they would help achieve West Germany's supreme foreign policy goal: reunification with East Germany and the recovery of vast stretches of German land lost to Poland and the Soviet Union after the war.

"The success of the exiles will positively influence carrying out German goals in their home states." Then Oberländer outlined those goals, writing in a vein that had an unusually strong revanchist tone: "The goals of the political exiles lie in a complex and mutual relationship to the German efforts for reunification and lifting the effects of the Potsdam Agreement in relation to the Oder-Neisse border."

Behind the bureaucratese was a crystal-clear message: West Germany wanted to redraw its border and regain its lost eastern territories, which lay beyond the Oder and Neisse rivers. For decades, the Oder-Neisse border was the most sensitive topic in German foreign policy. The two rivers separated East Germany from Poland. It had become the border after the 1945 Potsdam agreement had carved up Germany. The four major powers — Britain, France, the United States, and the USSR — each got a zone of occupation. Later, the Soviet zone would become East Germany, and the three western powers' zones would unite to form West Germany.

Less well known is that two other zones of occupation also existed, both of them east of the Oder and the Neisse. One was administered by Poland. It encompassed large parts of Prussia, Silesia, and Pomerania, and included Germany's third-largest city, Breslau (now known by its Polish name, Wroclaw). In addition, the Soviets received a slice of Germany, the eastern half of East Prussia, including the German city of Königsberg (renamed Kaliningrad).

Unlike the other zones, these two were never returned to German control after the war. Instead, they were annexed permanently by the Poles and the Soviets. The Poles didn't benefit much; the Soviets had already annexed parts of eastern Poland, so the German lands just compensated Poland for what it had lost. German territories, which had sprawled into eastern Europe for centuries, now ended at the Oder and the Neisse, which ran straight from the Baltic down to the Czechoslovakian border.

If it all looked neat on an armchair strategist's map, this redrawing of central Europe's borders added to the misery caused by the war. The lost German territories had been overwhelmingly populated by ethnic Germans. Within a matter of months, these people were murdered or brutally expelled, first by the Red Army and then by state-sanctioned pogroms. Together with ethnic Germans fleeing other countries, more than thirteen million German refugees, one of the largest refugee flows in modern times, were forcibly driven from their homes. Most ended up in what became West Germany, but hundreds of thousands died along the way.

Oberländer was the chief spokesman for these *Vertriebene*, the "expellees" or the "driven off." In the 1950s and '60s, they fought a rearguard action against those West Germans who wanted to establish diplomatic relations with the Soviet Union or recognize the Oder-Neisse border. Oberländer headed a key political party that kept attitudes firmly fixed on loss and grievance.

This was the same Oberländer who had participated in Hitler's failed beer-hall putsch of 1923 and who had led one of the first Wehrmacht units made up of Soviet minorities. Born in the Baltic, he realized the value of the non-Russian minorities. He had participated in pogroms against Jews but opposed the Nazis' policy toward the occupied territories—like von Mende, he thought Germany should be the non-Russians' ally. For that he had lost his position in the party and his military command. That setback became a blessing after the war, allowing him to position himself as a victim of the Nazis instead of a party insider who had fallen out because of infighting. That, along with his party's voting power, was enough to convince West Germany's first chancellor, Konrad Adenauer, to make Oberländer the cabinet minister in charge of refugees.

Oberländer was probably the farthest-right member of the West German government, and in later years he came to be considered the personification of the young democracy's Nazi roots. The memo he sent to von Mende illustrated this far-right bent: he wanted Germany's borders redrawn and von Mende's cooperation in keeping a firm grip on the assets he thought could help achieve that—the foreigners living on West German soil who had fought for Germany during the war.

Von Mende had most of the émigré groups firmly in hand. He financed Bulgarians and Rumanians, Ukrainians and Czechs. But the previous year's events showed that he was losing control of the Muslims. Compared to Amcomlib, his bureau was puny, and most of the Muslims were working for the Americans. Kuniholm's trip to Turkey and Europe emphasized Washington's more ambitious goal: using Muslims in its global propaganda wars.

West Germany and the United States were firm allies during the forty-year-long Cold War. America had supported West Germany's creation and its integration into the world community. West Germany became a steadfast military ally, providing the bulk of troops in the West's military alliance.

But the relationship wasn't always smooth, and this was a particularly trying time. West Germany had just regained full sovereignty. The country was making overtures to the Soviet Union, causing the United States to worry that it might accept a deal like the one offered to Austria: reunification of its eastern and western sections in exchange for neutrality. U.S officials even thought West Germany might expel Amcomlib and Radio Free Europe from Munich and discussed how to evacuate staff.

Oberländer's plan began to worry Washington. The U.S. intelligence community needed the Soviet minorities in Munich to staff Radio Liberty and Radio Free Europe — and to undertake covert activities. But this arrangement would fall apart if Bonn gained control of the minorities. As U.S. officials saw it, the driving force behind this policy was Oberländer and the diplomats in the Foreign Office, such as Otto Bräutigam, who, like Oberländer, had been heavily involved in the Nazi movement.

"They are not Nazis in the sense of seeking to put *Mein Kampf* back on every table in Germany," the State Department stated in a report on the group, "but they set the German national cause, in nationalist-imperialist fashion, higher than all other causes."

"Their chief agent is Professor Dr. Gerhard von Mende and their chief governmental tool is von Mende's Office for Homeless Aliens," a classified State Department cable said. "The von Mende mission is not concerned with the fate of 'satellite' peoples but with the fate of the Germans. He and his principals have no intention of allowing 'inexperienced' Americans to arbitrate in this area." The cable also stated that von Mende had been dealing with undemocratic émigré groups — "some of them rather shabby collaborators with the Nazis."

The CIA noted that von Mende had helped set up a group to help the émigrés — the Aid Society of Former Volunteer Units. It was made up of the German officers who had led the Soviet minority troops during the war and now were concerned about their fate in West Germany. Von Mende ran the group out of his offices in Düsseldorf, according to the CIA. While that might be an exaggeration, the group certainly did exist and its records show that it was made up primarily of ex-Wehrmacht and ex-SS officers who had led the minorities. And von Mende did have close ties to it. By late 1955, the CIA had decided to take action against the man they'd once tried to recruit.

"I have built up quite a small connection file on this gentleman and his associates," a CIA agent wrote in von Mende's file. "Perhaps we could launch an operation to subvert one of his people with the aim of getting microphotographs of his information files . . ."

But a few months later, the agent had another idea. Lodged in U.S. government files was a note from Amcomlib's Ike Patch, who a couple of months earlier had talked to von Mende. Patch reported that von Mende had been upset that West Germany was about to establish diplomatic relations with the Soviet Union. The unnamed CIA agent saw an opening: "I was 'stalking' von Mende with the idea of having his place and his files in Düsseldorf ransacked and possibly photographed but the latest information from you seems to me to indicate that we would do better to try to recruit him." The agent noted that this would be the third time in eleven years that U.S. intelligence would make overtures to von Mende, ruefully noting that they had a deal all but sealed in 1949. "The case was suddenly dropped at Munich because von Mende employed a methodical approach to the problem and [the CIA office in] Munich was immersed in a program of helter-skelter, planless recruitment of 'agents.'"

This time the CIA would do it von Mende's way. Attached to the formal recruitment plan was a list of von Mende's agents, including, of course, Veli Kayum. The agent wrote that Kayum had outed Rusi Nasar as having received CIA money for distributing U.S. propaganda during the Hajj. The CIA kept close tabs on von Mende and in March 1956 noted that the East German secret police and intelligence service, the Stasi (known by its German abbreviation, MfS), was seeking a map of his office. "This could be an indication that the MfS has some plans for Gerhard," the agent wrote.

Then, in early 1957, the CIA offices in Germany were asked to comment on Soviet plans to recruit Muslims. The request seems to have come after two U.S.-backed agents working with Muslims were exposed as spies; the CIA was trying to trace any further leaks in its operations. The Munich office responded by again proposing von Mende. "If von Mende is recruited, he can readily produce a 'Who's Who' of Moslems." But von Mende didn't seem to be interested in working for the Americans. Perhaps reflecting West Germany's growing self-confidence, von Mende was angry. He saw the minorities, including the Muslims, as *his* assets. And he had a plan to win them back.

In late March 1956, Nurredin Namangani landed in Munich. Survivor of the Soviet gulag, imam of an SS division, holder of high military awards, he was an ideal choice to bring Munich's Muslims into line.

At least that seems to have been von Mende's reasoning. In keeping with Oberländer's desire to gain control of the émigrés, von Mende had invited Namangani to Germany to head a new office aimed at unifying Germany's Muslims. Until then, the only organization in Germany that could claim to do so was Gacaoglu's Islam group, but it was now under strong U.S. influence. Namangani was one of von Mende's men, with a proven wartime record of loyalty to Germany.

Indeed, as Namangani's appointment was pushed through the bureaucracy, his long service to Germany appeared to be his main qualification. This was not a man who would hand out CARE packages for the Americans or front their press conferences. He was indeed a political creature, but one who would loyally serve West Germany, a salaried employee of the state.

Von Mende had been planning Namangani's arrival for a while. Earlier in 1956, Oberländer's ministry had contacted von Mende about funding Gacaoglu's group. Of all the exile groups in Germany, the Muslims seemed the most disorganized, and the ministry wondered if Gacaoglu wouldn't be the logical choice to unite them. When Gacaoglu wrote the Bavarian social-affairs ministry a year earlier asking for money, the officials noted that "the majority of the Mohammedans collected in the above-mentioned group served in the German Wehrmacht . . . therefore a favorable handling of the request is requested."

But von Mende pushed back. He wrote to the federal ministry that a one-time payment to Gacaoglu might "create a favorable echo in the Muslim countries of the Orient" but said that Germany needed more — a chief imam for its Muslims. One didn't exist in Germany, he wrote, but he knew someone who would be happy to return to Germany and "look after" the Muslims: Namangani.

Von Mende and Namangani were old friends. Namangani had been arrested by the Soviet secret police, the NKVD, in Turkestan and taken to a prison in western Russia. A month after the German invasion, the Wehrmacht overran his camp and he was liberated. Four months later he was the imam in the 450th Battalion during the pioneering Tiger B operation. During the war he rose to head imam of the SS division Osttürkischer Waffenverband, or Eastern Turkic Armed Formation. That unit helped suppress the Warsaw city uprising in 1944. For his service Namangani won the Iron Cross, first and second class, two of Germany's highest military awards.

At the war's end, Namangani spent two years in a U.S. prisoner-of-war camp in Italy and then lived in Germany. He was a regular at the von Mende home, coming over to cook Uzbek food and share stories with his patron. Later he went to Turkey, either to work among émigré groups or, according to his own account, to get theological training — these details of his biography are unclear, and no record exists of such study.

Friends remember him as strict and humorless. He criticized
one mixed Christian-Muslim family when the woman put up a
Christmas tree, arguing that the woman should convert and the
family become Muslim. A young Uzbek officer who met him in a
German prisoner-of-war camp in 1941 said that Namangani "commanded only a little appreciation from the men since his religious
fanaticism was so extreme." Namangani seemed to have little authority other than the fact that von Mende appointed him. In a letter to von Mende shortly after Namangani arrived, Veli Kayum
wrote that even before Namangani had left Istanbul, "denunciations" in Munich had started. Exactly why is not clear, but over the
next few years Namangani would be plagued by criticism for having been a hard-core Nazi and a bad leader—his poor German, for
example, made him unable to communicate with the ex-soldiers'
children.

Namangani's Nazi past might seem perfectly normal among men
who had almost all fought for the Germans. After all, this was the
1950s, a period of relative amnesia about the Nazi era, when people
wanted to forget and move on—dealing directly with the trauma
would get underway only in the 1960s. But Namangani had been
a highly politicized figure. As divisional imam, he had worked directly with the Nazi military leadership. That made him more than
a battlefield cleric; he was part of the political apparatus that had
led the men into a hopeless battle with an unsavory ally. Moreover,
Nazi ties weren't as unproblematic as we might assume. In 1960,
for example, Oberländer himself was brought down after his Nazi
past was brought to light. He was attacked in East German and
Soviet propaganda for participating in an anti-Jewish pogrom. The
charges stuck and he stepped down, spending the next forty years
trying to clear his name.

Just two months after Namangani arrived back in West Germany,
the Stasi was taking aim at von Mende too. It launched an investigation, probably on behalf of the Soviet Union—which likely had
asked for help in discovering why this small "research office" was

behind so much anti-Soviet propaganda. The Soviets were already attacking von Mende's most valuable employee, Baymirza Hayit. In July 1956, Radio Tashkent launched a well-informed attack against Hayit, recounting his wartime service and how he allegedly had planned for his own escape at the end of the war, leaving his men to their fate. In the end, the Stasi never launched a full assault on von Mende's operation, perhaps saving its powder for later or focusing on Oberländer. What is clear is that people like Namangani were vulnerable.

How could the West Germans, none of whom were Muslim, anoint a Muslim leader? That question never seemed to bother von Mende and his colleagues in the government. To them, the only issue was how to knock out Gacaoglu and the Americans. They treated it as a tactical issue and began casting around for ideas that would increase Namangani's appeal.

At first, von Mende stumbled because he was ill. Always a heavy smoker, he had a heart attack in 1956. Unable to work for a couple of months, he recuperated only slowly. During that time, Gacaoglu wrote letters to Oberländer, appealing for support. But by the end of the year, von Mende was back at work full-time and fought back forcefully. He blasted Gacaoglu for being an American stooge. "Because no German office could be found to finance [Gacaoglu], it seems that the American Committee is interested in the Society to use it as a launching pad for its political-propaganda activities among the emigrants of Muslim faith in the Federal Republic and further afield, in the Orient," he wrote in a letter to Oberländer's refugee ministry.

Proof, von Mende said, was the August press conference Gacaoglu and Sultan put together after their Hajj. Von Mende saw it as a turning point in Amcomlib's propaganda offensive in the third world. "Since their return, the American Committee is trying to start its own political-propagandistic campaign in the Muslim world." Now, he wrote sarcastically, Sultan had begun referring to

himself as "Hajj Sultan bin Garif," an honorific that cited his participation in the pilgrimage — inappropriate, von Mende implied, for
someone who went on the Hajj for nonreligious reasons. Sultan,
von Mende wrote, was also trying to take a leading position in
Gacaoglu's group, which needed to be stopped. Only Namangani
could do it.

The refugee ministry concurred and outlined Namangani's role.
"Mr. Namangani has the assignment, first to gather together into
a religious community the Muslim stateless foreigners and non-
German refugees, in order to eliminate the unwanted American influence, which can be harmful to the Federal Republic." Another
official wrote that the key problem was that the Muslims were not
conforming to West Germany's political goals: "I find it unbearable
that currently the stateless Islamic foreigners are being misused for
various intelligence and political intrigues, and that all this is taking place on the soil of the Federal Republic, whose prestige is being harmed," a Bonn official wrote. "If we succeed in building a real
religious community, we will also succeed in gaining political influence. More about this verbally." The main obstacle was Amcomlib,
according to the ministry. "Mr. Kelley from the local office of the
American Committee for Liberation from Bolshevism supposedly
said recently that the affair of the Muslim emigrants must not fall
into German hands."

The West Germans decided to put an end to the discussion about
Namangani, which had been going on for a year, by simply appointing him as the Muslims' chief imam. To do this, they needed the
main ethnic groups to back Namangani. The numbers didn't matter — simply the backing of several groups who appeared to represent Munich's Muslims would suffice. So in March 1958, a cadre of
Muslims close to von Mende — all had worked in the Ostministerium's national committees — held a meeting in Munich's Löwenbräukeller, a popular beer hall and restaurant.

The participants defined their group as an amalgam of ethnic
groups representing five areas of origin: North Caucasus, Azerbai-

jan, Turkestan, Volga-Ural, and the Crimea. Led by the veteran Turkestani activist Ali Kantemir, the members stated that they were equal in number to those Muslims who followed Gacaoglu, even though this claim was questionable. At the meeting they concluded that they needed an imam and that Namangani was their choice.

To do this they needed a legal instrument. So the group then created the Ecclesiastical Administration of Moslem Refugees in the German Federal Republic, with Namangani elected as its head. The Ecclesiastical Administration became a West German government office, financed directly by Oberländer's refugee ministry. Namangani got 650 marks per month, his assistant 150 marks, and his men another 400 marks, designated for travel and for direct aid to be doled out to impoverished Muslims. (The annual budget of 14,400 marks is equal to about $30,000 a year in today's money.)

Gacaoglu's response to the new government office was immediate and sarcastic. He called the March meeting of pro-Namangani forces "a group of professional politicians and a small band of like-minded people, who were specially drummed up for this meeting, elected to a so-called ecclesiastical leadership and claiming to represent the wishes of the Federal Republic." He had a point. The group was purely political, with no popular mandate. But bureaucrats in Bonn had anticipated this. A few months earlier the refugee ministry came up with an idea to give Namangani popular appeal: a central place of worship for Munich's Muslims.

Helping to build a mosque is one of the greatest acts of piety a Muslim can perform. When the prophet Muhammad left Mecca for exile in the city of Medina, his first act upon arriving there was to build one. He also constructed mosques in other cities he visited in order to better pray to God. Mosques do not have to be fancy, but they function as the center of the Muslim community; gathering Friday for weekly prayers symbolizes the unity of all people of faith.

If Namangani could be identified with this good deed, he had an excellent chance of uniting Munich's Muslims behind him—and behind West Germany. But the idea was not his, and it was not conceived of as an act of piety. Instead, the bureaucrats in Bonn had very concrete, political goals, as one official stated explicitly in a 1957 memo: "The existence of a centrally located prayer room for the Muslims should, in consideration of the fact that many foreigners of Muslim faith also pass through Munich, provide them in addition to those permanently in Bavaria, with the opportunity to attend Muslim services. [Thus] an impact on Muslim countries shouldn't miss its mark, which will benefit the Muslims living in Germany and be favorable to the relations between Germany and Islamic countries."

By late 1958, Namangani was no longer talking about just a prayer room. An entire mosque was needed. He received backing from a mercurial German officer from the war, Harun el-Raschid Bey. Born Wilhelm Hintersatz, Raschid was a convert who headed the SS's Osttürkischer Waffenverband, the unit in which Namangani had served as chief imam. The two knew each other well from the war and together were taken prisoner by the United States. Raschid wrote a letter to the federal president, Theodor Heuss, explaining that Namangani was a "true loyal friend of Germany" whose "love for Germany" caused him to return after studying Islam in Turkey. Writing occasionally in capital letters for effect, Raschid summed up West Germany's motivations and intentions.

The Muslims in Germany, MUNICH, lack a politically free MOSQUE WITH AN ATTACHED SMALL SCHOOL (which would serve as a MEETING ROOM) for religious and language training. The MUSLIMS—in contrast to the situation in other western countries like England, France, and Italy—LACK a dignified central religious and cultural center in Germany, GERMANY, which they still see as a true and altruistic friend of Islam.

Wouldn't it be an IDEALISTIC and, as a German dare I say, POLITICALLY SMART act to give such a site for these true

friends of Germany? I don't doubt that the countries of the Muslim Orient would give much credit to this sign of German-
MUSLIM FRIENDSHIP.

By the end of 1958, the preparations were complete. On December 22, Namangani called a meeting of the Dini Idare, the Turkish
name for the Ecclesiastical Administration. The goal of the meeting: building a mosque.

8

DR. RAMADAN ARRIVES

O NE DAY IN MARCH 1956, the law professor Gerhard Kegel was holding his weekly office hours at Cologne University
when a short, trim man appeared at the door, seeking advice on his doctoral thesis. After learning about the man's education, Kegel agreed to take him on. The visitor was Said Ramadan.
He presented himself as a lawyer from Cairo who had come to
Europe to study law. Many professors might have been bewildered,
but Kegel was a generous man, well known for accepting just about
anyone, especially foreigners. He averaged seven doctoral students
a year and over his long career would advise 450. German universities usually don't require course work for a doctorate so all one
needs is the equivalent of a master's degree.

At first, Kegel didn't have much contact with Ramadan. Just a
few weeks shy of his thirtieth birthday, Ramadan was more mature than most of Kegel's students and knew what he wanted to
write about — Islamic law. He set about doing so with energy and
verve. "He made a good impression. He was respectable and intelligent."

Ramadan was often abroad. At first, Kegel thought he was just
preparing his final move to Europe. But Ramadan kept his adviser
well informed about his movements, sending letters and post cards
from Geneva, Damascus, and Jerusalem. With time the affable pro-

fessor began to understand his student's real calling. It wasn't law. It was revolution.

For virtually all of the non-Western world, the nineteenth century was a time of profound crisis. Powered by advanced economic and political systems, Western countries invaded and subjugated vast stretches of the world. Peoples who had considered themselves the most advanced or cultured in the world were quickly defeated by Western military might. From China to Morocco, vast lands were colonized, elites toppled, and peoples subjected to foreign rule. Few felt this humiliation as keenly as did the Muslim world, a great civilization stretching back to the seventh century. Inspired by Islam, Arab conquerors had fanned out across the globe. The new faith spread rapidly, contributing to the rise of kingdoms that nurtured great philosophers, scientists, and artists. But by the early twentieth century, no predominantly Muslim country remained under Muslim leadership; Christians ruled almost every one, from the British in the Indian subcontinent to the Dutch in Indonesia and the French in North Africa. Only Turkey remained independent. But it had been drastically secularized, and the institution of the caliphate — the formal head of state of the Muslim world — was abolished. Islam had been divided and conquered.

As Muslims tried to grasp the reasons for this decline, only two conclusions seemed possible: Christians had discovered better political and economic systems than Muslims had, or true Islamic principles were not being followed. For many, only the latter made sense, and efforts were made to find out where the followers of Muhammad had gone astray. The West might have introduced some useful technologies, but its ideology was to be rejected, a view many Muslims shared with other peoples. In China, for example, the "self-strengthening movement" called for remaining loyal to Chinese systems of thought while adopting Western technology, especially weaponry. Left unexamined was the intellectual context in which this new technology was developed — what sort of scientific

process was at work and what it implied about the relationship between the individual and authority, be it political or religious.

The Muslim world began grappling with these ideas in the nineteenth century. In the early part of that century, scholars such as
Egypt's Rifa'a el-Tahtawi grappled with Western ideas by translat-
ing books and pushing to create a national consciousness. This gave
way to the more overt political and religious activism of figures
such as Jamal al-Din al-Afghani and Muhammad Abduh, who, for
example, published a newspaper calling for a return to the original Islamic ideals. A generation later, these thoughts were taken
up by men such as Rashid Rida, who blamed the Muslim world's
weakness on the rigidity of the intellectual class and the failure of
Muslims to adhere to Islam's true teachings. Rida published an influential magazine in the early twentieth century that inspired key
political activists.

As the twentieth century progressed, more explicitly political
programs sprang up. Some intellectual historians call this movement Islamism and its adherents Islamists. According to this school
of thought, Islamists differ from traditional Muslims because they
use their religion in pursuit of a political agenda, via either democracy or violence. Followers are mobilized by specific issues related
to Islam — such as the need to apply Islamic religious law, or sharia, in their societies. Implicit in Islamism is a rejection of Western
society and its values, which are seen as incompatible with Islam.
Some political analysts prefer to use "political Islam" to describe
this movement.

But the concept of Islamism is controversial because it implies
that earlier Islam was not political. In fact, from its start Islam was
an all-encompassing faith that did not reject worldly power. The
institution of the caliphate grew out of Muhammad's own life. He
was intensely involved in daily political and military affairs, himself
organizing a small state and launching campaigns against enemy
tribes. Also, the term *Islamist* carries negative connotations because
it was widely used after the 2001 attacks on New York and Washington as, in effect, a synonym for *terrorist*.

Yet in the twentieth century Islam was the wellspring of a remarkable amount of political activity. Transnational political activists claiming legitimacy as bearers of the true faith sought to impose
their version of Islam — usually the version that they imagined Muhammad practiced — on Muslims with roots in a particular location, who over the centuries often had evolved distinct religious
practices. Thus the spread of Arab robes and head coverings, bans
on Western music, and restrictions on women's roles in society.
These activists often interpreted the Koran literally, an approach
that ignored the sophisticated legal arguments developed by Islamic
scholars over the centuries. Instead, they advanced a very modern
idea: anyone could understand the Koran, and the traditional caste
of scholars was unnecessary, even detrimental. On the other hand,
the movement rejected other modern ideas, such as taking historical context into consideration when interpreting ancient texts. Like
many other literalists, the modern Islamic activists considered heretical the idea that certain rules might have made sense when the
Koran came into existence but now were not important to its central message. Thus some modern Muslim activists successfully argued that high school girls should not be permitted to take a class
trip because the distance involved was longer than a camel could
travel in a day. Back in the Prophet's time, this was judged a safe
distance for a woman to travel, but for the activists it became a
hard-and-fast rule, for all times and places.

The most influential political movement to come out of this tradition was the Muslim Brotherhood. Al-ikhwan al-muslimun, more
literally translated as the Society of Muslim Brothers (or Brethren),
was founded in 1928 by Hasan al-Banna, a schoolteacher from a
small town in the Nile Delta. At the time, Egypt was still under British colonial rule. It was also modernizing quickly, going through
wrenching economic and social changes: Cairo was industrializing,
the peasants were moving to cities, traditions were breaking up, and
social mores were in flux. An avid reader of Rashid Rida's magazine, Banna was appalled by this combination of national oppression and rapid social change. He began to organize and do some

writing of his own. Banna's works contained virulent attacks on the British but also on freethinking and immorality, especially the kinds that had arisen in the capital. Like Rida and the intellectuals before him, his answer was Islam. What made Banna unique was that he was a populist and political activist. Members of the Muslim Brotherhood did not aspire to become intellectuals like the old ulema, or community of Muslim scholars, and were more grass-roots-oriented than the modern intellectuals Afghani, Abduh, and Rida. They usually adopted Western dress and modern rhetoric, spoke in simple sentences, and shunned the pseudo-classical phrases of traditional scholars. Most important, they built up Western-style organizations such as political parties, youth groups, women's groups, and paramilitary wings. They became an alternative state, able to provide what the government could not. This allowed them to appeal to the Muslim world's rising middle class. They vocalized the anger of the poor but always drew their leadership from the educated classes who were frustrated at their countries' impoverishment and humiliation at the hands of Western countries. Not limited by race or nationality, the Brotherhood would spread from North Africa to Southeast Asia.

"Sheikh al-Banna wasn't like other sheikhs," recalled Farid Abdel Khalek, a long-time member of the Brotherhood who lives in Cairo. "He described Islam as something new." Khalek used to attend Banna's rallies in small towns and, later, in Cairo. He joined the group early, headed the student division in 1942, and served on its shura, or guidance council, in 1944. He paid dearly for his activism, spending twelve years in Egyptian prisons. "The others said do good things and you'll go to heaven, do bad and you'll go to hell. He said you had to do something good for your country. It was something in this world, in this reality. It was Islam as we didn't know it before; it wasn't tradition."

Banna's method to win converts was to identify a problem in a community and then solve it. The group would help build a new mosque or school or develop a local industry. This would convince people that his movement was solution-oriented and its people sincere. New members were recruited directly in mosques and also in coffee shops and the market.

Then as now, politics was a sensitive subject in Egypt, so Banna was careful to call the Brotherhood a movement, not a political party. But Banna became intensely involved in politics, opposing the monarchy, which had colluded with the British. This interest caused the first split in the movement in 1931, when one group seceded. Its members thought the Brotherhood should be a traditional welfare group and objected to the politicization of Islam. Later, the Brotherhood backed Gamal Nasser, the Egyptian military officer who led a coup against the monarchy in 1952.

By the 1930s, the Brotherhood went so far as to accept money from Nazi agents. According to documents seized by the British at the start of World War II, the Brotherhood received significant funds from a German journalist affiliated with the German legation in Cairo. The Nazi money was used to establish the Brotherhood's quasi-military "Special Apparatus." For Banna, the idea of a religious group having a military wing was not at all strange. The Brotherhood conceived of itself initially as a populist party that could take to the street to protest or fight. Even today it has not renounced violence — its leaders advocate terrorism against Israeli civilians and in certain other circumstances. But the Brotherhood has also positioned itself as pro-democracy. This allows the organization to be, at times, revolutionary and reformist in emphasis, depending on the circumstances. None of this political work violated Banna's sense of the religion. Muslims have always considered Islam a total package — covering traditional "religious" spheres and the secular world as well. In essence they have tried to apply God's law in this world. For most of its history, Islam has accommodated secular rulers, but at its heart the religion accepts nothing like the idea of separation of church and state.

Banna subscribed to the Koran's message that there is no division between state and religion, which was expressed in the group's most

famous slogan: THE KORAN IS OUR CONSTITUTION. JIHAD IS
OUR WAY. MARTYRDOM IS OUR DESIRE. In one tract, he wrote,
"If someone should say to you 'This is politics!' say: 'This is Islam
and we do not recognize such divisions.'" In another he said, "O ye
Brethren! Tell me, if Islam is something else than politics, society,
economy, law, and culture, what is it then? Is it only empty acts of
prostration, devoid of a pulsating heart?"

As the Brotherhood grew, this heart focused on two national
causes. One was anticolonialism, something that all Egyptians
could identify with. Another was opposition to Jewish immigration
to Israel. The Brotherhood collected money for Arabs in Palestine,
and in 1937 and 1938 the group attacked shops owned by Jews as
well as other targets in Cairo. That was the start of one of the defining characteristics of Brotherhood thought: anti-Semitism.

The term "Muslim world" is misleading; from the start, Islam has
never existed in a vacuum and always had to deal with other religions. When Islam was founded in the seventh century, its followers came into contact with Christians, Jews, and practitioners of a
variety of other religions, including polytheists. Islam had no place
for the latter, whom Muslims considered heathens, pagans, or idol-
aters. According to the Koran, their future was clear: "You and your
idols shall be the fuel of Hell."

Unlike polytheists, Christians and Jews were respected by Muhammad. Like Muslims, they practiced "revealed religions" — based
on God's revealed word. In addition, Islam worships the same God
and recognizes the same prophets as do Judaism and Christianity. In a way, they are seen as precursor religions to Islam. But the
two were not viewed as equal; Judaism is clearly of a lower status.
The classical Koran commentators agree on this. For example, the
ninth-century writer Muhammad al-Tabari stated that Christians
"are not like the Jews, who always scheme in order to murder the
emissaries and the prophet, and who oppose God in his positive
and negative commandments, and who corrupt His scripture which
He revealed in His books."

There are several reasons why Islam is less accepting of Jews. Christians might not think of Muhammad as a prophet, but at least Christians recognize Jesus, who is also an important prophet in Islam. So in a way, Christians are a step farther along the path than Jews, who do not recognize Christ. Jews are also accused of murdering or ignoring prophets. Perhaps the most important issue, however, is that Muhammad himself had unhappy experiences with Jews. When he fled Mecca to found the first Islamic society in Medina, he had hoped that the Jewish tribes there would welcome him. He was bitterly disappointed when they rejected his revelations and kept their own faith. When they allied themselves with his enemies, he launched a preemptive strike, massacring hundreds. The verses in the Koran describing this are bitter and angry — and have been used to justify attacks on Jews.

Many scholars rightly point out that despite all this, Islam provided protection for Jews and Christians. In theory, they were afforded a minority rank called *dhimmi,* which exempted them from many Islamic laws. For its time, *dhimmi* status was progressive, especially when contrasted with the treatment of Jews in medieval Christian Europe, with its ghettos and pogroms, not to mention the Holocaust in recent times. But it is also true that *dhimmi* status did not prevent mistreatment of minorities, especially Jews, in the Muslim world.

With the rise of modern Islamism, especially the Muslim Brotherhood, anti-Semitism was taken to a new level. Just as the Brotherhood made use of modern political structures, such as the fascist-style political party, the group also adopted Western anti-Semitic stereotypes and arguments, the principal one being that Jews are to blame for key problems in society. During the war, Nazi propaganda added fuel to this idea; German radio regularly beamed gross anti-Semitic slurs into the Middle East. Cairo, which once boasted a vibrant Jewish community and actually staged anti-Nazi demonstrations in 1933, was by 1945 a haven for ex-Nazis fleeing justice.

The Muslim Brotherhood was at the forefront of this rising anti-Semitism. Banna could not accept all Nazi ideas, especially not the concept that the Germans were a master race. But Nazi agents supported him, and anti-Semitism formed a key part of his political activity, which crystallized in the Brotherhood's close association with one of the more controversial figures in twentieth-century Arab history, Amin al-Hussaini. Better known as the Grand Mufti of Jerusalem, Hussaini was a popular leader in Palestine but also a rabid anti-Semite. He was the same figure who worked with von Mende on the possibility of setting up a religious hierarchy in the Crimea and who inspected Muslim troops fighting for the Nazis.

Hussaini was not a casual associate of the Nazis. Some biographers have glossed over his career in the 1930s and '40s, saying he acted at worst out of ill-advised opportunism. But he contacted the Nazis early — in 1933 — and specifically mentioned the need to get rid of Jewish influence in economics and politics. One can explain his views as a reaction to Zionism and Jewish immigration to Palestine, but from the start he displayed a fervent hatred of Jews, even citing *The Protocols of the Elders of Zion* — a notorious work of anti-Semitism — as testimony before a British commission in 1929.

Hussaini's collaboration with the Nazis involved more than advising von Mende on religious policy. He recruited soldiers for them and declared their cause just. Most famously, he warned the Nazis of plans to send about seventy thousand Jewish children in Rumania to Palestine, saying they would increase the territory's Jewish population. He argued that he had been a guest of the Nazis for three years, moving in the highest Nazi circles, so there's no doubt that he knew about the Holocaust and was fully aware that if the children did not leave Rumania they were doomed to die.

After the war, the French arrested Hussaini as a war criminal. He was allowed to return to Palestine because the British worried that trying him as a criminal would inflame Muslim passions. By 1948, he was again leading opposition to Jewish immigration. Despite what he had seen in Nazi Germany, he had no sympathy for those arriving, even though tens of thousands had barely escaped the Holocaust. Hussaini continued to associate with ex-Nazis, such as the propagandist Johann von Leers, who had moved to Cairo and changed his name to Amin Lahars. Von Mende's intelligence reports show that Lahars had contact with members of the German Muslim League, a Hamburg-based group of immigrants. One report stated that Lahars "intends through this society to start an anti-Semitic movement in the Federal Republic. Ex-Mufti of Jerusalem, Hajji Hussaini finances the plans of Amin Lahars . . . His goal: Anti-Semitism."

One could argue that Hussaini was an outlier. Yet he was a close associate of Banna and his successors. In all of his actions and his worldview, Hussaini behaved as a classic Islamist, bridging the Nazi and post-Nazi era. He pops up again and again in the Munich story, not only in von Mende's reports but also in the company of other players, such as the novelist, activist, and intelligence figure Ahmad Kamal.

Hussaini and the Brotherhood were probably in closest alliance when Arab armies attacked Israel in 1948. Desperate for soldiers, Hussaini turned to the head of the Brotherhood, Banna. "The Mufti told him, you have to do something," recalled Khalek, who by then was in the Brotherhood's shura. "They [the Jews] will take over this place and be cruel to Muslims." Banna agreed to help. The Brotherhood began to recruit soldiers to fight in Palestine. To head the operation, Banna turned to one of his rising stars, Said Ramadan. It was the start of a close cooperation that would last twenty years.

Said Ramadan first saw Banna speak at an outdoor revival-style meeting in 1940. After each such gathering, Banna would ask people to come up on the stage — almost like a pledge to the movement. After about five meetings, the fourteen-year-old Ramadan, not much over five feet tall but powerfully built from wrestling, finally decided to go forward.

"What took you so long?" Banna said. The sheikh had known all along that his future protégé was in the crowd. He had just been waiting for him to take the first step.

It was a story that Ramadan liked to tell his friends and acolytes. Banna, he felt, was often misunderstood as purely a political figure. The man had a deeply spiritual, mystic side as well and, as Ramadan tells it, he slept in a graveyard once a month to remind him of his ultimate fate. Disciples of the two often emphasized their physical power. Banna led members in physical exercises, adopting Western ideas of the body as being almost equal to the mind. Ramadan, slender and short — as an adult he stood five feet six inches tall — commanded immense respect, partly because he appeared virile and energetic. He had a strong jaw, highlighted by a trim beard. His eyes were soft but intense. People inevitably spoke of his physical attractiveness and presence in a room.

"Physically he was enormously strong," said Dawud Salahuddin, an African American convert to Islam who met Ramadan in 1976. "What I found about him so attractive is you rarely see men of that intellectual caliber have a physical side. He was a champion gymnast as a kid. There definitely was a charisma. When you're dealing with someone who can stand and talk for three hours then there's a physical aspect."

Like most Western-oriented people of his generation, Ramadan usually wore a suit and tie, reserving traditional Arab dress for special occasions. He spoke directly and always made eye contact.

After meeting Banna, Ramadan became active in the movement, helping to organize rallies. He studied law in college and became an attorney. In 1946 he was hired as Banna's personal secretary and married one of his daughters, cementing the bond. "He was a good speaker," recalls Khalek, who studied with Ramadan at Cairo University. "He had charisma. He was good to be sent to difficult places."

Accounts vary concerning his work in Palestine. Some say he was crucial to Jerusalem's defense against Israeli armies; others, that he had organized only a Brotherhood youth wing there. Some wrote that he established the Brotherhood's branch in neighboring Jordan, where he headquartered their efforts in the 1948 war. Jordan issued him a passport, which he used for years.

The Brotherhood's intense political work, however, was seen as a threat by many governments. Egypt banned the group in 1948, and Ramadan went to Pakistan for a year, where he worked closely with the government, which gave him a radio broadcast. Then, shortly after he returned to Egypt in 1949, Banna was assassinated. Ramadan, who was too young to be considered a successor to his father-in-law, continued his overseas organizing.

"If the Brotherhood had ministries, he'd have been the foreign minister," says Gamal al-Banna, brother of the movement's founder. "He was an eloquent orator and spoke English. He had many contacts overseas." Most of Ramadan's work was devoted to Islamic organization. The goal wasn't some sort of theological or ecumenical agreement among Islam's oft-warring factions. Instead it was political. In theory, Muslims should be ruled by a caliph, a secular ruler who would enforce Islamic law, sharia, in a temporal government. The last caliph resided in Istanbul, but Turkey abolished his office in 1924. Ever since, Islamic activists had dreamed of restoring it.

Starting in 1926, activists tried to unite Muslims through an ersatz caliphate: leagues and conferences. If the Muslim world was too fractured to be united by one leader, then a representative body might at least provide some sort of umbrella structure. In 1949, Ramadan and the Grand Mufti spearheaded efforts to create such a body and in 1951 succeeded in holding a meeting of the World Muslim Congress in the Pakistani city of Karachi. Ramadan was elected as one of the conference's three secretaries. He immediately attacked Turkey's secular government. Ramadan was also active with the Grand Mufti in the Islamic General Congress of Jerusalem. Another key player in these groups was Sayyid Qutb, the most influential Islamist theorist of the twentieth century, who held that anyone, even a Muslim, who didn't followed the Brotherhood's views was an apostate and thus could be killed.

A key goal Ramadan pursued at the conferences was the fight against communism. Although Western countries were seen as degenerate and corrupt, communist states banned or tightly proscribed religion. That made them worse and therefore the Islamists' first target. The Mufti was especially vociferous in opposing communism. According to a declassified U.S. War Department Strategic Services Unit assessment in 1946, "Source states that the Mufti has also sent messages to his followers reminding them that the principles of Communism are completely at variance with the teachings of the Koran."

This theme would come up again and again in CIA surveillance of the Mufti. He was a known anticommunist and thus attractive. But his Nazi past made him an unacceptable ally. Ramadan was a different matter.

The first brush between U.S. officials and Ramadan came in the summer of 1953. The White House received an urgent request: prominent Muslims were coming to Princeton University for an "Islamic Colloquium"; would the president meet them? At first, it seemed the encounter wouldn't happen because President Eisenhower was out of town. Then Abbott Washburn, deputy director of the U.S. Information Agency in charge of liaison with the White House, recalled the high priority that Eisenhower gave to religion in his personal life and in geopolitical strategy. The early discussions about using religion more effectively in global politics had already taken place, and Edward Lilly had just circulated his influential memo, "The Religious Factor." Although it's not clear from the record that Washburn saw his memo, the overall feeling was clear: the United States had to grab this chance.

Washburn sent a note to Eisenhower's psychological warfare whiz, C. D. Jackson. He told Jackson that the conference was sponsored by the USIA, the State Department's International Information Agency (IIA), Princeton, and the Library of Congress — a "four-way play," as he put it, to influence the Muslim world. "Hoped-for result," Washburn wrote, "is that the Muslims will be impressed with the moral and spiritual strength of America."

The White House hesitated. Washburn made one last pitch. He noted that President Eisenhower believed the United States had to push home its spiritual superiority over the USSR. "These individuals can exert a profound and far-reaching impact upon Moslem thinking. Their long-term influence may well outweigh that of the political leaders of their countries." The White House agreed, and eight days later the invitations went out. The meeting was entered into the president's appointment book: 23 September 1953, 11:30 A.M. One of the delegates would be "The Honorable Saeed Ramahdan, Delegate of the Muslim Brothers."

The meeting, Eisenhower officials made plain, was meant to complement the Princeton conference's purely political goals. Some of the attendees were scholars and did present papers, but the conference's principal aim was to show the United States feting Muslim intellectuals. "On the surface, the conference looks like an exercise in pure learning. This in effect is the impression desired," said a confidential memo forwarded to Eisenhower's secretary of state, John Foster Dulles. "IIA promoted the colloquium along these lines and has given it financial and other assistance because we consider that this psychological approach is an important contribution at this time to both short term and long term United States political objectives in the Moslem area."

Attached to the memo was an analysis of the upcoming conference. The goals were to guide and promote the Islamic "Renaissance," whose most influential group was the Muslim Brotherhood. Interestingly, the paper acknowledges that some of the attendees might be dicey — by law the IIA was supposed to promote cultural exchanges. The Muslim Brotherhood, an overtly political body, did not fit this definition, making it difficult for the IIA to fund Ramadan and other political leaders' participation. "Since the exchange program cannot give grants to some individuals whose presence at the colloquium would be desirable, it is hoped that outside sources may provide a small amount of financial assistance." Private sponsors stepped in. The U.S.-Saudi oil giant Aramco paid some travel costs. The IIA contributed too, paying for two Princeton professors to travel in the Middle East to invite candidates personally.

In July 1953, when most of the participants had been chosen, the U.S. embassy in Cairo was asked if Ramadan could attend. Ramadan wanted to visit Muslim centers in the United States. The embassy forwarded the request to Washington, along with a sanitized version of his career history — leaving out, for example, his close ties to the Grand Mufti and his battle against Israel. The embassy recommended that he attend.

The conference itself lasted ten days; speakers gave presentations on education, youth, art, and social reform. Compared to conferences today, the pace was leisurely, with only two to three panels scheduled per day and time for long, far-ranging discussions as well as socializing in the evening. The conference moved from New Jersey to Washington and ended as Ramadan and the other participants met President Eisenhower. The resulting photo op symbolizes this era's tentative steps toward harnessing the power of Islam. Ramadan, standing on the far right of the picture, looks on as Eisenhower gestures to make a point. The meetings went smoothly and the conference was deemed a success.

But Ramadan was not going to be an easy ally. In a CIA analysis after the conference, he came across as a political agitator. "Ramadan was invited at the urging of the Egyptian embassy. He was *the* [emphasis in original] most difficult element at the colloquium as he was concerned with political pressure rather than with cultural problems." According to the report, he refused to make small talk. At one evening gathering he was asked if Egyptian youth shouldn't be encouraged to engage in social work. "The only thing Egyptian youth is interested in is in getting the British out," he is reported to have said. The author of the report continued with a personal evaluation of Ramadan: "I felt that Ramadan was a political reactionary, a Phalangist or Fascist type, rather than a religious reactionary as in the case of the three sheiks who attended," the report's author wrote. "Ramadan seems to be a Fascist, interested in the grouping of individuals for power. He did not display many ideas except for those of the Brotherhood."

Ramadan, however, continued to pop up in U.S. diplomatic circles. In 1956, he met U.S. officials in Rabat, pressing home his demand that Jews be expelled from Palestine. These views made it impossible for Ramadan and the United States to cement a formal alliance. But the mutual attraction to fighting communism was obvious. Later that year, Ramadan and other leaders of the Islamic General Congress of Jerusalem — the Grand Mufti's group — pledged themselves to a tough anticommunist battle, stating that communism was antithetical to Islam. But he conceded that it would be a hard sell in the Middle East because communism was seen as anti-Western and most Arabs blamed the West for allowing the state of Israel to be created.

Ramadan had his own immediate problems as well. In 1954, Nasser cracked down on the Brotherhood after a botched assassination attempt, allegedly by one if its associates. Ramadan fled to Saudi Arabia, then to Syria, Pakistan, and Jordan. Cairo stripped Ramadan and a handful of other leaders of their citizenship and charged them with treason. Later Egyptian officials tried to defame him as a homosexual. Few countries wanted to antagonize Egypt, the most powerful nation in the region, and Ramadan had to keep on the move. Perhaps out of gratitude for his service in 1948, Jordan let him keep a diplomatic passport, and the small kingdom sent him to West Germany as ambassador-at-large. Then, perhaps out of genuine academic interest or as a cover for other activities, he showed up at Professor Kegel's door.

Five months after Kegel agreed to take Ramadan as his student, he received a letter from the young man, sent under the letterhead "World Muslim Congress Jerusalem" and datelined Damascus. "Dear Prof. Kegel, Again I need your help . . . I have not yet found a good material for a thesis," he wrote in English. "There is a clear new tendency towards what is called the 'Islamic law' in many newly independent Muslim countries. What about a thesis comparing efforts to implement Islamic law? Waiting for my Professor's word for this subject: yes or no!"

Kegel was unsure how to respond. The forty-four-year-old

scholar was already one of West Germany's most important legal minds because of his work on civil law. A rigorous academic, he liked his students to research traditional thesis topics. He wanted them to seek out court cases or some other form of empirical work and back up their ideas in footnotes. Ramadan was proposing something completely different: a guide to implementing sharia. If Ramadan was to become an academic, the thesis would have to stand up to intense scrutiny, and the young man's interests seemed to Kegel more like a hobby than a serious academic pursuit. But Kegel was nonetheless intrigued, and he gave his approval.

By late 1956, however, Ramadan moved back to the Middle East. He wrote a telegram to Kegel: "On the eve of my departure from Europe I felt I have to express my deep feelings of gratitude I shall always remember the decent reception and good hours I had in Köln." Ramadan continued working on his thesis as he flitted from one country to another, acting as secretary general of the World Muslim Congress. In June 1958, Ramadan wrote Kegel to say the "worsening situation" in Damascus caused him to move his family to Jerusalem. Later he wrote to say he was off to the Hajj to meet Egyptians — which supported Egyptian intelligence's belief that during this Hajj the exiled Brotherhood met and discussed strategy.

In August of that year, Ramadan decided to move back to Geneva. Swiss officials seemed unaware that he was moving permanently — a few years later they discussed the fact that he seemed ensconced in Geneva, concluded it was illegal, but decided to allow him to stay because of his strong anticommunist tendencies. Ramadan later explained that he moved because one of his sons needed medical treatment.

In late 1958, Ramadan completed his thesis. On December 15, Kegel gave him the mark *"sehr gut"* — equivalent to an A, or "honors." Kegel wrote that "the writer is a man who is capable," saying that Ramadan's dissertation was "head and shoulders" above others that he had read from the Near East and the Middle East. But Kegel also wrote in his two-page evaluation that it was an unusual thesis. It was more theological and political, he said, than law-oriented — an attempt to make Islamic law, or sharia, apply to the modern world.

"It was good. It was very well thought out," Kegel said in an interview, thinking back over forty-five years.

But Kegel began to wonder about Ramadan. When I asked him about Ramadan, Kegel's initial answer was snappy and short: "I would describe him as intelligent if also fanatical."

Ramadan was trying to build a religious utopia. Kegel didn't have anything against utopians, but he didn't like the venture's exclusionary nature — one religion above all else. Surely, Kegel thought, this was a recipe for intolerance. Kegel had been a young academic in the years before World War II. His teacher had been the famous Jewish legal scholar Ernst Rabel, who emigrated in 1939 after the Nazis made academic life for Jews impossible. "[Rabel] remained lifelong my greatest role model. He was a victim of fanaticism and I couldn't forget such a thing. I knew this kind of fanaticism and felt uncomfortable with it."

Despite Kegel's misgivings, he and Ramadan stayed friends, and Kegel's papers contain several of Ramadan's handwritten letters, which he sent as he traveled the Muslim world. Kegel also wrote a preface for Ramadan's thesis, which was eventually published in 1961. It was the best-selling thesis of any Kegel had supervised. Today *Islamic Law: Its Scope and Equity* is a standard of the Islamist scene. Translated widely, it is sold in mosques and cultural centers across Europe, wherever the Muslim Brotherhood's ideology has penetrated.

St. Paul's Church near Munich's main train station is a testament to an earlier, God-fearing age in Europe. Built in 1906, the church had six thousand members who were generous — and ambitious. They hired a popular architect who had just built the city's neo-Gothic town hall, and they asked him to build the tallest church in town, hoping to surpass the Marienkirche, the city's medieval landmark.

St. Paul's reflected the confidence and pride of the new imperial Germany. Only the intervention of the bishopric kept the spire at ninety-six meters in height, allowing the Marienkirche to keep its status as the city's tallest. During World War II, Allied bombers reduced the church to a shell. Its heavy stone walls withstood the blasts, but firebombs tore through the roof, gutting the interior. By 1958, it had been rebuilt, but in a more sober, almost traumatized-looking form. The roof and windows were replaced, but the church management chose not to reconstruct the ornate decorations. Instead it was outfitted with austere sculptures, clear glass, and raw brick. It became a reminder of ideology's destructive power, which had left the country weary of belief and suspicious of certainty.

It was to this church that upwards of fifty men trudged the day after Christmas in 1958. They arrived by streetcar and subway, braving a snowstorm and walking past the still-empty lots and shells of buildings left by the war. They were there not to praise Jesus but to participate in von Mende's effort to unite Muslims across Germany in building a mosque. Nurredin Namangani's Ecclesiastical Administration was gaining traction after von Mende had sidelined Gacaoglu's group. Now Namangani's association was claiming to represent all Muslims in Germany. Invitations printed in German and Turkish (in Arabic script) requested the attendance of not only the ex-soldiers but also "the other brothers — Germans, Pakistanis, Persians, Arabs, Turks — who live in your city to this meeting, because every Muslim who believes in Allah and his Prophet, Muhammad, must answer to Allah if he remains away or doesn't tell his brothers of it." The tone had nothing of the rebuilt church's measured sobriety. Instead, it was old-school apocalyptic: "The end of the world can happen any day and any hour. Therefore we cannot live in this world with closed eyes. We have slept enough and want now to rise up as one."

The meeting had been preceded on the twenty-second by a smaller session of the Ecclesiastical Administration, whose members decided to establish the Mosque Construction Commission with Namangani as chairman and the venerable Said Shamil — the Dagestani whose family had moved to Saudi Arabia years ago — as honorary chairman. Four days later, the group met again, this time with students and other Muslims present; Said Ramadan was guest of honor. Faisal Yazdani remembered the day well: "The room was full and it was an exciting feeling," he recalled; he was then a twenty-year-old medical student. "We felt we were doing something idealistic — building a mosque." It was to be a mosque for all Muslims from all over Germany. "Everyone was especially excited because of the presence of Dr. Ramadan. He was a great personality, the head of the Muslim Congress. He was really famous and here he was among us, helping us build a mosque."

Ramadan added to the buzz by showing off his financial connections. The group collected 1,125 marks in donations that day, 1,000 of which came from Ramadan. He was made honorary member of the Mosque Construction Commission. Ramadan had been invited to the meeting by a young Syrian student, Ghaleb Himmat, a self-described member of the Muslim Brotherhood.

"Himmat invited him to take over the leadership," said Obeidullah Mogaddedi, an Afghani medical student and the son of a famous Muslim leader. He attended the meeting and was close to Ramadan for the next few years, functioning as his de facto private secretary. "The idea was to have a famous guy head it."

As Mogaddedi recalled it, Ramadan said he was eager to spread his influence in Europe. Geneva was his base, but Munich, a day's drive away to the northeast, would make a good steppingstone. Mogaddedi was in awe of Ramadan, but — perhaps in hindsight, perhaps all along — he had qualms about bringing such a political personality on board.

"Personally I was against it, not against Said Ramadan as a person, but Dr. Ramadan was a member of the Muslim Brotherhood and a leader of the Muslim Brotherhood and was also a political figure and not only a religious figure," he said. "I thought it wouldn't be good if the center was stamped as a Muslim Brotherhood center. We should work for Islam and not a group, whether it's good or bad."

But Ramadan was a captivating, charismatic figure. Students, most of whom were impressionable nineteen- and twenty-year-olds, considered him a star, a man who was leading a renaissance of their ancient religion. He had taken on colonialists and dictators. They enthusiastically endorsed him as their champion.

"The students were all well educated," recalls Muhammad Abdul Karim Grimm, a German convert and long-time Muslim activist. They were especially well educated in Islamic issues — above all of the Muslim Brotherhood. "They had learned the lessons of Hasan al-Banna."

Ramadan realized that he had to pay a courtesy call on von Mende but had other business to attend to. So he sent Mogaddedi in his place. "After the meeting, I went to von Mende [in Düsseldorf] and told him about the meeting. It turned out that he knew about it already," Mogaddedi said, laughing. Mogaddedi hadn't realized that Namangani was von Mende's man and had been closely following the events. Ramadan, though, was a bit of a mystery. Von Mende quickly put out feelers. Was he an ally or a challenger? Soon von Mende's tidy card file had a new entry: "Said Ramadan, 36, head of the Muslim Brotherhood. R. drives a Cadillac, a gift from the Saudi government."

9

MARRIAGE OF CONVENIENCE

N THE SUMMER OF 1957, Bob Dreher finally got his chance to return to Munich, charged with shaking up Amcomlib and making more aggressive use of émigrés, especially Muslims. He had yearned for a chance to implement rollback and score some propaganda points against the Soviets. But he was driven by other impulses too. Behind the hard-driving CIA man was a nonconformist who disliked the confines of 1950s America. Thumping the communists was satisfying, but Dreher also saw Europe as a place to quench other desires.

His route to Munich reflected these impulses. Instead of flying directly, he landed in Paris and then traveled by train and boat to the Île du Levant, a nudist colony off the coast of France. He met old friends and made some new ones. Best of all were the photos: "Received my Kodachromes yesterday, and there are some prizes among them!"

He seemed to have little trouble attracting women. At six foot two and a trim 180 pounds, Dreher had the conventional good looks of 1950s Hollywood — slicked-back dark hair, a smooth handsome face, and a quick sense of humor. In every picture he is smiling, his perfect white teeth giving him a passing resemblance to Cary Grant.

"I'm not a one-woman man," he jokingly warned Karin West, a Baltic refugee who worked for Amcomlib's think tank on the Soviet Union. West wasn't bothered by Dreher's promiscuity; she was a platonic friend and confidante who posed as his wife in order to get the two of them into Germany's famed FKK nudist resorts. FKK — Freikörperkultur — was not meant for snap-happy singles like Dreher. It was an offshoot of the nineteenth-century back-to-nature movement, and visitors were meant to be sober, serious, and married. For Dreher, the spiritual context meant little.

At times, his lifestyle tortured him. In letters home, he would regale his family with studiously careful accounts of all the cute girls he'd met. The tone was of Bob in Europe, having fun, the eternal bachelor. But once, in a fit of remorse, he wrote, "Deep down inside I realize that it's I who am not in step, and I'm determined to get back to God's country and to do something about it."

During his second stint in Europe he seemed, according to the memories of his employees and colleagues, oddly split: wanting to pursue a tough path that few believed would be effective and often preoccupied with the travails of his exhausting bohemian life. His main problems seemed to be finding the right convertible (a Mercedes was too expensive; a VW was too plain), hi-fi system (German systems looked good but sounded bad), and women (all they want is to marry).

Many Amcomlib employees became specialists in the émigrés' cultures and languages, earning their respect. Not Dreher. When asked, on his CIA application, to rate his hobbies, he wrote that he was "very good" at dancing, dramatics, and Ping-Pong, "good" at tennis, sailing, and photography, but only "adequate" at reading. Language was another weak area: on paper he knew Russian and German, but he spoke broken German even after years of living in the country. What he had in abundance — and liked to show off to bewildered émigrés — were his Kodachromes. Some recall being repelled by the pictures. Dreher apparently didn't notice; they stayed framed on his desk. Strangely, it was this model of 1950s hedonism who decided to shake up Amcomlib. His method: partnering with Said Ramadan and the Muslim Brotherhood.

*   *   *

By Eisenhower's second term, the administration had decided to get more serious about Islam. In 1957, the Eisenhower Doctrine was announced; it promised U.S. armed intervention against aggression, actual or threatened. This was a response to what U.S. policy makers saw as growing Soviet influence in the Middle East, especially in Egypt. Privately, President Eisenhower seemed concerned about how to reach the Muslim world. He wrote to his confidant, the Presbyterian church leader Edward Elson, that Islam and the Middle East were always on his mind. "I assure you that I never fail in any communication with Arab leaders, oral or written, to stress the importance of the spiritual factor in our relationships. I have argued that belief in God should create between them and us the common purpose of opposing atheistic communism."

In White House meetings he was more blunt. Speaking with the CIA covert operations czar Frank Wisner and the Joint Chiefs of Staff, Eisenhower said that Arabs should dip into their own religion for inspiration in fighting communism.

"The President said he thought we should do everything possible to stress the 'holy war' aspect," according to a memo outlining the conversation. "Mr. Dulles commented that if the Arabs have a 'holy war' they would want it to be against Israel. The President recalled, however, that [King Ibn] Saud, after his visit here, had called on all Arabs to oppose Communism."

The Operations Coordinating Board — the body set up to implement covert plans by the CIA and other agencies — took up Islam. It had already produced a detailed study of Buddhism and how that religion could be used to further U.S. interests. In 1957, the board established an Ad Hoc Working Group on Islam that included officials from the U.S. Information Agency, the State Department, and the CIA. According to a memo on the group's first meeting, its goal was to take stock of what public and private U.S. organizations were doing in the field of Islam and come up with an "Outline Plan of Operations." The plan had two main components, both of which were echoed in CIA actions in Munich. First, the United States would shun traditional Muslims in favor of "reform" groups, like the Muslim Brotherhood. Then, as today, the Brotherhood's radical political agenda of a return to a mythic state of pure Islam was obfuscated by its members' use of modern symbols, such as Western clothing and rhetoric. "Both the Chairman and the CIA member felt that with the Islamic world being divided as it is between reactionary and reformist groups, it might be found profitable to place emphasis on programs which would strengthen the reformist groups."

In May, the coordination board passed the inventory and plan of action. Its statements were clear and simple: Islam is a natural ally, communists are exploiting Islam, and Islam affects the balance of power. The paper listed a dozen recommendations for strengthening ties with Islamic organizations, especially those with a strong anticommunist bent. As always, the operations were to be covert. "Programs which are indirect and unattributable are more likely to be effective and will avoid the charge that we are trying to use religion for political purposes," the report concluded. "Overt use of Islamic organizations for the inculcation of hard-line propaganda is to be avoided."

This was exactly the strategy pursued by Dreher and Amcomlib. Because the CIA files are still closed, it is impossible to say definitively that Amcomlib was directly financing the Muslim Brotherhood and Ramadan. But short of a CIA pay stub, every other indication points to the fact that Dreher and Amcomlib were using financial and political leverage to give the Brotherhood's man in Europe a leg up.

Before he left the United States for Munich, Bob Dreher worked as special assistant to Amcomlib's president. His task was to organize covert propaganda to convince Americans that a strong, independent movement of Soviet émigrés existed — when in fact it did not. He also sat in on Amcomlib board meetings.

This positioned him perfectly for his new job as coordinator of émigré relations at Radio Liberty. He was relieving Ike Patch, who had been sent over a few years earlier to unite the feuding Soviet ethnic groups and build a credible front to hide the CIA's financing and control of the operation. A career diplomat, Patch was seen as an affable consensus-builder, a family man who was well liked but lacked Dreher's aggressive ideas. Dreher was eager to reinvigorate émigré relations. Instead of using émigrés merely as on-air talent for Radio Liberty, he wanted to push covert propaganda measures like the operations in Bandung and Mecca.

Dreher's new colleagues were unimpressed. Amcomlib's New York headquarters was replete with intelligence types like Dreher, but Munich was different. There, people were mostly interested in running a radio station; they considered themselves journalists whose organization happened to have an unusual owner. Dreher was a reminder that they were participating in a CIA front operation. Staffers suspected his role was to make sure ideology didn't take a back seat to journalism. They were also suspicious of his tactics. During the Hungarian uprising in 1956, Radio Liberty's sister station, Radio Free Europe, had encouraged the rebels, only to watch the Soviets crush the revolt. To most in the Munich office, that failure exposed the concepts of liberation and rollback as empty rhetoric. Dreher didn't seem to learn that lesson. "We all thought the Soviet system would bring about its own downfall," says one of Dreher's deputies, Will Klump. "I'm not sure, however, that Bob Dreher did."

Dreher began to agitate for more aggressive use of the émigrés. He divided his tactics into "offensive" and "defensive." The latter meant defending against Soviet efforts to repatriate former Soviet citizens — the USSR had launched an aggressive publicity blitz to win back the refugees, promising amnesty and a job. Many were homesick and some went home; Moscow heralded their return as proof that the allure of the West was hollow.

Dreher's real interest, however, was offense. Early attempts in this vein — for example, by parachuting Soviet émigrés into the Soviet Union — had ended in disaster, but now, frustration with the pace of the Cold War led to a new emphasis on bold operations. Dreher's boss, Walpole Davis of the CIA's Office of Policy Coordination, strongly advocated such measures. Most émigrés were eager to go along — and Dreher clearly had the resources. He set up automatic payments, ensuring that money flowed regularly to émigré groups. The people who got the cash might have been unsavory — some possibly were killers — but the payments were made on time. Everyone knew that the paymaster was the CIA, and Dreher was its man in Munich.

In 1958, a second Bandung Conference was held. Unlike its predecessor in 1955, this meeting was a disaster for Washington. Although in hindsight Washington's fears seem overblown, the second meeting proved that the event in 1955 wasn't a one-off and that some sort of permanent grouping of nonaligned nations was inevitable. Indeed, the Non-Aligned Movement exerted some influence in the middle years of the Cold War. Although its relevance would fade, Washington saw the 1958 conference as the start of a dangerous new alliance, especially because it included a key role for communist China.

U.S. diplomats spent that year assessing why their country had done so poorly. They concluded that one of the saving graces had been their old reliables, such as Said Shamil, who wired to conference delegates petitions against the Soviet suppression of Islam. And Rusi Nasar, who had worked for Amcomlib on a Hajj as well as during the first Bandung Conference, attended this second meeting too; he had presented a blistering attack on the Soviet delegation, forcing it into a defensive posture. But the Americans needed more credible spokesmen. Shamil and Nasar were hardly at the leading edge of the Muslim world.

That was where Dreher came in, according to his assistant at the time, Edward A. Allworth. Now a professor emeritus at Columbia University, Allworth was then a budding scholar of Central Asian history who took off a year from his studies to put his language skills to work in Munich for Amcomlib. Allworth confirmed that Dreher was trying to make use of Ramadan, with Nasar functioning as a liaison between the two. (Nasar declined to comment on this.) "Rusi Nasar tried to link the World Muslim Congress with Munich and events in Southeast Asia," Allworth said in an interview.

It's not clear if this alliance was in place when Ramadan made his grand announcement at St. Paul's Church in 1958. Around this time, West German intelligence stated plainly in separate reports that the United States had secured Ramadan a Jordanian passport, allowing him to flee to Europe, while Swiss intelligence claimed that he was a U.S. agent. Ramadan's family will not comment on this, and the CIA still has its Ramadan file locked up. What is definite is that soon after Ramadan settled, he and Dreher were working together.

A clear sign of this arrangement came in February, when two people close to Amcomlib visited von Mende. One of the visitors was Ahmet Magoma, a long-time political activist and former Ostministerium employee. A few years earlier, he had asked Amcomlib's Eric Kuniholm for a job when Kuniholm made his big trip through Germany and Turkey. Accompanying him was Said Shamil, the venerable Dagestani leader with long-standing ties to Amcomlib. The two presented von Mende with an open letter. It called for Namangani's Ecclesiastical Administration to broaden, embracing not only the old soldiers but also all Muslims, especially Ramadan's students. The two also demanded a European congress on Islam, to be led by Said Ramadan. Magoma and Shamil said Namangani wasn't up to the task. Students who turned to him for religious instruction found that they knew more about Islam than did the ex-SS imam. Said Ramadan, they said, had a similar impression of Namangani.

Von Mende was outraged at the Americans' plan to back Ramadan at Namangani's expense: "I have the impression that this criticism was leveled on purpose and avoids the whole truth in order to limit Namangani's responsibilities and impact." As for Ramadan, von Mende put him down, saying — in a colossal misjudgment — that he had no influence in the Muslim world.

Shamil told von Mende that his concerns were irrelevant; the plan was already underway. He said that Dreher was willing to pay for the congress. All they needed from von Mende was his support in getting West Germany's Foreign Officee to issue visas to Muslims traveling to Munich to attend. Von Mende sent his notes on the meeting to the Foreign Office, writing that Shamil was known throughout the Middle East as a U.S. agent and that West Germany should be skeptical of the congress led by Ramadan "because it is obvious that the goal of Shamil's efforts is the creation of a new platform from which he [Ramadan] on behalf of the Americans can operate in the Near and Middle East." Apparently von Mende's concerns were ignored; Amcomlib was powerful in West Germany, and the Foreign Office issued the visas.

The West Germans were losing control of the situation. Von Mende got a report from a source that the Soviet embassy was recruiting Arab students and planning a party for Muslim students in Cologne at a popular beer hall, the Franziskanerkeller. East Germany was offering scholarships to Egyptian students and other Arabs. If von Mende didn't act, the Soviets would move into this large pool of potential recruits.

Then, almost at the same time, the Soviets struck at one of von Mende's key men. A certain Professor Abdullah arrived in Hamburg from Syria and phoned Namangani, asking whether he would like financing for his mosque. All it would take was a trip to Cairo. Namangani called Kayum for help, and he relayed the message to von Mende. Von Mende quickly pulled Namangani out of Munich and brought him and Kayum to Düsseldorf for a consultation. Von Mende figured the offer was Moscow's response to the Americans' bid to organize the congress. The Soviets wanted to undercut the Americans by funding the mosque themselves. Namangani was told not to go to Cairo.

To counter the superpowers, von Mende launched his own covert operation in the Middle East. During the Hajj season of 1959, he sent Namangani and Hayit on a trip through the Middle East to distribute anticommunist and pro–West German propaganda.

What he heard back bothered him. Thanks to Ramadan's involvement, the Muslim world was gaining the impression that the Munich mosque was the Americans' project, not the West Germans' — yet another sign that Ramadan was doing significant work on behalf of Amcomlib. Namangani reported to his boss that "we have difficulties with the 'American Committee for Liberation from Bolshevism'" that seemed "insurmountable." In this game, the West Germans were out of the superpowers' league. At heart, the Germans wanted the Muslims to play a role in a vaguely defined, quixotic quest — to help a united Germany recover its lost territory someday in the future. The superpowers, by contrast, had broad, strategic, and immediate goals for Islam. West Germany was simply their battleground.

Around this time, Ramadan was at the peak of his influence. While winning strong allies in Europe, he remained a force in the Muslim world too; for example, he revived the Muslim World Conference in Jerusalem. This body had been formed to unite Muslims around the world, but by the 1950s it had degenerated into a forum dominated by the Muslim Brotherhood and the Grand Mufti of Jerusalem. Few other Muslims attended, and its influence was stunted. But then Ramadan called the conference's third general meeting for January 1960 and scored a resounding success. In addition to the exiled Brotherhood members, the Indonesian premier Muhammad Nassir attended, as did representatives of twelve other Muslim countries. In addition, the meeting was backed by a group of notable intellectual and cultural leaders, including Said Shamil. Topics included Palestine and communism. The group condemned "Muslims under Communist rule" — a far cry from the 1955 Bandung Conference and its successor meeting in 1959, which produced only a grudging criticism of communism through the efforts of U.S. employees like Rusi Nasar. Ramadan's ideological sympathy with the American position can also be detected in a letter he wrote to one of the CIA's front organizations in Munich, the Institute for the Study of the USSR. Ramadan wrote to the institute's *Arabic Review,* saying how much he enjoyed the magazine and offering to distribute it throughout the Arab-speaking world. He said to send as many copies as possible to the World Muslim Congress's offices in Jerusalem.

Ramadan's base, though, was clearly shifting to Europe. Although a powerful figure among the Muslim populations of the Middle East, he felt unsafe there. He was living in Sudan in 1959 when he finally decided to move his family once and for all to Geneva. In a letter to Professor Kegel, he said he had had his fill of coups d'état and dictators.

His appearances in Germany multiplied. A month after his family arrived in Geneva, Ramadan participated in the European congress that Dreher financed, which was meant to represent all Muslims in Germany and Europe. Gacaoglu wrote a letter about it in April 1959; given his close ties to Amcomlib, it's no surprise that the content reflects Amcomlib's thinking. Gacaoglu describes Munich's future as the world center of Islam. Its mosque would be for all Muslims, not just followers of von Mende's Ecclesiastical Administration. "The mosque to be built shouldn't be aimed at an existing group; it should be above all a meeting point for Muslims of the entire world, a center of Islamic thinking, and a place where Islamic and German art can flow together," Gacaoglu wrote.

These goals were reflected in a new structure that Ramadan established. When the soldiers and students met in Munich on Christmas Eve in 1958, they set up the Mosque Construction Commission, with Namangani as chairman and Ramadan as honorary chairman. It remained an informal group until 1960, when it was registered at the local courthouse as an official organization. In Germany, that meant the group's name ended with the abbreviation "e.V." — *eingetragener Verein,* "registered association" — giving the commission certain legal rights and obligations. The benefits included official standing as a legal entity, meaning it could sue. The obligations entailed articles of association, an elected board of directors, minutes of its meetings, and a chairman — and that person was Ramadan.

It's not exactly clear how this happened. The commission was Namangani's idea, and he signed the letter notifying the court that Ramadan was the chairman. It could simply reflect the fact that early on, the two men were not opponents. Namangani may also have believed that the mosque commission was simply an appendage of the Ecclesiastical Administration, which he was still running. A few years later, however, Namangani acted as if he hadn't realized the implications of officially registering the commission — which is quite possible, given his low level of education. Ramadan, by contrast, had just completed his doctorate in law with Professor Kegel. In any case, Ramadan was suddenly at the helm of the legal entity charged with building the mosque — another sign that the Americans had backed the right man. (Namangani stayed in charge of the Ecclesiastical Administration, which was not in charge of the mosque.) The Germans, who had brought over Namangani and come up with the idea of a mosque, were suddenly on the outside.

Ramadan quickly took advantage of his new position. When Namangani first raised the idea of a mosque in 1958, no one had a plan for raising the hundreds of thousands of marks needed to finance such a building. Now, in mid-1960, Ramadan announced that he was off on the annual Hajj and would bring back money. The cost of building the mosque was now estimated at 1.2 million marks ($2.2 million in today's terms), and an architect had drawn up plans for an Arab-style building, complete with dome and minaret.

Ramadan continued to try to approach von Mende and win him over — probably a sign that the Americans were advising him to cultivate their old intelligence contact. Otherwise it isn't clear why Ramadan would have taken the initiative to do so. After the first meeting of the Mosque Construction Commission at the church, he had sent a young aide to seek von Mende's support. Now he met with Hayit, trying to push for the establishment of a broader organization to include all Muslims. Hayit reacted angrily. "Germany is a gate that no one controls because no gatekeeper exists," he wrote in a frustrated letter to von Mende in March 1960. "Everyone comes in and does what he pleases."

The next month, Hayit reported that the United States was again trying to change the focus of Namangani's group — broadening it so it could address global Islamic issues. The mosque was supposed to become an organ that would criticize Soviet Islam. Hayit wrote to von Mende, "One comes to the conviction that the American Committee for Liberation from Bolshevism is trying through its people to use this religious office for its propagandistic purposes."

The more the intelligence agencies looked into Ramadan, the less they understood him. Hayit wrote in one report to von Mende that Ramadan was planning a meeting with Sijauddin Babachanow, the mufti of Turkestan and a Soviet functionary. Babachanow promised money for the mosque. The plan went nowhere, but it underscored the difficulties surrounding the person Amcomlib had decided to back.

Dreher kept trying to bring the West Germans on board. He telephoned von Mende in May 1961 and advised him to see Ramadan. Von Mende was baffled because he knew Amcomlib had originally rejected Ramadan as "too reactionary-conservative" — as reflected in CIA comments some years earlier about Ramadan's being a "fascist." Dreher argued that there was no point in having competing Muslim organizations in West Germany, so why not back the better man? Ramadan had excellent contacts in the Middle East, and this could only benefit the free world's fight against communism.

Von Mende reluctantly agreed to see Ramadan, who traveled up to Düsseldorf. The two had a long discussion in von Mende's grand offices. The German was shocked at Ramadan's proposal, which was to send a "Muslim delegation" to the next meeting of the UN General Assembly. The delegation could plead for religious freedom — and, of course, attack the USSR. Ramadan would head the delegation, with two assistants, Gacaoglu and Shamil. Von Mende thought the idea ludicrous. He wrote, "The two gentlemen have not always been known positively from their work in Munich — Shamil's activities during and after the war are topics of conversation in the emigration. Therefore, the two men proposed by R. are not usable for the purposes he has for them."

He then wrote to his contact man in West German intelligence, saying he wondered "for which American agency Mr. Ramadan is active." Perhaps he didn't know Dreher's position as liaison to the CIA, although von Mende's files are full of notes from Amcomlib moles describing other aspects of the organization's internal workings.

Von Mende was also concerned about Ramadan's plans for the Hajj; he believed that the fund-raising work was just a platform to gain attention so Ramadan could more easily supplant Namangani. For Amcomlib, it would be a chance to attack the Soviet Union; Ramadan could also lobby on behalf of the oppressed Brotherhood and for his dream of a united Muslim world.

After Ramadan left, a worried von Mende wondered what to do. He had told "the gentlemen" from Amcomlib on several occasions that they hadn't chosen well in the Muslim émigrés they had backed. But if Dreher thought Ramadan had such great contacts and was worth backing, maybe von Mende himself should change his mind — perhaps he had been too hasty in writing off Ramadan?

Von Mende could think of only one way to test Dreher's judgment: break into Ramadan's office and steal his files. So he did what every good bureaucrat would: he wrote a memo outlining the problem and the solution. Ramadan, "who continually cooperates with Amcomlib," had "a small fanatical following among the Arabs" but was widely pigeonholed as a foe of the Egyptian strongman Gamal Nasser. His files, though, would show his influence in the Muslim world.

Von Mende spent some time figuring out the logistics of a burglary, writing that "Dr. H." — presumably Hayit — would organize the operation. He ran the idea past his contact man with West Germany's BND, its foreign intelligence agency, and he confirmed in writing that Ramadan was indeed working closely with the Americans: "At the same time, his expenses are financed from the American side." In the end, the burglary was called off, but von Mende had reason to worry. Ramadan had all but taken over the mosque project. As usual, it was his trusty right-hand man, Hayit, who brought the issue to von Mende's attention — and, as usual, the message was cast in his inimitably direct but broken German.

"It is astounding that yet another Islamic group has appeared, this time with Said Ramadan at the top. Too many societies but too little useful work seems to be the fashion." And then Hayit mentioned yet another group angling for control of Munich: JAI. It stood for Jami'at al Islam, a strange Muslim charity based in Washington and led by a rambunctious author, Ahmad Kamal.

10

THE NOVELIST'S TALE

BUREAUCRATS IN BAVARIA's refugee ministry were charged with helping the local Muslims, but by 1960 they were finding it hard to sort out the competing groups — the Americans, the politicians in Bonn, the ex-soldiers, and the Arabs like Ramadan. Then suddenly, they were faced with Ahmad Kamal. Author, adventurer, and spy, Ahmad Kamal was one of the most charismatic — and erratic — figures involved in America's efforts to harness Islam. He ranged from California to Turkestan and Indonesia to Algeria, always claiming to be a champion of downtrodden Muslims. Often, though, he was working for foreign intelligence agencies. He arrived in Munich not on his own, but instead cloaked in his latest creation, a charity called Jami'at al Islam. His goal: to control the Muslim community in Munich.

In January 1960, Jami'at officials announced that they were moving their operations from Austria to Munich. German officials were immediately bombarded with pamphlets and newsletters explaining the group's founding. Social-affairs bureaucrats were confused. "I hardly think it's possible to unify the rival groups, namely the Ecclesiastical Administration [von Mende's group], 'Islam' [Gacaoglu's group], and the newly arrived Jami'at al Islam," wrote an official from the displaced persons' ministry in Bonn to his Bavarian counterpart.

Von Mende's men had been trying to undercut Ramadan by asking Bavarian officials to stifle his efforts to build a mosque. The officials now seemed too busy with Kamal to respond to von Mende. Wittingly or not, Kamal's Jami'at was running interference for Ramadan, sowing confusion among low-level bureaucrats and allowing Ramadan to move forward unhindered.

The Bavarians' confusion becomes understandable in light of the content of Jami'at's brochures. They overflowed with articles about the group's strange history—almost surely a product of Kamal's novelistic imagination. He portrayed Jami'at as a millennial movement, a holy brotherhood forged in battle and now championing oppressed Muslims around the world. "Jami'at al Islam was founded in the years 1868 to 1869 in Turkestan during the time of the attack of czarist Russia against the defenders of Buchara and Khiva. Men of all social classes and professions united in this brotherhood, which considers as its holy task, to curb the Russian expansion in the lands of the Turkic peoples."

The story continues with the defenders losing to the czar's armies but taking Jami'at abroad and transforming it into a charity that also supported military insurgencies; for example, it sent observers to the Dutch East Indies as the region gained independence and became Indonesia. From Jakarta, Jami'at coordinated freedom fighters from Tunisia and Morocco, as well as other parts of Africa. Then the story gets even odder. Jami'at sent "expeditions" to Africa, where its associates collected 660 kilos of precious metals. This was added to the personal property of the old Central Asian warriors. By the end of 1957, Jami'at had assets worth $328,556.98 (about $2.4 million in today's terms). Then it set up operations to help Muslims in Jordan—primarily Palestinians—and opened an office in Vienna to coordinate aid for Muslims living there.

For all this action, Jami'at didn't seem to do much in the way of charity work. Its thirty-page newsletters included little concrete news about specific projects. Most of the essays expounded on the future of Islam and how Christian aid organizations were neglecting Muslims. The only real assistance Jami'at seemed to provide was to administer money for the U.S. Escapee Program, a classic Cold War project meant to encourage people to leave communist countries. This effort gave defectors money to support their resettlement once they arrived in the West. Jami'at seemed to aim at getting as many defectors and refugees as possible onto its rolls — thereby guaranteeing steady funding from U.S. aid agencies in addition to the UN High Commissioner for Refugees, which financed one of the group's projects. But Europe's refugee situation was improving, and Jami'at struggled to find more prospects, especially Muslims. That led to refugee poaching. According to one of Jami'at's officers, while the charity was working in Italy it ran afoul of Catholic agencies when its members tried to sign up Muslims who were already on the Catholic agencies' rolls. In Austria, Jami'at got into a dispute with the Office of Refugee and Migration Affairs, an agency of the U.S. State Department, concerning the number of cases it oversaw. The office cut Jami'at's funding and then restored it after Kamal organized a protest led by Muslim leaders. When Jami'at arrived in Munich, its representative's first act was to visit the displaced persons' camps around the city. Kamal had himself photographed in front of a shack with a health warning affixed to it. Given the rapidly dwindling refugee problem, this seemed like a stunt.

Despite all this, Jami'at was taken seriously. Kamal implied that his group was endorsed by the U.S. government, emphasizing that it was the only Muslim charity recognized by the American Council of Voluntary Agencies. This U.S. advisory board registered — but did not vet or endorse — charities. But it sounded official and letters from Jami'at always emphasized this tie, as well as the group's tax-exempt status in the United States and its relations with the UN High Commissioner for Refugees. Politicians lent their backing. When Pakistan's president, Field Marshal Ayub Khan, visited Germany in 1961, he met Kamal in Munich and promised to support Jami'at. That same year, Jami'at organized a large conference in Munich on Islam and the West, featuring top Jami'at officials and senior politicians, such as Bavaria's labor minister, Walter Stain. Von Mende fell for it too. His Ecclesiastical Administration encouraged its members to sign up with Jami'at. In a letter to them, Namangani said Jami'at was the only officially recognized Muslim charity in the world.

Within less than a year, Jami'at was so successful that the local media assumed it was running the mosque project. In early 1961, the *Münchener Merkur* matter-of-factly described the mosque as Jami'at's project and ran a picture of a Jami'at official inspecting plans for Munich's mosque.

"The Bavarian capital has recently become the center for Muslims living in western Europe," the *Merkur* noted, citing Jami'at's move to Munich as key proof. "The Islamic organization has taken on the cultural support of its brothers in faith. In Munich, a mosque, a culture center, and a kindergarten are to be built."

From today's perspective, all of this might seem like an elaborate hoax. But it wasn't. Jami'at was almost certainly backed by U.S. intelligence, and Kamal had most likely been sent to Munich as a backup to Ramadan — to make sure that a U.S. organization influenced Muslim religious life in Munich. What U.S. officials didn't know is that Kamal wasn't just brilliant — he was also unstable. They also probably didn't realize that his entire life story was as fictional as his novels.

Figuring out the true biographical facts about anyone involved in intelligence work is tough enough, but Kamal's public life makes it harder. While people like Dreher and von Mende hoped for nothing more than anonymity, Kamal didn't shy away from publicity — for the better part of a decade he worked as a novelist and wanted to sell books. But he created such a bizarre public persona that the real man is almost lost.

The official story is exotic but straightforward. On the back cover of Kamal's novels — the reprint editions, which his son published in 2000 — is a short biography of the author. We learn that Ahmad

Kamal was born on a Colorado Indian reservation in 1914 to "Turco-Tatar" nationalists who had fled persecution in czarist Russia. "Kamal's genetic makeup imprinted all his endeavors, be they as deep sea diver, combat pilot, horseman, warrior, or as exponent of national self-determination," goes the blurb.

When he came of age, according to the story, Kamal traveled to his ancestral homeland of Turkestan. There, he "commanded" the Basmaci rebellion against the Soviets, who were reasserting czarist-era colonial control over the region. Later, he fought alongside Muslim rebels in western China. He also supported the independence of Indonesia and Algeria and was "commanding general of the Muslim liberation forces of the Union of Burma in the 1980s."

This summary contains much that is true. But even a cursory glance at it raises questions. If Kamal was born in 1914, then how could he have participated in, let alone "commanded," the Basmaci rebellion in the 1920s? Archival records raise even more fundamental issues, such as Kamal's actual name and the ethnic makeup that supposedly motivated him.

According to Kamal's Federal Bureau of Investigation file, he was born Cimarron Hathaway on February 2, 1914, in the affluent Denver suburb of Arvada. His father was James Worth Hathaway and his mother Caroline Hathaway. His mother's maiden name was Grossmann, and no typical Central Asian facial features are apparent in her photo. As for his father, Kamal's passport applications stated for years that his father's surname was Hathaway. But in a 1952 application he listed his father as Qara Yusuf. According to Kamal's daughter, Kamal's father had been much older than his mother — sixty-four years old versus sixteen for the bride — and had wives back in Turkestan. He had left Kamal's mother and returned home, possibly to fight in the Basmaci rebellion. That could explain the presence of a man named James Worth Hathaway — perhaps he was a stepfather whom Kamal's mother married after being abandoned or widowed by the older man?

FBI records do show that in about 1935 Cimarron Hathaway went to Central Asia. Here his fiction may provide clues to fill out the biography, or at least help us understand his motives for traveling. The autobiographical narrator in one of his novels goes to find his father and converts to Islam. By 1935, however, the Basmaci rebellion had long been extinguished. Perhaps Hathaway met some of the defeated fighters and imagined that he had participated along with them. According to his FBI file, he married while in Central Asia, but his seventeen-year-old wife died after one month, a victim of some unspecified violent act in the Chinese province of Xinjiang, where a rebellion against Chinese rule was underway. Accused of being a spy, Hathaway was arrested by Chinese authorities in the city of Hami but escaped from prison.

When Hathaway returned to the United States, he published his first book, an extravagantly imaginative work called *The Seven Questions of Timur*. It is a retelling of a legend about Tamerlane, the fourteenth-century Turco-Mongolian ruler whose armies conquered vast tracts of the Eurasian continent. Tamerlane poses questions about the universe and receives answers from a simple young soldier — perhaps in this story the young Hathaway imagined a relationship with his father. Using a familiar storytelling convention, Hathaway sets himself up as the simple translator of an ancient text, adding this explanation on the title page: "From an Original Turki Manuscript by Ahmad, Descended of Karu Yusuf Ibn Kara Yakub." This Karu Yusuf echoes the Qara Yusuf on Kamal's passport application. The book, sumptuously illustrated with fanciful art nouveau–style drawings of Timur and his Tatar court, was published by a small arts press in Santa Anna. Only several hundred copies were printed, and they were hand-numbered. Aside from the single volume housed in the Library of Congress, the book is almost impossible to find. At this point, Cimarron Hathaway is well on his way to transforming himself into Ahmad Kamal. The book's copyright is held by C.A.K. Hathaway — Cimarron Ahmad Kamal Hathaway, presumably. On November 1, 1938, a court in Hollywood approved the name change once and for all, so the former Hathaway was thereafter Ahmad Kamal.

Soon Kamal began to distance himself from his mother, coming to scorn her. When she died many years later, Kamal's daughter found him in his study, crying. She asked him why — she thought her father had never loved his mother. "I'm crying for what wasn't," he replied. The difficulty in their relationship probably belongs at the therapist's office, but it is telling that on one passport application later in life, Kamal put his mother's name as Caroline Kamal Hathaway — was he imagining a Muslim identity for her? Did he resent the fact that she didn't raise him as a Muslim and that he had to leave home to find his father, who had died? Could this explain his passionate, even violent, support for Muslim causes?

In 1940, Kamal published a tough adventure story set in Turkestan. And he did so in high style, signing with one of America's most prominent houses at the time, Charles Scribner's, publisher of Ernest Hemingway. *Land Without Laughter* starts as a conventional tale of hardship, with a character named Kamal traveling in the dead of winter through mountain passes from India through Tibet and finally into eastern Turkestan, known today as Xinjiang. This is probably a retelling of Kamal's own trip back to Turkestan in 1935 to find his father. He recounts in fascinating detail — too much, it seems, to spring entirely from the imagination — his encounter in Chinese Turkestan with the rebel general Ma Hsi-jung, who was challenging the tottering Kuomintang government for control of the region. The character Kamal serves as an officer in Ma's army and then is sent to buy weapons abroad. As he tries to make his way overland to eastern China in order to embark on a ship back to America, he is betrayed and thrown in jail, only to escape and finally make his way home. The book received a long write-up in the *New York Times*, which called it "swash-buckling, boastful — and sometimes oddly ingratiating." Yet as the writing of an advocate of all things Muslim, it certainly seems odd. Like an ignorant outsider, Kamal conflates ethnic groups, calling them all Tatars. These people are invariably brutal and rough and speak in strangely stilted language — exoticisms designed to appeal to Western readers.

Kamal claimed that in 1941 he returned to Turkestan to retrieve documents; war broke out, and the Japanese interned him. He had already met his second wife, a Tatar journalist and linguist named Amina, who had been living with White Russian exiles in Tianjin. The two spent the internment writing, an activity that Kamal hid from his Japanese guards by copying his works in a Turkic dialect and claiming that they constituted a rendering of the Koran — at least this is the story Kamal told the *Los Angeles Times* when he arrived back home in 1945. A photo of Kamal accompanies the article: with an intense expression on his face, he hovers over his mother, who is inspecting the fake Koran.

Physical and mental intensity are what contemporaries remember about Kamal. Like Said Ramadan, he wasn't tall or imposing, but people always remarked on his presence — the power that he radiated. He was about five foot eight and slender but strong. Until his thirties he had red hair that flamed from his head; he wore it trimmed so short, his head looked shaved. He eventually went bald, which made him even more intense-looking. His face was set off by a small mustache, his skull stood out prominently beneath his taut skin, and his eyes burned like the tips of two hot pokers. On his right cheek was a small V-shaped scar. He appeared timeless and hardly seemed to age through his thirties into his seventies.

Kamal brooked no opposition, not even within his family. A disciplinarian, he matter-of-factly told his children that he had killed people, including a mullah who had opposed him. His daughter, Tura, thought this was a boast or exaggeration, but she came to believe him after she left home and talked to people who knew him. "He definitely killed people," Tura Kamal-Haller said. "I thought maybe he was just telling me stories because this seems so foreign to us in our lives here. But others told me the same thing."

Whatever he had been writing in China, Kamal came back to the United States brimming with ideas. Over a four-year span he published three books. Curiously, for a man who had started out with romantic ideas of Turkestan and his ethnic heritage, he produced commercial books and signed them with mainstream publishers such as Doubleday and Random House. The works have little in common. One novel describes Greek immigrant sponge divers in Tarpon Springs, Florida; another book is a memoir about a dog. The third, *The Excommunicated,* is a romantic thriller set in Shanghai, cowritten with Charles G. Booth, a British author who had lived for years in California, writing hard-boiled fiction and screenplays. The reviews were favorable, and screenwriting jobs were coming Kamal's way. His writing career was blossoming — and then it stopped. The 1950 publication of *The Excommunicated* marked the end of Kamal's popular writing career. As far as the mainstream public was concerned, he disappeared.

In fact, just two years later he produced another book, one that holds a clue to Kamal's intelligence career. *The Sacred Journey* was initially published in Arabic. In this book Kamal tried to describe a Hajj as accurately and undogmatically as possible. The book did not appear in English until 1961. The delay seems strange, especially because in 1953, Kamal had announced in the *Saturday Evening Post* that he was writing a book on Mecca. Perhaps it has to do with the book's tone. Kamal's earlier works were adventure stories. *The Sacred Journey* is almost anthropological in its painstaking commitment to accuracy, giving a day-by-day account of a typical pilgrimage to Mecca. Compared to his other books, it is extremely boring, a dry recitation of facts. It cannot have excited many New York editors and indeed was published by a relatively small house.

In Kamal's note to the English edition, he says he wrote the manuscript while living in Bandung, the Indonesian city that would host the famous conference in 1955. A Jami'at brochure claimed that the group used Jakarta as a base for aiding revolutionaries. That could have been true; Kamal might instead have been observing Islamist groups, perhaps for U.S. intelligence. Before he left the United States, he told a friend he was going there to work for the U.S. government. His FBI file also records a debt of $1,877.40 that he owed the U.S. embassy in the Indonesian capital of Jakarta for money the government had advanced him for moving costs. He was clearly cooperating with U.S. officials before he left home.

This was the view of West German intelligence. Von Mende's files from 1955 contain a report on Indonesia. At the time, the young country was a battleground where pro- and anticommunist parties competed for influence. The anticommunists consisted of an Islamic bloc led by a former government minister, who used money he kept in Swiss banks to finance acts of sabotage against supporters of the communists. The minister's overseas contact man, according to the Germans, was Kamal. The report states that Kamal suffered two assassination attempts in Jakarta and fled to Barcelona.

Interestingly, the German report says Kamal rejected an offer to work directly with the CIA because he considered the agency tainted by the infiltration of many Soviet agents. Then the U.S. government made another overture, asking Kamal to work directly for Vice President Richard Nixon, who also headed the National Security Council. Kamal accepted this position, according to the Germans. While this development might seem far-fetched, the NSC oversaw intelligence and psychological warfare through the Psychological Strategy Board and its successor, the Operations Coordinating Board. It's possible that the intelligence report simplified the chain of command, putting Kamal directly under Nixon. Although the archives of both bodies contain nothing on Kamal, this is not unusual — agents' names are typically excised from all documents, even those approved for declassification. Kamal certainly was pursuing U.S. objectives in Indonesia. Besides helping the anticommunist insurgents, he used his influence in the government to try to cancel the Bandung Conference, according to the West German report. He showed up in Bandung during the event but stayed for only twenty-four hours because of security concerns.

By then, Kamal was living in Franco's Spain. His family learned Spanish and his son took music lessons from the celebrated Spanish guitarist Andrés Segovia. Spain might seem an odd choice for a place to live, but U.S. intelligence had extensive contacts there — Radio Liberty, for example, had situated a large transmitter in Spain. Likewise, Kamal used it as a safe base. His goal: support for the uprisings across the Mediterranean in North Africa and the Muslims of Munich. To accomplish this, he needed to recruit a loyal lieutenant.

Touhami Louahala grew up in a large Algerian family. His father sent him to work when he was fourteen. Good with numbers, he won a small scholarship to study aircraft design in France in 1949. There, he began to associate with other Algerian students and realized he had to help in the effort to rid his homeland of French colonial rule. He began to work as a courier, driving to Sweden to pick up propaganda material from the Algerian resistance group FLN. In 1956, he took a shortcut on his way back down to Marseille and drove through Switzerland. Swiss border police were waiting for him and he was thrown in jail.

Help soon came — from Ahmad Kamal. After hearing from others in the FLN that Louahala had been arrested, Kamal arranged for a lawyer to represent him. This legal counsel successfully cast Louahala as a victim of an overzealous Swiss attorney general (who later committed suicide in response to allegations that he had fed information on Egyptian and Algerian spies to France). On January 1, 1957, Louahala was freed and flown straight to Libya, again courtesy of Kamal.

"We couldn't communicate because he didn't speak much French or Arabic, and I didn't speak English," said Louahala in an interview at his home outside the French city of Montélimar. "So he said, 'Look, Touhami, if we're going to communicate, you must learn English.'"

Kamal got Louahala a Libyan passport and then sent him to London to learn English. Louahala would have been at a loss in a foreign city, unable to speak the language, but Kamal had thought of that too. He flew over his Jami'at representative in Washington, James Price, to help Louahala get organized. The two spent a couple of days setting up bank accounts, renting an apartment, and registering Louahala for classes. Price even took him to Marks & Spencer to buy him a suit and an umbrella. Over time Kamal tutored Louahala in how to run an organization. "He was very strict but he was diplomatic. He wouldn't shout, but you would know what to do. He was like that."

Kamal liked good scotch and red wine. Louahala drank alcohol too, defending this behavior through his own interpretation of the Koran: it says that you cannot pray when your thinking is impaired, but not that you should abstain completely. The men shared this take on a typical prohibition of their faith, and over time Kamal became a mentor to Louahala. The younger man made his children get up at 6 A.M. and repeat Arabic, English, and Spanish phrases in a rote drill for an hour before school because this is how he remembers Kamal teaching his children in Madrid. Louahala became one of Kamal's most trusted officers. He was sent to Italy, Lebanon, Vienna, and then Munich. He is cagey about what he did. In Lebanon he claims he oversaw a sewing class, whose proceeds went to help refugees in Algeria.

A French journalist of that era saw it otherwise. Serge Bromberger, a correspondent for the French newspaper *Le Figaro* and the author of the 1958 book *Les rebelles algériens,* wrote that Jami'at was a cover for funding insurgencies from Indonesia to Algeria. When France and Britain invaded Egypt in 1956, Bromberger wrote, Egypt was unable to supply the FLN with arms. Jami'at then stepped in and began sending weapons — hence, perhaps, the sewing classes worked as a cover for gun running. Certainly this scenario fits the overall time frame and Kamal's ongoing agitation on behalf of Muslims. It also wasn't incompatible with U.S. aims; many in Washington thought France should leave Algeria and probably wouldn't have cared too much if Kamal was aiding the FLN. The problem with Bromberger is accuracy. He confuses Jami'at with the much more famous Pakistani group of a similar name. And none of his assertions are proven — as a reviewer in 1959 put it, "It is difficult always to be sure what is fact and what is fiction."

Louahala categorically denies that Jami'at sent weapons to Algeria. But he does not rule out the possibility that Kamal's money was used for weapons. "He did not raise money directly for guns. He raised it for humanitarian purposes. It was sent there and . . ." Louahala shrugged his shoulders. As for the CIA, Louahala stated that the agency was fully aware of Jami'at's actions. "The CIA had him [Kamal] in their sights," Louahala said.

I asked him about Kamal's reaction.

"He did something very smart. He asked a CIA agent to work for him."

Who was that?

"That was Mr. James Price."

The person who had flown over to London to help him? A CIA man was working for Kamal?

"Yes, he worked for them. But this meant nothing to Kamal. He said, 'You can see what we do. We have nothing to hide. You can send someone to work with us and see everything. Everything. See what we are doing and inform your superiors. Then you will know we are not hiding anything.'"

That is one possibility. Another is that Kamal was already working closely with the CIA, and Price was his handler. Price later worked for the Library of Congress, where he authored a favorable report on Radio Liberty after its CIA connections had been exposed. It's clear he had a close relationship with officials in Munich — Amcomlib staff expressed relief when they heard that Price was authoring the report, and archival material shows that he discussed it with them in letters before it was released. But the larger issues are harder to confirm: the CIA refuses to release information on Jami'at, citing the blanket "national security" exemption to the Freedom of Information Act. Price is still alive but refused several requests for an interview.

Louahala arrived in Munich just as pro-French terrorists were targeting West German businessmen for selling weapons to Algerian rebels. On October 17, 1960, the Munich businessman Wilhelm Beisner stepped into his car, turned the ignition, and was almost blown through the roof. A bomb wired to the ignition had detonated, severing his legs and injuring passers-by. Miraculously, Beisner did not die, but a message had been sent: West German businessmen should stop selling weapons to anti-French Muslim insurgents in North Africa. Beisner was one of West Germany's most notorious arms dealers, a former high-ranking Nazi who U.S. diplomats believed was now delivering matériel to North African insurgents. Louahala says he had nothing to do with exporting weapons. He was there, he says, to replace Jami'at's local representative, Ahmet Balagija, who had allegedly been telling the Germans that Jami'at was a front for covert activities.

Over the next year, Kamal's group began to act more and more unpredictably. In 1961, Jami'at pulled out of Jordan, stating in a newsletter that the kingdom had banned the group because its members had cooperated with Jewish charities. This explanation does not ring true because U.S. government files show no other U.S. charity being banned in Jordan. Instead, Kamal might have been pushed out because of his work on behalf of Palestinian nationalists. In several of his writings, Kamal emphasized that he was aiding Palestinians. This would have worried Jordan, which had plans to annex the West Bank and wouldn't look favorably on a group pushing Palestinian rights. Kamal also had close ties to the Grand Mufti of Jerusalem. He asked him to write an endorsement of *The Sacred Journey* and had hired a person with close ties to the Mufti, Mahmoud K. Muftic, who von Mende thought was the Mufti's man in Germany. These are far more convincing explanations for Jami'at's troubles than any ties with Jewish groups.

Then, in late 1961, Jami'at issued an angry letter "To All Members." It said that over the past few years, Jami'at had been cautious and measured in its approach, especially toward churches. But Western religious groups had spurned Jami'at. "The conditions force Jami'at al Islam-International to admit that all in all its restraint was a mistake." Jami'at's board had met on October 17 in the New York Sheraton, the letter said, and Kamal had decided "that JAI has withdrawn its declaration to refrain from extreme methods." The group also warned Western authorities to change their tactics or lose the support of the Muslim people. The next day, Jami'at announced that Balagija had been fired "for cause," effective immediately.

From the ordinary Bavarian bureaucrats' point of view, Jami'at's actions were incomprehensible. Because Balagija had been so active, everyone believed that Jami'at was running the mosque project. His barrage of letters, visits, and media activity made the Bavarians think they were dealing with a major Muslim organization and not a one-man front operation. The Germans trusted Balagija, a former soldier in one of the Muslim units in World War II. The officials were right to wonder about Jami'at's actions; Balagija's firing coincided with Jami'at's disintegration.

Perhaps trying to rein Kamal in — or perhaps by coincidence — Washington ordered an audit of Jami'at's management of the escapee program. The group had charged the cost of its brochures and grandiloquent histories to the U.S. Escapee Program and now had to pay it back, as well as half the salary of the European director and money used for administrative costs that didn't have to do with refugees.

Concerned officials in Munich were kept apprised of the situation and finally asked von Mende for help. He called Balagija and his successor up to Düsseldorf individually. The successor made vague charges that Balagija had been corrupt. Balagija said that Jami'at had claimed a caseload of four thousand refugees to milk money out of the U.S. Escapee Program, whereas in fact, Jami'at had handled only four hundred. Balagija also warned Bavarian officials to stop funding Jami'at "because the group will only use this money for the purposes of its propaganda, including anti-Christian." Von Mende wrote a memo saying that Balagija probably had been fired because he was more loyal to the Germans than to the Americans. As if to underscore that point, he wrote another letter a few days later saying Balagija was going to open a small restaurant for Muslims and was willing to cooperate with West German officials in providing information.

In March 1962, Jami'at made another strange announcement: just two years after the organization had arrived in Germany, it was leaving and would change its focus to sub-Saharan Africa. Effective immediately, Jami'at was closing all offices and advised that any correspondence should be sent to San Francisco. German and U.S. officials were relieved. "I think," wrote the Council of Voluntary Agencies to its German counterpart, "that we've been spared a common worry." But Jami'at didn't move to Africa; it vanished. Louahala returned to Algeria to join the FLN government. A few years later, Kamal would move back to California to continue his covert work. In 1969, he offered the Burmese opposition leader U Nu $2 million if he would depose the country's dictator, Ne Win.

It's hard to know what to make of this strange episode. Kamal probably believed in his messianic description of Jami'at and his role as a savior to the Muslims; he likely felt that taking U.S. money was just a means of helping his people. Perhaps when his actions became too erratic—agitating on the West Bank or sending too many weapons to Algeria—the United States pulled the plug. Yet it's also true that he didn't stop collaborating with U.S. intelligence and that in some way he helped the United States by running interference for Ramadan. Kamal might simply have been an insurance policy in Munich—a fallback plan in case Ramadan didn't work out—but by 1961 he either was no longer necessary or was simply out of control. In any case, the project ended and JAI vanished.

With one American down, the West Germans received more good news. Balagija wrote to von Mende, telling him that the soldiers were fed up with Ramadan and wanted to elect as mosque head Ali Kantemir, an old, widely respected fighter from the North Caucasus and a von Mende loyalist. He could unite the factions and get the mosque built. Ramadan's plans for a grandiose mosque would be scrapped and a smaller, more affordable prayer room would be built instead. The Germans were thrilled. Finally, it seemed that Ramadan and the Americans could be stopped.

11

WINNING THE MOSQUE

S AID RAMADAN HAD NO serious competitors in the fight for control of Munich's mosque project. Men like Ali Kantemir might have been respected in their communities, but they had been broken by World War II. Kantemir was almost blind and got by on a few hundred marks per month, which he earned by editing Amcomlib's *Arabic Review*. Ramadan, by contrast, was jetting around the globe, helping to lead an Islamic revolution.

"Dear Professor Kegel," he wrote in July 1960, "I am just back from Saudi Arabia and East Africa. It was a very interesting trip indeed. In Somalia, I attended the quiet birth of its Republic and was happy to see my old Somalian friends of exile back at constructive work in their homeland. One of them has already become first president of the Republic and another one already has been the leader of the Opposition." Ramadan returned to Europe just long enough to find a publisher for his book and then was off on a Hajj; next he journeyed back to Europe for a short time before finding his way to Turkey and Pakistan.

During one stop in Europe in 1960, Ramadan addressed the Mosque Construction Commission, telling of his fund-raising success. He had had a personal audience with the Saudi ruler, King Ibn Saud, who had promised a large sum for the mosque. So had King Hussein of Jordan and businessmen in Libya and Turkey. Ramadan told the commission that he had set up "branches" for its work in Mecca, Medina, Jeddah, and Beirut — probably he had appointed honorary consuls who would collect money for the project. The members of the mosque commission were stunned and thanked him profusely.

Some, however, were worried. Hassan Kassajep, an old battalion commander from the 162nd (Turkestani) Infantry Division, spoke up. He had married, started a family, and was now a carpet dealer. He had taken the job as the commission's manager simply because he wanted a mosque. He wasn't so sure about kings and princes or secret political affiliations. Like other commission members, he hadn't even realized that Ramadan had gone to the Middle East. Kassajep asked how the two had paid for the trip. Ramadan's answer was that the mosque project had "branch" offices in various countries, which had financed it. This answer implies that the project had something of a wide following in the Muslim world, perhaps among the Brotherhood's followers. Kassajep warned that the group shouldn't get too political. "Our task is to build a mosque in Munich," Kassajep said at the meeting, "but not to get involved at all politically."

These concerns brewed throughout the year as Ramadan continued his high-profile tactics, flying here and there, speaking at conferences and attacking communism — all in the name of the Mosque Construction Commission and Germany's Muslims. Kassajep and Namangani wrote to the Bavarian social-affairs ministry, asking that it help guide the commission back to its original goal. But it was just at this time that the Bavarians were overwhelmed by Jami'at's sudden arrival. Kassajep and Namangani's letters apparently went unanswered. The situation festered into 1961. In February, Kassajep met with Bavarian officials and said Ramadan was a problem for a number of reasons. Because of his political activities, Ramadan was persona non grata in many Arab countries. Even though he was a star of the Islamist scene, he couldn't actually raise money, Kassajep said, and the money promised during the previous year's Hajj hadn't materialized. In fact, the Mosque Construction Commission had only 78,890 marks (about $145,000 in 2008 money) in the bank, and the total project was estimated at 1.2 million marks ($2.2 million). Kassajep said he hoped Ramadan would be replaced.

It was around this time, in 1961, that Dreher sent Ramadan to meet von Mende and that von Mende considered breaking into Ramadan's office. Von Mende's BND contact had talked him out of this plan, but turmoil in von Mende's office also probably played a role in his abandonment of the idea. His plan had called for Hayit to break in, but Hayit and von Mende's other star agent, Kayum, were at loggerheads. Kayum started the trouble by visiting Hayit at his home in Cologne and telling him that he knew all about his work for the West German government. Hayit ran to von Mende, who wrote to his contact at the BND, expressing his concern that Kayum was aware of the arrangement. (Interestingly, von Mende did not dispute that Hayit worked for the BND.)

Salary was another concern for the skimpily funded von Mende — another sign of the West Germans' inability to compete with the Amcomlib juggernaut. Hayit complained to von Mende that his skills were unappreciated even though he had been working for the Germans since his stint in the Zeppelin unit, which was a group of Soviet minorities who had collaborated with the Germans beginning in 1942. West Germany had plenty of money but spent too little of it on Muslims, he wrote, adding, "And then we demand that these Muslims remains [sic] friends. Paradox!" Kayum too was constantly writing to von Mende about money woes. In 1961, von Mende gave him a monthly salary of 450 marks "in recognition of his earlier services for Germany."

Von Mende finally got Kayum and Hayit to work on a report about Ramadan. Presciently, they focused on Ramadan's right-hand man, Ghaleb Himmat, who would later head the mosque for thirty years and transform it into a national network and a center of international Islamism. His influence was evident in the early 1960s, but only to a sharp observer. It had been Himmat's idea, while a student, to invite Ramadan to Munich to take over the mosque project from von Mende and the soldiers. He was now treasurer of the Mosque Construction Commission and had accompanied Ramadan on his big fund-raising trip to the Middle East. By mid-1961, he was setting up Ramadan's appointments with Bavarian officials during his trips from Geneva. He was constantly at his side and filled in for Ramadan when he was away. Kayum and Hayit wrote in their report to von Mende that Himmat distributed a procommunist Lebanese newspaper, *Al-Mujtamah*, implying that Himmat had procommunist sympathies. It is unclear if this is true, but it was an early sign that Himmat had his own international ties and interests.

Even though von Mende's operation was puny compared to Amcomlib, he did have influence in the West German bureaucracy. Bavarian social-affairs officials started to ask Ramadan tough questions, reflecting the ex-soldiers' concerns. In one meeting, they asked Ramadan how much money he really had raised. Ramadan repeated the figure of one million marks but refused to say who had pledged it. When the officials suggested to Ramadan that he was the problem — polarizing the group while not actually raising any money — he wrote back offering to resign. The mosque, he assured them, was not to be political.

But the mosque was already politicized. Begun by the West Germans as a political project, it was now divided internally. For over two years Arab students had been bad-mouthing the ex-soldiers; Namangani received especially sharp criticism. Finally, Namangani had had enough. On November 7, he sent Ramadan a short letter resigning as vice chairman of the Mosque Construction Commission. He said the commission was not professional enough and criticized Ramadan for not adequately explaining his fund-raising trip to the Arab world. He also said that Ramadan had threatened to sue him when he had raised this point in the past. The commission was due to meet later that month. Namangani asked Ramadan

to appear and answer questions about the trip. It was to be the final
showdown over control of the mosque.

After numerous delays and cancellations, the Mosque Construction
Commission finally met on November 26. All thirty ex-soldiers
and students who made up the commission were present. Ramadan
gave a long talk justifying his controversial tenure as head of the
group. Money was flowing in, he said, and the mosque was all but
financed. He now identified the donor of one million marks — it
was a Saudi businessman. Along with a flurry of smaller donations,
it would put them near their mark. Many of the commissioners
were skeptical. Word had gotten out that Himmat had lost donation receipts during the past year's Hajj, implying that he had issued
the receipts and accepted money but then claimed he had lost the
receipts and not issued them. That way he could account for the
missing receipts and pocket the money. Himmat replied that he had
lost only a few blank receipt books. The soldiers on the commission
demanded to know how Himmat and Ramadan had paid for the
trip — who was backing them?

At this, Ramadan made a savvy political move. Instead of an-
swering any questions, he resigned and walked out. If he wasn't appreciated, then so be it. The commission held a vote on a new chairman, and the students nominated Ramadan in his absence. But this
time the ex-soldiers had shown up in force. The confusion over the
date of the meeting — it had been scheduled for October, then early
November — worked against the young members of the Muslim brotherhood, who were scattered across southern Germany.
Instead of winning a new mandate, as he had figured he would,
Ramadan lost by two votes. In his place, the old North Caucasus
soldier Ali Kantemir was elected, putting von Mende's men back in
control of the mosque project. Ramadan had by then returned to
the meeting, expecting to hear of his own reelection; when he saw
the result, he stormed out and went to his hotel nearby. He claimed
that he was a victim of "intrigues" and flew back that day to Ge-

neva. Ramadan seemed finished: he was losing friends in the Middle East — just the month before, Jordan had withdrawn his diplomatic passport as the country tried to patch up relations with Egypt — and now his plans for a center in Munich with a young cadre of idealistic students seemed thwarted as well. But he was not as weak as he seemed. Kantemir had won the vote, but the commission statutes required that the chairman be elected with a two-thirds majority. Even though Ramadan hadn't rallied all the students to the meeting, he had secured enough votes to block Kantemir after all. Ramadan hadn't been aware of the discrepancy until a sharp-eyed German bureaucrat scrawled in the margin of the meeting's minutes, "No two-thirds!" Kantemir had failed to win the vote, and Ramadan was still chairman.

That effectively ended the ex-soldiers' presence on the commission. They decided they couldn't win against Ramadan. Kassajep resigned as secretary, and the soldiers refused to participate further. That left the students in control and, so it seemed, the Americans too. It was strange: the West Germans' influence on the commission ended because of a technicality caught by a West German bureaucrat. Von Mende had assiduously used the bureaucracy to bring over Namangani, create his group, and pave the way for a mosque, all in hopes of creating a core of loyal Muslims for West German political purposes. Now he had been bested by an even sharper player.

Von Mende's mistake was to rely heavily on people with a tainted past: ex-functionaries of the Ostministerium. Their former service guaranteed that they would be loyal to von Mende and the German cause, but they were badly tarnished by their Nazi-era activities and easily discredited. In the third world, Soviet propaganda labeled them Nazis, while Islamists like Ramadan looked down on their weak religious credentials. Even old Gacaoglu had landed many blows against Namangani, labeling him a Nazi marionette. That had made it easy for Ramadan to step in and dazzle with his international connections and the promise of a shiny new mosque.

The failed vote was a turning point in the history of the mosque. Dreher and the rest of his U.S. cohorts had tied themselves to Ramadan, hoping he would give the West a credible voice in the Muslim world. The mosque was meant to be his platform. To that end, U.S. intelligence reportedly had pressured Jordan to give Ramadan a passport and financed projects to raise his profile, such as the European Islam conference that Dreher had organized. Now these plans had succeeded. The Brotherhood controlled the mosque project. The question now was whether Ramadan would help his old friends or go his own way.

With the ex-soldiers gone, Ramadan moved quickly. First, he filled the position of secretary of the Mosque Construction Commission, which Kassajep had vacated, with Achmed Schmiede, a young German convert who had been publishing a magazine, *Al-Islam*, since 1958. *Al-Islam* became the commission's official organ, an important part of Ramadan's vision for creating a Muslim Brotherhood–type structure. This called for an array of institutions, not just a mosque. One was a propaganda organ, a role *Al-Islam* filled perfectly.

In March 1962, Ramadan united the Muslim students in Germany under an organization called the Council of Islamic Communities and Societies in Germany. The choice to use students to set up the council was typical: as with the mosque, he wasn't interested in old-fashioned Muslims like the ex-soldiers, who might indulge in the occasional drink or forget the odd prayer. Like all Islamists, he wanted to create a cadre of new and better Muslims. That meant linking up with students, who were younger, less set in their ways, and generally more impressionable. The council's meeting was held in the city of Mainz on March 17 and 18, with student groups from a dozen West German cities. About fifty representatives attended and elected Schmiede as secretary to coordinate their work. According to von Mende's sources, Ramadan financed the meeting, but that begs the question of who financed Ramadan. The records do not say. A key goal of the meeting was to criticize Ramadan's two main enemies: Nasser's Egypt and Israel. His article on Nasser must have thrilled Ramadan's U.S. backers, but it's hard to know what they made of his criticism of Israel. Ties between Washington and Tel Aviv were not as strong then as now; perhaps the agency was willing to accept Ramadan's position on Israel in order to have a strong anticommunist in its corner.

With his German base secure, Ramadan went back on the offensive internationally. In May, Ramadan and Schmiede traveled to Mecca to help launch what today is still the most important Muslim organization in the world: the Muslim World League. This was the culmination of decades of effort to unite all Muslims — if not under a caliph as in days past, then in a worldwide body that could issue guidelines and speak for Muslims. Ramadan played an important role in the league's founding, helping to draw up the bylaws. He led the "neo-salafiya" faction at the conference — essentially the Muslim Brotherhood's group. Its goal was to make the league more explicitly political, particularly by attacking Israel. Ramadan wore several hats at the meeting. He attended as head of the Muslim World Conference in Jerusalem, the group that he, along with the Grand Mufti of Jerusalem, had revived. He was also a representative of the Muslims in West Germany. Signifying how important the league's founding was, von Mende had sent Kayum there to gather information. He sent back a detailed memo on the new body but had little luck in asserting West German influence: when the meeting concluded, sixteen top Saudi officials did visit West Germany, but they came to see Ramadan, not von Mende or other government bureaucrats. Though little is known about this trip, it did show how Ramadan had internationalized the German Muslims and the mosque to a degree von Mende could not have imagined.

Ramadan's new visibility seemed good for the United States, but Washington was not likely aware of everything Ramadan was doing. Dreher, especially, seemed happy to pay for Ramadan's conferences but probably had scant knowledge of the young Islamists' activities and little idea that Ramadan was a stubbornly independent

man who would not be controlled by anyone — not by a Muslim
organization, let alone a non-Muslim one. But in the short term,
Ramadan's involvement in the Muslim World League helped
strengthen the group's anticommunist credentials, which was exactly what Washington wanted. Although many observers at the
time thought that Islam was a natural enemy of communism, it
was not a foregone conclusion. Just nine days after the league was
founded, for example, a rival group, the World Muslim Congress,
met in Baghdad. At the time the most important Muslim group in
the world, the congress's meeting was sponsored by the Iraqi leader
Abdul Karim Qassim, a left-leaning military dictator who had over-
thrown the monarchy in 1958. Normally, because of his interest in
organizing Muslims, Ramadan would have attended the conference
and might even have stood for office. But Qassim was steering a
pro-Soviet course, so much so that Ramadan felt it was physically
dangerous for him to attend. In his place he sent his ally Mahmoud
K. Muftic — a former Bosnian SS soldier with ties to the Grand
Mufti and the Deutsche Muslim Liga in Hamburg.

This was probably the most dangerous time in Ramadan's life.
Nasser had proclaimed that Ramadan was a leader of the Muslim
Brotherhood, and Swiss police believed that a group of six men
had been sent to Switzerland to assassinate Ramadan. Police detained some members of the group and the attempt failed, but Ramadan wasn't taking any chances. According to Swiss investigators,
he asked his former assistant to buy him a concealable handgun, a
Walther PPK. Fearing for his life, he didn't attend the Baghdad conference, but he was still able to help Amcomlib slip in one of its best
Muslim agitators — Garip Sultan.

Sultan had been honing his covert propaganda skills for Amcomlib
back in the United States. A typical operation was a talk he gave
at Philadelphia's venerable International House, a nonprofit institution founded in 1919 as a place for international scholars to congregate and share ideas. He appeared there as a Tatar scholar, reading a
nineteen-page paper, "Modern Forms of Colonialism."

Sultan started by attacking colonialism, a line of thinking with which all students from the developing world could agree. But he then broadened the idea to include the Soviet Union, which had enslaved a dozen countries. The discussion was lively. A few days later, Sultan wrote a memo on it to Ike Patch, who was heading Amcomlib's "Special Projects" department in New York, since Dreher had bumped him out of Munich.

"As far as I am able to judge, the report fulfilled its objective," Sultan wrote. "Heated discussions based upon the report took place. I was left with the impression that these students, although they are studying at American universities, for some reason have adopted the Soviet viewpoint instead of the American one. Or perhaps they have no idea of the American viewpoint." Sultan was now a U.S. citizen. He had emigrated from Munich to the United States in 1957, leaving Munich without a camera-ready Muslim able to smooth over Gacaoglu's rough spots — a crisis that in part led to Dreher's courting of Ramadan. But Sultan hadn't been completely out of the picture. He had continued to work with Amcomlib on special projects, deployed behind his own lines to fight communism on the home front. His guises were numerous and imaginative, always hewing as close to the truth as possible to create believable front organizations. During his appearance at International House, he was introduced as a fellow at the Institute for the Study of the USSR, one of Amcomlib's front operations. But he was also an authorized representative of the United Republican and Democratic Voters Club, a freelance writer for the American Federation of Labor's *Trade Union Courier,* and the founder of a raft of fancifully named organizations, such as the National-Liberation Revolutionary Organizations of the Islamic Peoples of the USSR and the Organization of Muslim Refugees from the Soviet Union. As head of the "Writers' Section" of the latter group, Sultan went to Cairo in 1962 to give a talk called "Soviet Asiatic Writers and the Problem of Creativity."

In a display of networking skill, Sultan finagled an invitation to the Baghdad conference by exploiting his Pakistani contacts. He wrote to Manzooruddin Ahmad at the Central Institute for the Study of Islam, asking if he would be interested in being point man for a conference on self-determination. Sultan then mailed Ahmad a $200 check from the Committee for Self-Determination, Inc., a covert propaganda organization run by Amcomlib's sister organization, the National Committee for a Free Europe. Sultan also wrote saying he'd like to attend the Baghdad conference. Ahmad answered that getting Sultan an invitation was proving tricky because the Iraqi dictator, Qassim, opposed allowing any Americans to attend. But he promised to lobby a personal friend, Inamullah Khan, the Baghdad conference's secretary general. Sultan then contacted Ramadan, who promised to ask his allies to lobby on Sultan's behalf. Qassim eventually consented, letting Sultan in as the sole U.S. representative.

Sultan made full use of the stay. He held private sessions with Muslim notables to convince them of the evils of communism, interviewed the head of the Soviet delegation, gave interviews on Baghdad television, and of course presented a talk blasting the Soviets and Chinese for their colonialist practices in Central Asia. But the situation in Baghdad was volatile, and Sultan was warned to leave. "Someone said I was to be kidnapped or assassinated," Sultan said in an interview. He left Baghdad early, but the conference remains one of the high points of his career and of U.S. deployment of Islam in the 1950s, thanks in part to Ramadan's work.

The big losers in all this were Munich's Muslims. Initially, West German officials were keen to support the mosque project — after all, it had been von Mende's idea and carried out by his protégé, the SS imam Namangani. Later, when Ramadan took charge of the project, von Mende still thought that West Germany should support it because of the positive public relations it would garner. He blamed Ramadan for problems with the commission but concluded that West Germany should go ahead with the project, secure a plot of land, and donate 100,000 marks to get it done.

But as it became obvious that von Mende's ex-soldier friends were completely cut out of the plan, West Germany's generosity evaporated. When Schmiede, Himmat, and Ramadan's other lieutenants contacted the Bavarian social-affairs ministry in 1962 for help with finding land, they were politely rejected. The social ministry had been involved, they were told, because the project had been meant for refugees. Now that refugees were no longer members of the commission, it did not need government support. West Germany guaranteed freedom of religion so the students were free to pursue their goals, but they wouldn't get state support. Rebuffing Ramadan might have felt good, but it underscored the fact that von Mende and his allies in Bavaria and Bonn had failed. A year later, Namangani reported that St. Paul's Church — where the whole idea had begun on the snowy night after Christmas in 1958 — no longer provided room for the ex-soldiers to use for prayer. That meant they didn't even have a prayer room, let alone a mosque.

Namangani was bitter. Four months after the blowup meeting, when Namangani and the ex-soldiers failed to dislodge Ramadan, the old SS imam finally wrote up his version of events. Someone — perhaps von Mende, but probably the German wife of Namangani's trusty friend, Hassan Kassajep — polished the text. It was laced with sarcastic swipes at Ramadan; for example, it said that "he clung to the Mosque Construction Commission as apparently a last hope." Despite the rhetoric, Namangani's comments were prescient, showing great insight into the actions and motives of Ramadan — and, really, of Islamic radicals over several decades.

Namangani said Ramadan had criticized the refugees for their lack of knowledge of Islam and their thirst for alcohol. Ramadan, Namangani said, should have been more humane in trying to understand the ex-soldiers. Their ignorance wasn't surprising, considering that they came from a communist land that systematically had tried to destroy their religion. Instead of offering sympathy and gentle guidance, Ramadan had lectured Namangani on how he should behave and threatened to write a letter to the authorities pointing out his faults; he told Namangani that he had only refrained from doing so to spare the Germans' feelings over having picked such an incompetent imam. Although Ramadan had led celebrations at Muslim festivities, he pointedly disappeared when Namangani did the same. He had no respect for the older man, one of the clearest signs that his revolution wanted nothing to do with tradition. In Ramadan's view, Namangani was a reactionary, and Namangani knew something about that sort of accusation. He had been called that once before — in the Soviet Union, when he had been thrown in the gulag for not being revolutionary enough.

"In one of his writings," Namangani wrote of Ramadan, "he declared that the Muslims studying in Germany would be the future rulers of the Muslim world and to whom we, the refugees, would do best to submit." He also said Ramadan had told him that these older men could never return to their home countries because they weren't real Muslims. If they went back, they'd just create crises. The Soviet Union was better off without them.

It is impossible, of course, to know at this juncture what Ramadan really said. These accounts reflect Namangani's perspective. But they match the recollections of Ramadan's young acolytes, who admit to having disdained the ex-soldiers. Interviews with some surviving students indicate that they had problems with the soldiers' version of Islam. Ramadan's arguments encapsulated pure Islamist thinking, in the best tradition of Sayyid Qutb or, later, Osama bin Laden. Saying the ex-soldiers didn't deserve to go back home — that they were worse than the communists — was in keeping with radical Islam, which holds that anyone who doesn't subscribe to fundamentalist views is an apostate and can be mistreated or killed without compunction.

As usual, blunt-speaking Gacaoglu reminded the community of its loss. The brusque, poorly educated imam, who had started West Germany's first group in support of the refugees a decade earlier, had been cut out first by the Germans for accepting American aid and then by the Americans in favor of the more polished Ramadan. He had been used by political operatives, but all along his main aim had been to help the Muslim refugees in southern Germany. Undiplomatic as ever, he laid the blame on von Mende for bringing over Namangani five years earlier.

"It is very shameful for our Society Islam when we receive calls from foreign guests asking about a prayer room, a mosque, or something similar and we must answer that it doesn't exist. The Federal Republic is trying to make reparations for damages that the German people caused in the Second World War. Why is it precisely the Islamic refugees, who lost everything in the last war, who are being so neglected?"

12

LOSING CONTROL

I T WAS MIDNIGHT, and the party celebrating Bob Dreher's forty-fifth birthday was coming to an end. Several dozen friends and colleagues had danced and drunk for a few hours. Then Dreher's old nudist-colony buddy, Karin West, stood up and began to recite a bit of doggerel she had written for the occasion.

> *Much beloved Bobby Dreher*
> *We're so sad and turning grayer*
> *'Cause you want to go back home*
> *An leave us here to cry and moan.*

It was at this point that most people realized that the gathering was also a farewell party. After four years in Munich as head of émigré relations, Dreher had decided to call it quits and go back to "headquarters" — the CIA in Washington. He preferred the lifestyle in Munich. He loved the city, the people, and his annual ritual of growing a beard for carnival. But his tour was up.

> *Your job was always weird;*
> *It let you wear a beard.*
> *From left to right you'd look and blink*
> *And laugh so secret like the Sphinx.*
> *In the desert of frustrations*

Lost in those Far-Eastern nations:
Balts, Caucasians, and Tatars,
Ukrainians, Russians, and Adschars,
Kyrgyz, Turks, and those Tungus,
Krassavitsi who seduce,
Christians, Muslims, Hindus, Buddhists,
Princes, dancers, maybe nudists.

Various émigrés stood up to thank Dreher. Most were from the old crowd — the Soviet exiles who worked at Radio Liberty. Ramadan and Dreher's new Muslims probably wouldn't have felt at home at such a fete. Eventually Dreher tried to find the right words, using his clumsy German. "I think that we are all people with the same goal." The audience groaned. A Georgian duke interjected with a laugh, "I didn't want it to get political!"

From all nations so exotic,
Even some quite idiotic.
All came to pay respect to you
Because the bucks came only through
Your cornucopian operations:
Director, Émigré Relations!
  Others were just like us,
  Wanting nothing but to trust.
  We wondered quietly from afar:
  What's he doing, our blazing star?
  What is it that he'd convey,
  Our little Bobby from the U.S.A.?

It was a question many of Dreher's colleagues had wondered about. Unlike his predecessor, Ike Patch, Dreher had cultivated new groups as part of a more aggressive strategy. The Muslim students and Ramadan — all had been supported in ways unimaginable a few years earlier. Only weeks before the farewell party on December 16, 1961, Ramadan had survived von Mende's ex-soldiers' attempted takeover and was now the unchallenged head of the

Mosque Construction Commission. That was in some measure due to Dreher's help: he had financed Ramadan's conferences and backed him, creating a platform for the Egyptian Islamist in Europe while also enlisting the support of former German collaborators, such as the Caucasian leader Magoma and the old Dagestani leader Said Shamil. In the past, the United States had tried to recruit von Mende to run the émigrés, but Dreher had essentially brushed von Mende aside. And then there was Dreher's probable role in helping Ramadan get settled in Europe — his visa, for example. That showed initiative and energy — exactly what one would have expected from Bob Dreher, the cold warrior, the veteran of Odessa and Moscow, the CIA man eager to shake up the wannabe radio journalists in Munich.

Yet what had all this accomplished for America? Dreher had clearly won over an important ally. In terms of fighting communism, the Muslim Brotherhood and the United States were on the same page. In late 1961, for example, Ramadan sent a letter to Arthur Schlesinger Jr., a key adviser to the newly elected president, John F. Kennedy. "When the enemy is armed with a totalitarian ideology and served by regiments of devoted believers, those with opposing policies must compete at the popular level of action," Ramadan wrote Schlesinger, "and the essence of their tactics must be counter-faith and counter-devotion. Only popular forces, genuinely involved and genuinely reacting on their own behalf, can meet the infiltrating threat of Communism." The letter was most likely a request to the new Kennedy administration to continue the strategic partnership between the United States and Islamists like Ramadan.

But the events unfolding in Munich cast doubt on the value of such an alliance. Ramadan was now in charge of the mosque project, but he was operating independently of the United States. The Germans and the Americans had the same idea: control the mosque, control the local Muslims, and then use them to fight communism. The local Muslims were still in Munich and to that extent could still be used for covert propaganda purposes, but Ramadan was not going to be their leader on the world stage. It seems that Ramadan hadn't cared about uniting Muslims to fight communism, as the Americans had intended. The CIA analysis from 1953 put it best: he was mostly interested in grouping people around him for power — power that he wanted to use to spread the Muslim Brotherhood's vision of Islam. He pushed aside those who didn't help him achieve this goal. Most of the Muslims in Munich were useless to him. They were old ex-soldiers with limited religious knowledge. More important, they were mature men, too worldly, too focused on their homelands, and too stubborn. Ramadan wanted a cadre of impressionable young men to spread his world revolution. He was leading a new movement, one that sought to heal the world's problems through religion. No wonder he didn't unite Munich's Muslims; that had been the furthest thing from his mind. He didn't want an umbrella group; he wanted a cell.

The Americans, meanwhile, were pulling back. Amcomlib decided not to replace Dreher. Instead, his new deputy, Will Klump, would keep up the payments to the old émigré groups but would cultivate no new talent and lose contact with Ramadan, who was focused on the Brotherhood. The Americans in Munich were of no more use to him, and no one there took the initiative to rekindle the relationship. Ramadan's letter to Schlesinger went unanswered. The émigré relations department would eventually be disbanded, and Amcomlib would make a symbolic but telling change. In 1964, like so many times in the past, it would be renamed: the Radio Liberty Committee. From then on, its emphasis would be broadcasting. Later, when the CIA's role in the organization was exposed in the early 1970s, Radio Liberty was separated from the CIA and merged with its sister radio station, Radio Free Europe. The two stations were put under the supervision of the Board for International Broadcasting, which in turn was run by the State Department.

Symbolic of America's changing priorities, Dreher was deployed to Vietnam. There, he helped the South Vietnamese run covert radio stations as part of the clandestine CIA-backed special forces unit, the Military Assistance Command, Vietnam, Studies and Observation Group. Dreher worked in the unit's covert propaganda unit, serving one tour. As in Munich, Dreher seemed out of touch with his surroundings and unaware of the impact of his work. He spoke no Vietnamese and had no idea of what was being broadcast. He was stationed there as an adviser, helping to channel millions of dollars into an effort he didn't understand.

In 1972 Dreher retired at age fifty-six, after more than thirty years in government service. He kept his stunning apartment in Virginia, with its distant view of the Capitol. His trips overseas stopped, a phase of his life that had dwindled away. He died in 2004 at a nursing home from complications related to a fall.

In September 1962, the Middle East Institute in Washington held a star-studded meeting on Islam in the Soviet Union. This field of study, once obscure, was growing in importance. Held at the luxurious Statler Hilton, the event was partly financed by the State Department and was meant to "open the door to the study of Central Asia" in the United States. Everyone important in the field was there — Sultan, Hayit, and key academics from around the world. Everyone except Gerhard von Mende.

"I myself didn't receive an invitation, presumably for the reasons that you told me," von Mende wrote to Sultan, hoping he could use his Amcomlib contacts to get an invitation. "On the other hand, Herr Dr. Hayit was invited, who is an employee of Research Service East Europe, which I, as an allegedly big Nazi, run . . . I find this course of action at least unfair."

Fair or not, it marked the beginning of a new era, one in which it was increasingly difficult to overlook the strong Nazi sympathies of someone like von Mende. Adolf Eichmann, one of the architects of the Holocaust, had just been executed in Jerusalem, and Raul Hilberg had recently published his pathbreaking book *The Destruction of the European Jews*. In the 1940s and '50s, the Holocaust had been an almost taboo topic — a strange embarrassment that most people ignored or chose to forget. Now it had become a serious field of study and people were becoming aware of who had participated. "He was known as a Nazi and definitely that's why he wasn't invited," recalled Richard Pipes, then a young Harvard professor who helped organize the conference. "His reputation was pretty clear."

Von Mende was increasingly cut out of the mosque project as well. He now had no contacts in the Mosque Construction Commission. In early 1963, the ex-soldiers announced their withdrawal from the group, formalizing what had been a fact for over a year. Ramadan, meanwhile, moved forward. Underscoring his broader ambitions for the group, he changed its name from the Mosque Construction Commission to the Islamic Community of Southern Germany.

In 1963, von Mende suffered another loss. Ali Kantemir, the seventy-five-year-old leader from the Caucasus who had been put up as a candidate against Ramadan and had lost by a few votes, died. For years, von Mende had been helping the half-blind leader. Now he sent a note to his intelligence contacts, asking them to help erase traces of this assistance. "Mr. Alichan Kantemir, with whom I was personally befriended, worked for several years with German agencies and for this was also financed by the German side. Therefore in my view a direct German interest exists to obtain and search through the part of his estate that touches on this cooperation."

Von Mende's impotence was underscored by a query about Turkish "guest workers," or *Gastarbeiter.* Since the 1960s, West Germany's booming economy had been attracting foreign laborers. Now, with their numbers rising, one of von Mende's intelligence contacts was writing to ask about their potential for unrest. It was an ironic question: for years, von Mende had been formulating grand strategies to use Islam without having many Muslims at his disposal. Now numerous Muslims were arriving in West Germany, but he had lost control of the mosque, the instrument that would allow him to influence them. Von Mende tried to establish new contacts. Hayit infiltrated a Muslim student group in Cologne, and von Mende began channeling money there. But he was working on the periphery. Ramadan had won.

The Stasi seemed to take note of von Mende's marginalization. On January 16, 1962, its agents stopped Operation Asiatische Emigration, their seven-year surveillance of von Mende's organization. Perhaps the Stasi was satisfied at taking down von Mende's old boss, Theodor Oberländer; maybe the organization had simply gotten enough mileage out of bashing the Ostministerium group. In any case, von Mende was no longer important. Even his own government had changing priorities. West Germany was hoping to improve relations with the East — the first seeds of détente. Hayit would be sent to another congress, this time in Delhi, but the West German Foreign Office told him to tone down the rhetoric. A few years earlier, such instructions would have been unthinkable.

Von Mende's nerves began to act up. He had suffered a serious stroke in 1956 and his doctor had ordered him to stop smoking. In 1963 he took it up again. The strain of running what was essentially a two-man show — himself and Hayit — was taking its toll. On a Monday in mid-December, von Mende was in his office overlooking the Rhine, reading one of the many intelligence reports that came across his desk. This one was a summary of recent events in the Soviet Union. With the file open before him on his desk, he suffered a massive heart attack and died immediately.

As an intelligence entrepreneur, von Mende didn't fit the usual paradigms. He didn't work for West Germany's foreign intelligence service, the BND, or its domestic counterpart, the Office for Protection of the Constitution. Instead, he had money coming from all sides. The Office for Protection of the Constitution funded him, but so did West Germany's Foreign Office. His operation was more akin to a typical German *Mittelstand* company — such midsize family businesses formed the backbone of the West German economy.

His office was located just downstairs from his apartment. His wife, Karo, played a big role in his work, especially when it came to dealing with the English-speaking world or the all-important socializing with the traditional folk of the Soviet Union. His children helped with clerical work.

The foreign ministry agreed to pick up the tab for von Mende's funeral "in consideration of the great service that the deceased gave as head of the Office for Homeless Foreigners and the Research Service Eastern Europe." But the ministry required one condition: "It is requested to treat this affair confidentially and to take special care that the Foreign Office does not appear publicly as financial backer."

Finding a successor to von Mende proved tricky. The federal government considered his old BND contact, Siegfried Ungermann, but this possibility was rejected as too complicated to organize — von Mende's institution was supposed to give the appearance of being independent of the government, and Ungermann had been a civil servant. Many émigré groups lobbied for Ungermann — or indeed anyone — to replace von Mende. Eventually, the government decided to close the operation.

That precipitated an ugly scene: it turned out that von Mende's children had been on the payroll, and now they demanded compensation. His son also claimed that family goods had been taken from the office. Later, his wife asked if she could use the name Research Service Eastern Europe — apparently she wanted to keep the organization going as a family business. The foreign ministry said no. Even von Mende's files were subject to dispute. Nearly a year after he died, the papers remained in unsecured filing cabinets in his grand office overlooking the Rhine. Officials worried that the mass of papers, most of them marked *Geheim,* "secret," would fall into enemy hands.

His children kept his personal papers, even though many were related to work. Von Mende's working papers, about one hundred thick binders in all, ended up not in the intelligence services' archives — where, like CIA files, they would have been kept under lock and key, if not outright destroyed. Instead, after complicated bureaucratic wrangling, they ended up with the German Foreign Office. After a few decades they were declassified and are now part of the public record.

With Dreher's departure and von Mende's death, the two western competitors had exited the stage. U.S. interests had shifted elsewhere — especially to Vietnam. Its interest in Islam as a Cold War weapon would not be revived until fifteen years later, when the Soviet Union invaded Afghanistan. Then, the Pentagon's Office of Net Assessment would commission the Rand Corporation to write a report on von Mende's use of Muslims. An enterprising research fellow named Alex Alexiev wrote about the Ostministerium in a classified report. He pointed out the obvious implications for the United States as it embarked on arming Soviet Muslims against Moscow. "This study should be of interest to military and strategic planners who are beginning to address the Soviet nationality issue in a strategic perspective," the report stated. Alexiev recounted the story of the Ostministerium and how the Germans had been effective in exploiting the Soviet Union's ethnic divisions. Since many of these ethnic groups formed part of the Soviet army that had just invaded Afghanistan, the United States had a chance to repeat the Germans' tactics and avoid their mistakes. He also noted that many of these Muslim ethnic groups were also living in Afghanistan, giving them a potent reason to fight Moscow.

Alexiev's study was part of a larger discussion that led to the arming of Muslim holy warriors to fight the Soviets. It was very similar to the Germans' pioneering use of them; the Germans had cultivated the Grand Mufti of Jerusalem, set up imam-training schools, and tried to appoint religious leaders in Soviet Muslim areas, all with an eye toward motivating Muslim troops to fight. On another level, Washington had an even clearer precedent for its support of Afghani holy warriors — its support of the Mufti's allies, the Muslim Brotherhood. In backing Said Ramadan, Washington had allied itself with the ur-Islamist group, the inspiration for the holy warriors in Afghanistan who would become known as the mujahideen. Lacking access to the CIA files, we can't draw a causal link between Munich and Afghanistan, but it is probable that the earlier use of the Muslim Brotherhood made it easier for U.S. intelligence to arm the Afghanis. When that support ran its course two decades later after the 9/11 attacks, most would look to Afghanistan for the historical basis of that assault. That was not incorrect — but few realized that its prototype was Munich.

West Germany was already moving toward rapprochement with the eastern bloc, and its officials had little use for Muslims. Von Mende's death effectively ended West German surveillance of radical Islamic groups until the 1990s, when the rise of Al Qaeda and Islamic terrorism caused united Germany's domestic intelligence to refocus on those groups. Only then did the Munich mosque and its Arab students — now adults — again come under scrutiny.

But one group was left onstage: the Muslim Brotherhood. Its members did not lose interest or focus. They grasped the small foothold prepared for them by West German and U.S. intelligence. Quietly, they turned the Munich mosque into a beachhead for expansion into the Western world.

MODERN WARS

———

To solve the labyrinthine quest

I spun out the thread guiding me best:

Did you feel the sense in the tale I told,

That I'm not just one but doubled-souled?

13

THE BROTHERHOOD TRIUMPHANT

O N AUGUST 24, 1973, it finally happened: a muezzin stood inside the bright new Islamic Center of Munich and issued a call to prayer. It was the first documented call to prayer inside a mosque in Bavarian history, and the mosque itself was just the sixth in all of West Germany. It stood bright and modern, a three-million-mark ($5 million in 2009 terms) structure in the pan-Islamic style: a dazzlingly slender 115-foot minaret crowned with a golden half-moon. A spiral staircase wound up to the muezzin's balcony, although this was just a symbolic piece of architecture; the Muslims didn't want to irritate their German neighbors with public calls to prayer. The prayer room was lodged inside an oval structure — nicknamed the "atomic egg" — made of steel-reinforced concrete and covered with cobalt and azure tiles. Nestled inside were meeting rooms, offices, and a library. It was the work of a Turkish-German architect, who had labored long to design something appealing but affordable.

About two hundred dignitaries and diplomats attended the opening, including many of the once-young students who had seized control of the project fifteen years earlier. But for anyone who had followed the history of the mosque, the scene presented a strange anomaly. When it came time for the head of the mosque to present the chief benefactor with a golden key, it wasn't Said Ramadan who picked up the Saffian leather case and handed it to a sheikh from afar. Instead, a Pakistani student did the honors. Ramadan wasn't just absent. He had left the project in disgust and was about to be expelled from the commission.

Ramadan's power had peaked eleven years earlier, when he helped set up the Muslim World League. He had worked tirelessly for decades to unite Muslims around the world in a common cause. With the league's foundation, he had succeeded in setting up a lasting institution. Ramadan was so influential at the decisive meeting that, according to one account, he personally handed King Saud the official proposal to found the league.

Ramadan had wanted to end national boundaries and allow Islam to rule supreme. But, as the founding ceremony revealed, the Saudis dominated the league from the start. The kingdom controlled all the top posts and funded the group. Many in the Muslim Brotherhood made their peace with the Saudis. The kingdom was the site of Islam's holiest places. The country was rich, so it could support almost any endeavor, from libraries and schools to training centers and an international missionary movement. Moreover, the ruling house supported a conservative strain of Islam that in some ways was similar to the Brotherhood's. Many members of the Brotherhood who were persecuted at home found refuge in Saudi Arabia. Almost all accepted Saudi money. Ramadan, however, stubbornly held out, determined to remain independent even as the Saudis pushed him hard. In 1963, the Muslim World League asked Ramadan to make his Islamic Center of Geneva its first overseas office. Ramadan refused, also rejecting efforts to turn his magazine, *Al-Muslimoon,* into an official league organ. The letter he sent to rebuff the league's offer of money was signed and dated with the fictive place name "Islamistan" — a signal that he wanted no country to control him or his work. The Saudis didn't cut ties with Ramadan right away. He still held a diplomatic passport with the title ambassador-at-large for the Muslim World League. Later, probably reflecting his growing frustration with the Saudis, he traveled on a Pakistani passport.

As power shifted in the Muslim world, the students moved away from Ramadan. A few factors contributed to this, money especially. Namangani might have been biased in saying Ramadan talked big and delivered little, but he had a point: Ramadan was so controversial that few who pledged money actually came through with the donation. He'd gotten his biggest pledge from a Saudi businessman — small chance that he would pay, now that Ramadan was splitting with the Saudis.

The Brutus in this drama was Ramadan's protégé, Ghaleb Himmat. Some fellow students speculate that national identity might have contributed to the trouble — Himmat was a Syrian and Ramadan an Egyptian. Syria had the second-most-vibrant branch of the Muslim Brotherhood, and its chief, Issam al-Attar, had arrived in Europe in the early 1960s, in exile. Himmat might have wanted to bring Attar, instead of Ramadan, to Munich. (He would later marry Attar's daughter.) Attar, however, refused, settling in the German city of Aachen and founding an Islamic center there. Others posit that the real problem lay in the fact that Himmat didn't share Ramadan's idealism. Ramadan hoped to spread the Islamist vision through education and teaching. Himmat was more political — and, in fact, would lead the center toward a violent, turbulent future. "Said Ramadan was a traditional Islamist. He knew the teachings of Imam al-Banna — he lived in his home," says Kamal al-Helbawy, the Muslim Brotherhood's official spokesman during the 1990s and an acquaintance of both men. "Maybe some new members tended to be more political and not enough interested in education. Maybe some people didn't pay attention to the full teachings of Imam al-Banna."

By the mid-1960s, Ramadan had had his fill of the students, says Obeidullah Mogaddedi, one of Ramadan's early followers in Germany who stayed on at the mosque after Ramadan left. "The [students] disgusted him and he said, 'I won't have anything more to do with you.'"

Himmat recalls it differently. He said Ramadan's departure had nothing to do with nationalism or different ambitions. Ramadan, he said, had never played much of a role in the mosque project and later was too busy for it: "He was in a few meetings. After a while he apologized and said he couldn't go on any longer. I don't know why. It was a burden for him to struggle for us in Munich."

Before he left Munich for the last time, in about 1966, Ramadan warned Faisal Yazdani, the young Pakistani who became his successor, that he was surrounded by political opportunists. Ramadan half-jokingly warned him about political intrigues—and the likelihood that the Arabs viewed themselves as superior to other Muslims: "Now you'll know what the Arabs are like."

At first, the students seemed cursed. After losing Ramadan, they had no experienced organizer. They had no idea how to lobby for money and lacked the resources for fund-raising trips. The ex-soldiers' departure also hobbled them. When von Mende's men were still part of the plan, the Muslims could count on getting a plot of land for free and government recognition of their venture as a charity—meaning that donations would be tax-free. German officials, however, now withheld both concessions. For two years, the students tried fruitlessly to raise money.

Faisal Yazdani stepped in to help. Ramadan had asked him to join the Mosque Construction Commission in 1960, seeing in him a capable idealist. Yazdani came from a good family, well connected in the Muslim world. Ramadan, ever the internationalist, probably didn't want the project to be dominated by Arabs. He made a wise choice; the young man proved to be devoted to the cause. His father had sent him to Germany to study medicine, but he gave up his studies to work on the mosque, becoming chairman of the Islamic Community of Southern Germany (the new name of the Mosque Construction Commission) in 1965, after Ramadan left. Through his father, a successful Pakistani businessman, Yazdani received introductions to the Pakistani ambassador in West Germany and through him to the embassies of other Muslim countries. Protests from these embassies caused the West German Foreign Office to pressure Bavarian officials into granting the society tax-exempt status. This valuable privilege was worth tens of thousands of dollars over the next thirty-five years.

Eventually, the students raised enough money to buy land on the outskirts of Munich and hire an architect. The land wasn't desirable — it had a high water table, and the mosque's basement would lie underwater, requiring costly modifications. But they were making progress. In 1967, the cornerstone was laid, and the Pakistani ambassador made a speech. Completion seemed just around the corner.

Then, another crisis occurred. Yazdani's main source of money had been the kingdom of Libya. Himmat had contacts there through the Muslim Brotherhood, and the court was expected to finance the project. The building's foundation was laid, the concrete shell erected, and even the heating pipes and radiators installed. Muammar al-Qaddafi's coup d'état in 1969, however, ended the Libyan monarchy and cut the flow of money. The mosque, still a shell, stood exposed to the elements. The pipes began to rust. In desperation, Yazdani went back to the Libyan embassy, now under Qaddafi's control, and pleaded for money. The ambassador sent a secretary to Munich to survey the site. Eager to burnish his credentials in the Muslim world, Qaddafi agreed to pay the balance, about 1.5 million marks. By 1971, the money was flowing, and the mosque opened two years later.

A few months later, members of the Islamic Community of Southern Germany gathered again in Munich. This meeting would shape the mosque's character for decades to come, putting it firmly in the hands of the politically expansionist, Saudi-financed wing of the Muslim Brotherhood — in other words, in Himmat's hands. As at every one of the group's biannual meetings, the key decision was who got to be chairman. Yazdani had held the office since 1965 and seemed a shoo-in. Together with Achmed Schmiede, the German convert whom Ramadan had taken to the founding of the Muslim

World League in 1962, he had almost exclusively raised the funds for building the mosque.

Yazdani, however, was not present. His father had been ill, and he had returned to Pakistan to be with him. In his absence, someone started a whispering campaign implying that Yazdani had enriched himself on the project. These charges were later proven groundless, or at least dropped. All the major contractors had been paid directly by the Libyan embassy, which would have made it hard for anyone to skim off money. But the rumors made Yazdani vulnerable, and a faction of the Arab students mobilized against him. Just as it happened a decade earlier, when the Arab students had forced out the émigré Muslims, the vote this time was close and controversial. The Arabs ran two candidates, Himmat and an Egyptian. In the first round, none of the candidates got the two-thirds majority. Then the Egyptian stepped aside, and Himmat won, with the Arabs united behind him. When Yazdani found out about the decision, he was crushed.

"I have to say that I'm happy that it's built," says Yazdani. "But at times I am still a little disappointed at how it turned out. It wasn't as idealistic as I thought it should have been." One problem, he said, was the emphasis on Arabs over other Muslims. "I talked to them about having different Muslims, but they didn't want it. They wanted just one group, Arabs."

The idea that Arabs banded together to expel a Pakistani might sound conspiratorial — or like the complaints of a sore loser. Perhaps the resemblance to the earlier expulsion of the Central Asian ex-soldiers is coincidental. But events the next year showed the group's exclusionary nature. In 1974, one hundred Turkish guest workers filed a grievance with the Islamic Community of Southern Germany. The Turks claimed that they and others had been consistently denied membership, even though the group's own bylaws stated, "Any Muslim can be a member who supports the purpose and goals of the society." The Turks said they did so. They had supported building the mosque and now wanted to help run it. A Turk had even designed the building. But the group voted against the Turks' joining, saying it would hurt cohesion.

In 1975 the Turks tried again, this time supported by Yazdani, who was still formally a member of the mosque. The meeting was closed to outsiders. Yazdani asked that everyone present on the mosque grounds be allowed to attend the meeting — many Turks had come, hoping to crash the Arabs-only party, and Yazdani was hoping for a show of support. But Himmat and his supporters voted to keep the meeting closed. Yazdani then filed a motion charging that the mosque had been hijacked by the Muslim Brotherhood. Himmat and his followers, according to their minutes of the meeting, said this accusation was ridiculous. Yazdani had no proof, they said. He was voted out of the group, and that was the end of his involvement with the mosque. Over the coming years, he would work as a court translator and distance himself from the mosque.

The mosque society then again took up the issue of whether Turks could join. Many of those waiting outside were guest workers — part of a new, unprecedented wave of Muslim immigration to Europe. They said they had been told they could attend the meeting. Germany had few mosques; most houses of worship were small prayer rooms rented by the immigrants. These people were eager to join a real mosque with a dome and minaret, one, in fact, modeled on the Ottoman style. In addition, the Islamic Community of Southern Germany had expanded to include mosques in Nuremberg and Ulm — this growth was the reason for its name change. The Turks felt that it should have a broader base than just the few dozen students who had been running the project for the past fifteen years.

The leadership rejected this bid for inclusion. Then the group moved to change its constitution to limit membership. Previously, the constitution stated that anyone interested in the mosque could join; now it was changed to create two classes of people: ordinary members who could attend the mosque and a group who ran it. The decision meant the Turks could pray and donate money but not vote. In a bitter irony, it reflected their role in German society: guest workers but not full citizens.

The official account of the meeting states that the core group wanted to remain small so it could take action more effectively, even at a moment's notice. At the time of the meeting, the Islamic Community of Southern Germany had just forty-one members, about the same number as a decade earlier, when it was called the Mosque Construction Commission and focused entirely on building the Munich mosque. Now it had members across southern Germany but had kept the same central leadership.

Over the next twenty-five years, Himmat would make good use of this cohesion, leading the Islamic Center of Munich down an adventurous path. It would eventually grow into a national organization, send shoots across the Atlantic, and lay the cornerstone for European organizations that endure today, ensuring that the Brotherhood's version of Islam would come to be the most influential one in the West. The mosque would be bombed and burned; it would become a focal point for jihad, recruiting young Muslims to fight in Bosnia. Men later convicted of terrorism would seek it out as their mosque of choice, and Himmat himself would one day be forced to resign from its leadership, when he was accused of financing Al Qaeda.

But before all this would happen, Himmat found a partner to balance his weaknesses. Himmat was reclusive, living far from the mosque and rarely appearing in public. Photos of him are hard to find, and over the years he turned down all interview requests. Youssef Nada was his opposite: flamboyant, outgoing, and publicity hungry. He also brought valuable contacts to Himmat. He was several years older, a veteran of the Muslim Brotherhood who secured money for the mosque and international contacts with the Brotherhood back in Egypt. If Ramadan had been the visionary and Himmat its new titular head, Nada was its *Macher,* the man who put the people and the money together.

* * *

Youssef Nada had joined the Brotherhood as a youngster in his hometown of Alexandria, a city in the Nile Delta, the same area that had produced the movement's founder, Hasan al-Banna. He remembers as a child how out on the street two groups of boys were fighting. The Brotherhood's youth wing — an organization similar to the Boy Scouts — stepped in and broke up the conflict. Nada joined soon after, in 1948, the same year that Banna was assassinated. He became a committed member, seeing in the Brotherhood a path to national salvation. When he was twenty-three years old, he was arrested and thrown in jail. It was 1954, and Nasser was rounding up anyone associated with the Brotherhood, banning the group and sending its members far and wide. It was the same wave of arrests that Ramadan had narrowly escaped, but Nada wasn't so lucky and was imprisoned for years. "I witnessed electrical shocks, fire, ice baths, whips, hanging from ceiling upside down, and dogs," Nada says of that time. While in prison, however, he met many senior leaders of the Muslim Brotherhood, ties that would last the rest of his life.

At first, he concentrated on business, working in the family dairy. But he found life under Nasser unbearable. Nada still felt close to the Brotherhood, but the group was banned, and he felt the weight of close surveillance. He sought a way out and finally, in 1960, went to Austria to study cheese making, which he hoped to launch as a business venture back in Egypt. He also set up a business exporting Emmentaler cheese to Egypt. In Austria Nada quickly got in touch with exiled members of the Brotherhood and heard about the students in Munich. In 1960, he drove from his new home in Graz to Munich to participate in the students' Bairam festival.

That was the beginning of his contact with Himmat. At first, the two men met infrequently. Nada would go to Munich once in a while but was not an essential part of the group. Links with Munich became even less frequent when he developed somewhat odd business ties with Libya. "Students there [in Libya] were eating tunafish sandwiches. I convinced the court they should eat processed cheese.

Tunafish is messy, but processed cheese is neater. You spill less oil on your books when you eat processed cheese." With this insight, Nada packed up and moved to Tripoli. It was there that he helped the students in Munich secure initial financing for the mosque.

The Libyan court so valued Nada's advice, he says, that it asked him to be the country's agricultural adviser. "I said, 'I am ready.'" He also won a concession to import building materials from Austria. Like most of Nada's successful ventures it was a quasi monopoly, one that relied on good contacts. During the Qaddafi coup in 1969, those contacts evaporated, and Nada fled. He claims he had to be smuggled out of the country, so tight had he been with the monarchy. He fled first to Tunis and then to Greece and finally Germany. His business in ruins, Nada had a nervous breakdown and went to a clinic in the German spa town of Wiesbaden. It was there he became close friends with Himmat, who was still in Munich, a couple of hours away. Nada decided to make Europe his home and set out to find a permanent base. He moved to Campione d'Italia, an Italian enclave in Switzerland near Lake Lugano. By then, Nada and Himmat were inseparable. Himmat asked Nada to join the Islamic Community of Southern Germany, and in 1971 he did. Soon, Himmat was also living in Campione, just a few doors down from Nada.

When the group met again in 1973, he traveled down from Campione — and for the next three decades the mosque and its ever-growing network of Islamic centers in Germany would be run out of the Italian enclave. At the 1973 meeting, Ramadan was officially kicked out based on his unexcused absences; Nada voted in support of the action.

Nada helped guide the mosque into the Saudi Brotherhood network. He still had close ties with the Brotherhood in Egypt, and he says that for decades he functioned as the group's unofficial foreign minister. It's hard to know how credible this claim is, but he did undertake missions for the Brotherhood to Iran during the Islamic revolution and to Afghanistan to help the mujahideen. Nada wanted to make peace with national governments. He had big business plans that required cooperation, not conflict, with authorities. In this sense, Nada was unlike Ramadan, who never shied away from confronting governments. But in other ways, Nada was more revolutionary than Ramadan. While Ramadan remained in Geneva, isolated and cut off, Nada's frenetic business and diplomatic efforts took place at the center of a worldwide revolution in Islamist activity. The marriage of Saudi money and the Muslim Brotherhood's ideology had set the stage for the spread of Islamist thinking, not only across the Muslim world but into the West too. Nada, Himmat, and the Islamic Center of Munich would be its epicenter.

14

BEYOND MUNICH

R UST FLAKING OFF window grilles, paint peeling off the walls — in every way the apartment block is typical of middle-class Cairo, except for the two police cars parked outside. Inside them, officers note the people entering and leaving one particular apartment: the headquarters of the Muslim Brotherhood.

Banned in 1954, the Muslim Brotherhood is still illegal in Egypt, but it is tolerated. Authorities launch sporadic crackdowns, but members are allowed to meet and issue position papers. The group has also been permitted to put up candidates for parliament; in one recent election it won 19 percent of the vote. Foreign governments reckon that in a country like Egypt, where half a century of dictatorships has systematically destroyed organized opposition, the Brotherhood is the last remaining truly independent group of any stature. Its message of religious revival is one that Egyptian governments once shunned but over time have slowly embraced, seeing their support of Islam as a way to legitimize their rule. The Brotherhood is simply too influential to be done away with completely.

Inside the apartment, the group's militancy is apparent. Pictures of martyred brothers hang on the wall, such as Sheikh Ahmed Yassin, the head of Hamas killed by Israel in 2004. Young men come and go, bringing reports and sending out policy papers to the group's thousands of cells around the country. The man in charge is the Muslim Brotherhood's "supreme guide," Mahdi Akef. He is a

short, elfin figure, born in 1928 and a member of the Brotherhood
since he heard Hasan al-Banna speak in 1939. His office is the apartment's master bedroom. In it are crammed a desk, two sofas, and
the ubiquitous Islamic map of the world, with each country colored
to indicate the extent of its Muslim population, and the whole map
ringed by famous mosques — similar to the one I saw in the London bookstore. "From this small place we run Islam in the world,"
Akef says, an exaggeration, but understandable coming from a man
who heads such an influential group.

Like Himmat and Nada, Akef represents a strand of the Brotherhood that has tried to make peace with authorities. Unlike Ramadan or more radical theorists, Akef is keen to be accepted by governments and wants the Brotherhood to participate in the political
system. He still wants to impose Islamic law, or sharia, in Egypt, but
says he would do so slowly, building up support at the grassroots
level rather than imposing it from above, as was done in Iran. Like
many veterans of the movement, Akef spent years in jail, in his case,
a staggering twenty-three years. The first twenty stretched from
1954, after the initial crackdown on the Brotherhood, until 1974,
when President Anwar Sadat announced an amnesty for all members of the group. The second stint ran from 1996 to 1999, when
Sadat's successor, Hosni Mubarak, acted to suppress the Brotherhood, as he did periodically.

After his release in 1974, Akef quickly linked up with other prag-
matists from the movement, such as Youssef Qaradawi, now famous
around the Muslim world for his television broadcasts and books.
Akef identified with a journal that Sadat allowed to be published,
known as *Al-Da'wa*. It commented on news events, hewing to four
basic principles: anti-Semitism, anti-"Crusaders" (that is, anti-
Christianity), anticommunism, and antisecularism. But it didn't
challenge the government, and many of its backers were fabulously
wealthy, having escaped Nasser's and Sadat's prisons and settled in
Saudi Arabia. This journal signaled the start of a new, more prag-
matic Muslim Brotherhood, one that made itself more acceptable
to authorities by toning down violent rhetoric against the state.

Also close to this group were Himmat and Nada. The Islamic studies scholar Gilles Kepel calls this group the "neo–Muslim Brotherhood."

One of Akef's goals was to reconstruct the Brotherhood's organization, which had been damaged by the crackdowns and the exile
of its key members. That involved careful grassroots work, which
brought about the Brotherhood's phenomenal ascent; it is now the
most influential political movement in Egypt. But Akef also wanted
a carefully wrought international network of organizations that
would be impervious to any single tyrant, such as Nasser. That took
him to Himmat and Nada in Munich.

From 1984 to 1987 Akef lived in Munich as head imam of the
mosque. The timing wasn't accidental. The years following Sadat's
assassination in 1981 were particularly harsh for the Brotherhood.
The Islamic Center of Munich was Akef's refuge. He was its spiritual head while Himmat ran the legal organization from his home
in Campione d'Italia. "The Muslim Brotherhood has a large Islamic
Center in Munich," he says, gazing at the map of the world.

It was a happy time for Akef. He had studied physical education
and now went swimming almost every day. He emphasizes the fact
that he swam with Germans. He has nothing against the local people, he says, although he faults them for placing the mosque next to
a garbage dump and sewage treatment plant. He ascribes the fact
to prejudice rather than the students' lack of money: "This was the
only place the government would approve." The dump was eventually beautified through a costly government program and now
features jogging and biking paths. To him it's another triumph for
the Brotherhood. "We made this dump beautiful and now it's full
of trees," Akef says, his voice trailing off. "It's one of the most beautiful parts of Germany." Whatever his role in urban renewal, Akef
helped drive an unprecedented surge in the organizing of Islam
throughout Europe.

Just a few months before the Munich mosque opened in 1973, the
Islamic Cultural Centres and Bodies in Europe met in London's

theater district, with the purpose of establishing a network of like-minded groups. Several dozen activists attended, including Himmat, the newly minted head of the Islamic Community of Southern Germany. Reflecting Saudi Arabia's efforts to dominate organized Islam, the chairman was Saudi. Himmat was elected to the governing council, along with Khurshid Ahmad, an influential Pakistani activist. The London meeting didn't immediately succeed in setting up a European network. But it was a first step.

Four years later, the Brotherhood scored a success. The 1977 meeting was held at the Swiss lakeside resort of Lugano, just up the street from the homes of Himmat and Nada. Nada welcomed the participants, many of whom he knew personally or would later become his business partners, to Switzerland. One of the most impressive was Qaradawi, who at around this time was with the magazine *Al-Da'wa.* Now widely known as the Brotherhood's spiritual leader, he had been an important figure as early as the 1950s. In 1955, for example, Nada recalls that when he was in prison along with the other members of the Brotherhood, their jailers allowed them to pray. When the call to prayer went out, he said, "I couldn't believe it. [It was] the first time I'd heard it in prison. Qaradawi led the prayers."

Far away now from such travails, the group meeting at Lake Lugano began the arduous process of rebuilding the Brotherhood's organization. Here in Europe, protected by laws and democratic institutions, they were free to set up lasting structures. Their first was the International Institute of Islamic Thought. Despite IIIT's name, its function was not theological. Its goal was to provide the theoretical underpinnings for the spread of Islamism in the West. It would hold conferences and allow leaders of the Brotherhood and similar groups to meet and exchange ideas. It would also publish papers and books, helping to nurture the global rise of Islamist philosophy. A year later, the group met in Saudi Arabia and decided to locate IIIT in the United States. Ismail Faruqi, a leading Islamist thinker who had also been at the Lugano meeting, was instructed to open the center in Pennsylvania, near Temple University, where he held a teaching post.

The Lugano meeting was also attended by two Muslims important to the spread of the Brotherhood in the United States: Jamal Barzinji and Ahmad Totonji. When Faruqi opened IIIT in 1980, Barzinji signed the papers of registration. The two had close links with Nada. Barzinji was an officer in one of Nada's companies starting in 1978; he worked for him for five years. Nada also nurtured another stalwart of political Islam in the United States, Hisham Altalib. He worked for Nada's companies, and Nada sponsored him for membership in the Islamic Community of Southern Germany. At a meeting in 1978 at the Islamic Center of Munich, Nada put Altalib forward as a candidate to be a voting member in the mosque, even though he didn't even live in Europe, let alone Munich.

Totonji, Barzinji, and Altalib all came from Iraq, studied in Britain, and then went to the United States in the early 1960s. Totonji and others helped found the Muslim Student Association in 1962, widely regarded as the first Brotherhood organization in the United States. So their participation in the Lake Lugano meeting is a sign that parallel to events in Europe, the Brotherhood was gaining a foothold in the United States. Their work for Nada and participation in the mosque show that transatlantic ties were strengthening, as did the fact that Nada lived in the United States for a while; in fact, three of his children were born there, between 1978 and 1982. Nada lived in Indianapolis, where Barzinji, Totonji, and the others were turning their student group into a national movement. In many ways they repeated the process that Nada and Himmat had pioneered in Germany: form a student group, go national, and then build an organization with Saudi money and Muslim Brotherhood ideology. Just as he had done in Munich, Nada apparently helped organize financing of the Indianapolis headquarters. The forty-two-acre site soon boasted a mosque, classrooms, residences, a gymnasium, and an eighty-thousand-volume library. By the 1980s it formed the headquarters of the North American Islamic Trust, the Muslim Student Association, and the newly created national group, the Islamic Society of North America.

Meanwhile, the Islamic Center of Munich continued to grow in importance. In 1982 its name was changed to the Islamic Community of Germany, reflecting its growth across the country. The Islamic Center of Munich was now headquarters to a national group that oversaw a chain of mosques and cultural centers. The exact number in the early 1980s is not clear from the historical record, but it had branches in all major West German cities.

Reflecting its international importance, the group continued to add members from abroad, turning membership in the mosque into a mark of honor. Just a few years after having kicked out a Pakistani and rejected Turks as full members, the organization accepted a group of non-Arabs — the difference being that these were famous Islamist activists, not run-of-the-mill believers. Khurshid Ahmad, for example, joined. He had attended the London meeting in 1973 and was the most important representative in Europe of Jamaat-e-Islamiya, the Pakistani version of the Muslim Brotherhood. Another key new member was Issam al-Attar, the charismatic head of the Muslim Brotherhood's Syrian branch, who had moved to Belgium in the early 1960s and settled in the West German city of Aachen in 1968. These two men symbolized the Islamist movement's ability to internationalize and overcome the ethnic divisions that split the Muslim world. Although men like Himmat, Attar, and Ahmad had their ideological and personal differences, in Europe they had far more in common than they did with non-Muslims. From their point of view, they were the vanguard of a new wave of Islamist activity in the West, minorities in Christian lands. But of course they did not live in Munich or have anything to do with the mosque there; it was just a vehicle for their struggle. Himmat highlighted the group's lack of connection with West Germany when he sent in the minutes of the 1982 meeting by registered mail from his villa overlooking Lake Lugano, 250 miles away from Munich.

Like Akef's office in Cairo, the center of this painstaking effort to build a network of institutions appears a bit anticlimactic. The Brotherhood's European base is now located in the Markfield Conference Centre, a former training ground for ambulance crews on the outskirts of Markfield, a tiny bedroom community with one church and three pubs situated outside Leicester, itself a faded textile mill city, two hours north of London. Far from Europe's great centers of Muslim population, it looks like a small campus: rolling lawns dotted with dormitories, an auditorium, and a bookstore. One of the buildings houses the Federation of Islamic Organizations in Europe and its chief, Ahmed al-Rawi.

Rawi was born in 1947 in a small Iraqi town of the same name. The Brotherhood was an important part of community life there; its members were among the most progressive residents. In an interview, Rawi said he used to consider himself a member of the Brotherhood, although he emphasizes that he has never formally joined. The rise of a military dictatorship in the late 1960s made Iraq increasingly inhospitable and in 1975, Rawi went to Britain to study structural engineering. He got his doctorate in Dundee and later settled in Loughborough, a town near Markfield. As a driving force behind the Brotherhood in Britain and Europe for thirty years, he was able to choose the federation's home, although he takes pains to emphasize the logic of the choice. "This is the Midlands," he says, "and so we are in the middle of things. We have an airport. It is not so remote."

There is another reason too. The Markfield Conference Centre is owned by the Islamic Foundation, whose founders and organizers are close to Jamaat-e-Islamiya. The foundation promotes interreligious dialogue, and even Prince Charles has visited. But that was before it became widely known that the foundation's lecturers have backed the terrorist group Hamas and that its bookstore is stocked with the classic authors of Islamist literature: Sayyid Qutb, Harun Yahya, and of course the Brotherhood's ubiquitous spiritual leader, Youssef Qaradawi. Rawi fits into this intellectual universe. Like Qaradawi, he believes that suicide bombing is justified as long as it is aimed at Israeli Jews — even if children become victims. The argument, as explicitly set forth by Qaradawi, is that Israeli children grow up to be Israeli adults and thus are fair game. Rawi has signed petitions condoning suicide bombings in Israel and has stated that Western soldiers are appropriate targets for suicide bombers in his homeland.

Rawi's office is a small room dominated by the regulation Islamist map of the world, with predominantly Muslim countries colored green and others in varying shades. Rawi is a short, trim man with a silver beard and clear, friendly eyes. Still struggling with English, he shrugs his shoulders to emphasize the rationality of his position: "It is not suicide. Anyone can agree in general that they have the right to resistance. We can't deny them the right to resistance. Like Iraq is occupied by the U.S. We prefer peaceful resistance and civil disobedience but they have the right to defend themselves. It is like the French resistance."

Rawi represents what some call "engineer Islam" — the control of the Islamist movement by men with professional training but no deep education, religious or otherwise, who exert control over the Islamist movement. Indeed, from Hasan al-Banna to the present, the people who built the Brotherhood have had little or no formal religious education. Rawi is a narrowly focused functionary, able to organize interreligious dialogues but with little real understanding of his own religion or others.

His views have been honed by decades of organizational work. In 1977, two years after he arrived in Britain, he headed the Muslim Student Association. In 1984, the same year Akef came to Germany to head the center, Rawi served as a delegate from Britain to the "big circle," a meeting with representatives of eight countries. The German representative was the Islamic Community of Germany, headquartered at the Munich mosque. Five years later, the federation was founded with the eight original countries plus seven others. "We realized we weren't students anymore. We are living here and we need to deal with society as locals and shouldn't treat it as foreigners."

The federation has become an umbrella group for more than two dozen national Muslim groups, all with intellectual or organizational ties to the Muslim Brotherhood. Rawi himself confirmed the ties. "We are part of nobody outside of Europe, but we have good relations with the Brotherhood. We have our own ideas and mission and they know it. We are interlinked with them with a common point of view," he says, meshing the fingers of each hand together like teeth on a gear. "We have a good, close relationship."

A rash of organization building followed the federation's founding. The next year, 1990, the federation set up the Institute for the Study of Human Sciences, which was designed to train imams and Muslim elites. In 1997, it set up the European Council for Fatwa and Research, aimed at spreading the Brotherhood's religious views across the continent. It also established the European Trust to raise money for the movement's activities. Besides serving as a holding company for these groups, the federation also has a public role as the only transcontinental lobbying group for Europe's Muslims. It has held meetings with the Vatican and the European Union. The chief financier is the Maktoum Charity Foundation, a group based in Qatar, with ties to the Brotherhood.

This frenzy of organizing highlights an important point about the Brotherhood: it is not a religious society with theological goals. It has had one or two important thinkers, but their main point has been simple: the Koran should be interpreted in a relatively literal fashion in order to shape every aspect of temporal society. The Brotherhood's primary goal is to implement this vision, and for that it needs institutions. Back in Egypt, before it was banned, the Brotherhood operated political parties, newspapers, youth associations, women's groups, and a quasi-military wing that imitated the style of fascist parties of the 1930s. In Europe, much of this structure (minus the military wing) has been duplicated. The main difference is that the Brotherhood is operating as a minority religion, so it uses its structures not to Islamicize mainstream society — which is too ambitious a task at this point — but to dominate the West's Muslim communities. It aims to shield them from the West's secular society, provide an alternative reality for its members, and convert other Muslims into "better" Muslims, who follow the Brotherhood's narrow vision of Islam.

As modern-day Islam has no formal religious structure, a group that sets up an organization and claims to speak for Muslims is hard to challenge; creating a rival group seems the only way to do so. The Brotherhood, with its organizational prowess, has been faster on the draw than other Muslim groups — from Ramadan's pan-European Muslim conference, sponsored by the CIA in the 1960s, to Rawi's federation today. It's no coincidence that in both cases — and everything in between — outsiders have financed the Brotherhood's activities. That is because at its heart, the Brotherhood outside of Egypt is not a mass organization. It is a group of elite organizers who have set up the structures to define Islam in the West. The Islamic Center of Munich and all its successor organizations have never had more than a few dozen official members. These people did not serve Munich's Muslims — indeed, the Turkish population that made up 90 percent of the Muslims in Munich by the 1970s was explicitly denied membership. Instead, the leadership was obsessed with organizing. In the Cold War, these groups had relatively little influence on the world stage except as pawns in the fight against communism. But as they developed, something unexpected happened: Europe, once outside the Muslim world, became central to its future. And the Brotherhood, after years of laborious organizational work, was suddenly poised to lead it.

15

DEFINING THE DEBATE

S PEAKING IN 1966 to a group of Turks about to leave from Istanbul to work in Cologne, a West German official made this prophecy: "Many of you are going to build new lives for yourselves in Germany. You will put down roots and visit your homeland only as guests."

At the time, few on either side of the equation would have agreed. For the West Germans, the Turks filled an urgent need for labor, which their economic miracle had created. West German unemployment was virtually at zero, and companies were expanding rapidly. In this era before globalization, which allows firms to hopscotch around the globe to open factories near labor and markets, West German companies needed workers where their factories were situated. The country had already imported laborers from Italy, Spain, and Greece and would do so in the coming years from Portugal, Tunisia, Morocco, and Yugoslavia. In all cases the "guest workers" — *Gastarbeiter* — were seen as temporary because they were rotated in and out after a few years.

The Turkish laborers also thought they were taking temporary jobs. Most came from nonindustrialized parts of Turkey, especially the rural stretches of central Anatolia. For them, this was the chance of a lifetime — a union job in West Germany, where as semiskilled laborers they could make many times the money they could earn at home. Their goals were simple: to help their families and perhaps retire to the Black Sea and live in a home paid for with their savings from Germany. And indeed, for years the workers lived simply and sent money home. No one thought of building a house in West Germany.

Over time, the concept of guest workers began to lose favor. Employers complained about the high costs of training new employees, and workers wanted to stay on. So regulations were relaxed, and the foreign workforce, instead of rotating in and out, was allowed to stay. In addition, the West German government began to let workers bring their families along. By the time West Germany stopped importing labor in 1971, more than 700,000 Turks were living there. In the following years, immigration actually continued because Turks were permitted to move to West Germany to be reunited with family members living there. For the first time in German history, a sizable number of Muslims resided in the country. Today, roughly 2 million people of Turkish origin live in Germany, most of them Muslim. Another 1.5 million Muslims from other parts of the world, especially Bosnia and North Africa, also make their homes there.

Across Europe, similar demographics were in play. Islam's great era of conquests had left large Muslim populations on Europe's fringes — in Kosovo and Bosnia, for example, and the Crimea; for many centuries, the Muslim Umayyad caliphate ruled much of modern-day Spain as Al-Andalus. Interactions with the Muslim world had a profound impact, reintroducing to the West works of science, literature, philosophy, and mathematics lost to Europe after the fall of the Roman Empire but preserved in the great Islamic libraries. Yet overall, Islam and its people had seemed distant, far removed. Since the fifteenth century, when the last Muslim emirate, Grenada, was conquered by Spain, almost no Muslims had lived in western Europe. They became the ultimate outsiders, close enough to be worrisome but far enough away to be exotic. At times viewed with dread (for their slave galleys and scimitars, their reputed des-

potism and cruelty), Muslims later became a subject of frivolous
fascination (for their harems and genies, flying carpets and tur-
bans).

After the postwar immigration, the stereotypes remained, but
real Muslims were suddenly living in the midst of western Europe-
ans. As it had in West Germany, economics drove countries to import laborers. Some preferred subjects from former colonies. Sometimes that meant non-Muslims, such as Hindus from India, who
went to Britain, or animists and Christians from central Africa,
who went to Belgium. But most immigrants were Muslims. With
eastern Europe cut off by the iron curtain, low-wage workers were
most easily found to Europe's south — across the Mediterranean in
Muslim North Africa and Turkey.

In France, the effects of decolonization and the Algerian Civil
War increased the number of Muslims in that country from a sta-
tistically insignificant number before World War II to more than
four million today. By some counts the number is as high as six
million, or 10 percent of the population. (As in many European
countries, French census takers do not ask about religion or race.)
In Britain, Muslims who had arrived during the colonial era, primarily as traders, formed small enclaves. After World War II, India's civil war triggered a flood of immigration as people fled the
subcontinent. The number of Muslims in Britain grew from 23,000
at the end of World War II to 360,000 in 1971 and nearly two million today. In western Europe, Muslims number fifteen to twenty
million, about four times the number living in the United States,
which has roughly the same size population.

At first, religion did not play a major role in the Muslim guest
workers' daily lives. Companies occasionally accommodated the
faith of their new employees, creating some of the first places of
worship for the new arrivals. In 1965, for example, the Mannes-
mann smelter in Duisburg, a city in the Ruhr Valley, set up prayer
rooms. Workers fulfilled the role of imams themselves, with the
person with the best voice and most religious knowledge leading

prayers. Over time, however, the desire grew for a normal religious life. Most Muslim immigrants were not wealthy and so couldn't afford to build mosques, so they rented commercial space and converted it into prayer rooms. These hidden mosques are often taken as proof of discrimination against Muslims. While it is certainly true that many local governments have hindered or prevented efforts to build visible mosques, it is also the case that the immigrants were (and in fact still are) working their way up the economic ladder and lacked the financial means to build large, costly places of worship.

For many groups, religion was still tied to the homeland. Turks in Germany brought with them groups such as the Süleymans and the followers of Necmettin Erbakan. The former were archconservative pietists who formed the Union of Islamic Cultural Centers (known by its German acronym, VIKZ), which offered schooling in the Koran to youngsters. The latter set up the religious community Milli Görüs, a Turkish variation of the Muslim Brotherhood. Back home, the government kept these groups in check, but in the West, where religious thought was not circumscribed, they spread freely. Worried that religious zealotry was infecting Turks in Germany and that the problem would spread back home, the Turkish officials set up an organization in West Germany known as Ditib, a branch of the Turkish government's religious authority, Diyanet. Over the years it financed many large mosques in Germany and provided the country with imams. In 2007, Germany and Turkey signed a treaty formalizing this process. The situation in other European countries is similar. In France, the Grande Mosquée de Paris is headed by an Algerian civil servant. Britain has lavish mosques paid for by Persian Gulf sheikhs. In another era, immigrants might have taken decades to leave an architectural mark; in twentieth-century Europe, it happened quickly.

This demographic shift was not lost on the Muslim world. When Said Ramadan first landed in Europe in the 1950s, it was a haven precisely because it was not part of the Muslim world. Europe was separate and safe. Organization building was primarily a reaction to oppression back home. But as Europe gained a sizable Muslim population, it regained its historical position as a part of the Muslim world. Traditionally, Islamic thinkers have viewed the world as divided into two areas. In the Dar al-Islam, or House of Islam, the word of God reigns supreme. Its opposite is the Dar al-Harb, or House of Infidels. For centuries, Europe was in the latter camp. But now, with millions of Muslims living there, it had rejoined the Muslim world. Whether through luck or brilliant foresight, the Brotherhood was already firmly planted in the West just as this historical transformation was taking place.

In a small hotel on the edge of London in 2004, Mohammad Hawari was addressing a panel of men practicing the ancient art of Islamic jurisprudence. The men were helping European Muslims integrate into the West by reconciling the demands of Islam with the secular laws of their host countries. Because Islam regulates many temporal matters — such as finances, times for prayer, and food — the need for concrete, practical advice is arguably greater than it is in most other religions. Questions range from the complex (Can I pay into a pension system that is based on interest, which is forbidden by Islam?) to the practical (When do sunset prayers take place during the summer solstice in northern Scandinavia, when the sun doesn't set?) and the mundane (What if I cannot find halal food?). Hawari and the scholars were ready to provide answers. These particular questions had answers that were seemingly simple but had far-reaching implications. Yes, pay into pension plans that have interest, but do not accept the interest. For parts of the world where times of sunrise and sunset vary significantly by season, timetables for prayer are provided. And regarding halal food, Islam is a practical religion and makes exemptions for hardship. If you are truly hungry, eat whatever you can find.

At this session, the panel had decided to tackle family life. Hawari, a prosperous scientist from the German city of Aachen, was addressing a key problem familiar to any modern parent or grand-parent: sex. Muslim children, the sixty-three-year-old said, were being waylaid by the West's sexual revolution. They had to stay pure and chaste, saving sexual relations for marriage. It was a normal plea for traditional virtues, one that can be heard countless times a week in mosques, churches, and temples around the world.

Then came a disturbing turn in the discussion. The cause of the sexual revolution, Hawari informed the group, was Jews. They had a secret plan to take over the world by weakening families of other faiths. This was no idle speculation on his part, Hawari told the scholars, all of them taking notes and listening attentively. He had found proof: the minutes of a meeting, which he now read aloud to the group.

"We should seek to collapse morals everywhere to facilitate our control," Hawari read. "Freud is one of us. He will continue to high-light sexual relations in order for them to cease to be sacred in the eyes of the youth, until their major concern becomes satisfying their sexual desire and then their morals collapse." The citation came from *The Protocols of the Elders of Zion,* one of the most noto-rious works of anti-Semitism in Western history. The protocols are purported to be an account of Jewish conspirators plotting to take over the world by undermining Western civilization. The book was the creation of czarist agents in the nineteenth century, who were at the forefront of a new, more dangerous form of anti-Semitism. Maybe more stunning than Hawari's use of the book was the re-sponse it elicited: nothing.

It was a meeting of the European Council for Fatwa and Re-search. The men discussed a series of questions that European Mus-lims had posed to them. Hawari and other counselors responded, issuing religious opinions known as fatwas. The council is the most influential body involved in shaping Islamic religious opinion in Europe and, through a sister organization, in the United States. It helps set the tone of religious discussion, defining what Muslims are allowed and not allowed to do. Its opinions are not binding, but they are available online and published in books, which are distributed to mosques throughout Europe. Imams take courses in the council's thinking and are advised to use its methods of argumentation when local worshipers raise questions. The council's role in Europe might seem like a bit of bad luck — perhaps a typical case of immigrants bringing with them the regressive social mores or traditions of their homeland. But that view would be mistaken. As we saw in the previous chapter, the council is a creation of the Federation of Islamic Organizations in Europe, a direct descendant of the Munich mosque.

One could argue that the federation, the fatwa council, and any of the other creations of the Muslim Brotherhood are simply minority enclaves. Every society has groups like this: think of the Mennonites and the Amish in the United States. They live according to rules meant to re-create an idealized past, cut off from the mainstream. So what if a few Islamists strive to create a similar community for themselves? This might have held true but for the size of the Muslim immigration to Europe: it completely changed the parameters. Far from setting up rules to govern a fringe group, the fatwa council issues guidelines aimed at tens of millions of European citizens and residents — members of Europe's second-biggest religion. The fatwa council's parent group, the federation, likewise lobbies European politicians, trying to create the impression that its vision of Islam — for example, requiring headscarves for women — is the authentic one; Muslims who choose to dress differently are cast as "assimilated" and inauthentic. Also, groups like the Mennonites have not given rise to terrorist organizations, as has the Brotherhood.

Although the Brotherhood says it supports terrorism only in certain cases — usually against Israel — it does more than target Jews. It creates a mental preconditioning for terrorism. This mindset divides the world into two camps, those to be protected (a small number of "good" Muslims) and the rest (including many other Muslims), who can be destroyed. Some other religious groups see the world in similar Manichaean terms, but few have given rise over the past decades to so much violence. Thus, when groups like the fatwa council make a decision, it matters.

Hawari, for example, wasn't citing an anti-Semitic tract for effect; that speech was given as the theoretical foundation for a fatwa, an answer to a question concerning the practice of religion. In this case the question was about the legality of a divorce. A French Muslim had written to the council, asking if she was indeed divorced after her husband had shouted "I divorce you" three times, in a drunken rage. According to Islamic law, saying the sentence three times is enough to secure a divorce. The issue for the council was the man's sobriety; the scholars carefully considered his level of intoxication, weighing his ability to think clearly and realize what he was saying. They decided he knew what he had said, and thus the divorce stood. But the scholars never included a more fundamental consideration: the marital dispute had taken place in France. Under French law, a divorce requires a ruling by a French court. Thus the man's rantings were largely irrelevant.

Hawari's citing of the *Protocols* is another example of his group's disconnection from the broader society. One of the West's greatest traumas is the Holocaust, and at least since the mid-twentieth century most educated people have developed a sensitive understanding of anti-Semitism and can recognize the false claims and scare tactics that inform it. Hawari's ignorance of this — whether a self-chosen blindness or a true lack of knowledge — and the council's failure to upbraid him for using such literature was a clear sign that the group itself is not integrated into mainstream Western thought. In this regard, it also fits the fabric of the Brotherhood. The current head of the organization (and past head of the Islamic Center of Munich), Mahdi Akef, has called the Holocaust a myth and expressed solidarity with Iran's leader, who also has questioned it.

Given the council's makeup, its members' acceptance of these ideas is not surprising. Of the council's thirty-five members, two thirds are Muslim Brotherhood activists from the Middle East or Africa. Its head is Youssef Qaradawi, the man who helped rebuild the Brotherhood in the 1970s, along with Akef. Qaradawi is often considered the Muslim Brotherhood's chief imam — not in a rigid, hierarchical sense, but in recognition of his charisma and influence. He is arguably the most influential religious figure in the entire Muslim world, not just the Brotherhood, and has a popular website and television show. His views are often considered mainstream or even progressive by Middle Eastern standards; he encourages women to work and permits music, which fundamentalists frown upon. But he also sanctions suicide bombings against Israeli civilians and the stoning of homosexuals. He denies that he practices anti-Semitism, but he associates with only a few Jews — those who belong to an extremist faction called Neturei Karta. This small group of Orthodox Jews opposes the existence of the state of Israel. They sometimes appear in public with Qaradawi, court jesters used to display his tolerance: Jews have a role in our vision of Islam, so long as they know their place.

For years, the Brotherhood pushed this kind of Islam in Europe, not only through the fatwa council but also at scores of conventions, seminars, and workshops. In most major European countries, Brotherhood groups are among the most influential — the Union of French Islamic Organizations (known by its French acronym, UOIF), the Muslim Association of Britain, and the Islamic Community of Germany, with its ideological Turkish twin, Milli Görüs. Throughout Islamic communities, the Brotherhood was helping to define who was a Muslim and what was considered proper behavior for a Muslim. Invariably, these guidelines were based on a more fundamentalist interpretation of the Koran than the people had previously subscribed to.

Mourad Amriou slowly warmed up the crowd inside a small mosque on the outskirts of Paris, giving the congregation a pep talk after the Friday evening prayer. "Just nearby here are Fatimas and Mohammeds who are drinking," said the beefy twenty-six-year-old former rapper, using generic names for Muslim women and men. "Can you believe it? Just around the corner, going to nightclubs. Do you accept it?"

Murmurs of disapproval arose from the crowd as he continued. Life, he said, should center on mosques. Not just for prayer, but for everything from language classes for children to social life. Otherwise, he said, Muslims will become indistinguishable from their French neighbors. "Society has to be based on Islam," he told the gathering.

Amriou was a young Muslim I'd come to know over several months. He did not work for the UOIF but went to its offices for training and for networking with other activists. He read the decisions of the fatwa council and held Qaradawi to be the most profound thinker of the present day. He lived apart from French society, orbiting Paris in a tiny Fiat Punto on the aptly named *périphérique* ring road around Paris.

On this day, Amriou was in the slum suburb of Aubervilliers, doing a quick "intervention," his term for a pep talk at which he rallies the crowd to the Islamist cause. Before entering the mosque he affectionately tousled the hair of a couple of young boys collecting money in black-and-white Palestinian scarves. The money was for a charity that helps Palestinian orphans.

"Zap zap zap, I go in and say my piece and am out," he said. "I go to all sorts of mosques to pray. Speed speed speed. I'm on the go all the time. Each time of the day a different mosque. But I like the UOIF. I like the stuff they do. I know some of the leadership here and some of their works."

Amriou grew up in Paris, the youngest of nine children born to Algerian immigrants. He got involved in drugs, cut an album as the rapper HLM System, and served time in prison. Five years ago he was "converted" from the streets back to Islam by a local member of the Tablighi Jamaat, a rigorously apolitical pietistic group. He still wears thick, hooded sweatshirts from his pre-Islamist era, but they are now balanced by a skullcap and, sometimes, a knee-length cotton gown.

Jews hold a special fascination for him. Typical of Islamists, Amriou compares the lot of Muslims with that of Jews in pre–World War II Europe, the implication being that another Holocaust is around the corner. He says his neighborhood of Paris had no mosques but contained six synagogues, "even though we were far more numerous than they were." He doesn't consider that Jews have been in France for centuries and have fought for a place in society; for Mourad, the Jews' success is a sign that society is unfair.

Recently, one of Amriou's heroes, the charismatic preacher Hassan Iquioussen, was criticized in the media for making anti-Semitic comments. He gave a lecture, recorded and sold widely at mosques across France, in which he repeated typical Islamist anti-Semitic claims: Jews had benefited from numerous prophets but ignored God; thus they deserved whatever they got; they were "vipers" who had "no scruples against killing their prophets; in one morning they killed seventy of them. In one morning." And so on.

For Amriou, the media's reaction to the tape was proof that mainstream society was against Muslims. He considered it a smear campaign based on something absolutely atypical in the speech. "If he's a radical, then we're finished. The UOIF didn't care about that at all. They just laughed when it came out. Everyone there thought it was a joke. A three-year-old tape and he just slipped up. Everyone says that sort of thing."

Amriou's speech to the crowd is short but moving. He recounts his story, the drugs, the nights he'd sleep in the basement of the apartment block to avoid his parents. One old man in the front row begins to cry, probably recognizing in the story a family member, maybe his own son. Then Amriou launches into his critique of Muslims who have lost their way, the men who dance and socialize, the women who do not wear headscarves and associate with men. The crowd of 150 men listens, murmuring approval. At the end, they applaud the speaker and send him off with a glass of tea and a handful of sweets. He hops into his Fiat and heads home. It is 10 P.M., and he will be lucky to get six hours of sleep before morning prayers, a bit of work, and then more rounds.

The work of Muslim Brotherhood activists like Amriou picked up in pace throughout the 1990s and into the new century. Largely shielded from public view, the Brotherhood's grassroots work helped define Islam in Europe. But then an apparent disaster changed everything: the 9/11 attacks, with their links to the Brotherhood's European network. After decades of operating quietly, the Brotherhood was once again at the center of attention.

In the 1950s and '60s, German domestic intelligence had kept an eye on the ex-soldiers and Arab students struggling to control the mosque project. The Bavarian branch of the Office for Protection of the Constitution, which monitors domestic extremism, had paid von Mende to keep tabs on the mosque. But after von Mende died, this surveillance stopped. West Germany essentially missed the transformation of the Islamic Center of Munich into a hub of the Islamist world.

One of the few people close to the mosque who drew outside attention was Ahmad von Denffer. He published *Al-Islam*, the official organ of the mosque and the broader organization, the Islamic Community of Germany. Founded by Achmed Schmiede in the 1950s, the magazine was taken over by the mosque and run by Schmiede and then von Denffer until 2003, when it suspended publication. (It is now a website.) Von Denffer was strongly influenced by Khurshid Ahmad, the head of the Pakistani version of the Brotherhood, Jamaat-e-Islamiya. Von Denffer encountered Ahmad after he joined the mosque's governing board in the early 1980s. Later, von Denffer went to Britain to study at the Jamaat-influenced Islamic Foundation, writing several books in English and German, all of which reflect classic Islamist thinking — that all problems can be solved only by Islam. In the 1980s, he cofounded a charity that channeled money to Afghanistan. Von Denffer has denied that the charity money supported the mujahideen warriors, but at this time Pakistan-based Afghan charities were synonymous with holy war. For the first time in two decades, German domestic intelligence put the mosque on its informal watch list.

Soon, more signs hinted at the mosque's importance. In 1990, an expert on Islam alleged that the Munich mosque was where policy was being formulated for the entire Muslim world, a claim that drew a sharp rebuke from *Al-Islam*. Von Denffer and others close to the center also participated in overseas conferences with well-known Muslim Brotherhood leaders, such as a conference in Sudan led by a powerful Islamist political leader there, Hasan al-Turabi. The center also got into a dispute with one of the most important centers of Islamic studies in Germany, the Orient-Institut in Hamburg. One of the institute's affiliates wrote that von Denffer's writings had "clear tendencies of anti-German, anti-Jewish, anti-democratic, misogynist, racist, anti-integration, and Islamistic polemic."

The Munich mosque was also developing disturbing links to terrorism, although at the time they were discounted as one-off events or coincidences. In the 1980s, Mahmoud Abouhalima was a regular at the mosque and sought spiritual counseling from Ahmed el-Khalifa, then the chief imam there. Abouhalima soon after went to the United States, where he was convicted and jailed for helping in the attempt to blow up the World Trade Center in 1993. Then there was the case of Mamdouh Mahmud Salim, widely thought to be Al Qaeda's finance chief and bin Laden's personal mentor. He was arrested in 1998 in a small town near the mosque while on a business trip to Germany. Before being extradited to the United States, he called Khalifa and asked for spiritual counseling. (He was later put on trial in New York and sentenced to thirty-two years.) Khalifa confirmed meeting both men but said it was a bit of bad luck — he can't know everyone who passes through town, and he is available to all.

German intelligence was nevertheless alarmed and launched an all-out investigation into Salim's contacts. One, particularly, stood out: Mamoun Darkazanli, a Syrian businessman living in Hamburg. He attended a small mosque there called the Al-Quds. German police bugged Darkazanli's home and observed his contacts at the mosque, including one particular man, Mohammed Atta. After a while, the police weren't sure what they had, so they dropped the investigation. Two years later, in 2001, Atta flew the first plane into the World Trade Center. The Al-Quds mosque turned out to be the place where the hijackers had been radicalized. Darkazanli was never prosecuted, but he was another less-than-glorious link between the Islamic Center of Munich and extremism.

Shocked by the 9/11 attacks, the U.S. government swung hard against the Brotherhood. Investigators were especially fascinated by one of Nada's investment vehicles, Banque al-Taqwa. Himmat sat on its board, and seemingly every Islamist in Europe had bought shares in it, making its shareholder list a who's who of the Muslim Brotherhood in Europe. Nada had set up the bank as one of the first to operate in conformity with Islamic law. Instead of offering depositors interest, the bank called its customers investors and offered them profits from money it lent out. But he had invested the money amateurishly — Nada himself said he put most of it in Malaysian businesses shortly before the 1997 Asian financial crisis — and the bank went under. American prosecutors, however, said the bank was a conduit for terrorist money. Washington declared Nada and Himmat terrorist financiers and had the designation endorsed by the United Nations. Both men's bank accounts were frozen.

The Islamic Community of Germany suddenly faced a financial crisis. As the community's chief officer, Himmat signed the group's checks, but now anything he touched was frozen. (The group had already lost its status as a charity, for which Yazdani had struggled so vigorously in the 1960s. This action was unrelated to the attacks; it occurred in 1998 when mosque officials failed to fill out the proper forms to extend the status.) Then a painful interview was published in *Al-Islam,* in which Khalifa tried to justify why Himmat, who had not lived in Munich in decades, was running the group. After twenty-nine years, Himmat resigned in early 2002.

Terrorist attacks in Madrid and London followed over the next few years. Investigators were shocked that key suspects were young second- or third-generation Muslims born in Europe. In most cases, the young men had begun their careers as radicals through contact with Brotherhood ideology, attracted to its utopian message and learning through it to separate the world into two classes of people: believers and infidels. Ties to the terrorists seemed to mark the end of the Brotherhood. Its mother mosque shorn of leadership, its champions accused of terrorism, the Brotherhood's European beachhead seemed about to collapse. But then something happened. Just as in the 1950s, Western governments' repulsion began to turn to infatuation. Anti-democratic, anti-Western factions of Islam became fashionable — then to fight communism, now to fight terrorism and combat extremism.

16

1950s REDUX

YOUSSEF NADA SITS in regal splendor, slouched in a faux-ancien-régime chair next to a window overlooking Europe. His villa is perched on a hill next to Lake Lugano, whose dark green waters snake between alpine foothills. Thick forests run down to the lake's edge; this primordial view is marred only by a few towns cut into the banks. Nada's picture windows are decorated with trophies from his trips around the world on behalf of the Muslim Brotherhood. On one table stands a deep-blue glass vase from Pakistan; on another are silver candelabras from North Africa. A strange pewter peanut graces a third — a memorial to his days in agriculture. The furniture is an assortment of Eastern and Western styles, set next to giant handwoven rugs from Central Asia. Nada is now frail but still dapper in a gray shirt with French cuffs, a flowered tie, a black blazer, and gray flannels. His eyes are dark and drawn, his goatee thin. He appears exhausted, but then he leans forward, eager to explain who he is.

"Engineer, I am engineer.

"Businessman, I am businessman.

"Banker, I am a banker.

"Intellectual, I am intellectual.

"Politician, I am a politician.

"Activist, I am activist.

"Islamist, I am Islamist.

"Terrorist, I am not."

It's hard to argue with that bullet-point résumé. In hindsight, the charges of terrorism leveled against Nada seem like an act of desperation by the U.S. government, fulfilling a need to do something, anything, after the 9/11 attacks. A case of *Aktionismus,* a German word that means "a love of action": action for action's sake. Despite Nada's extensive contact over the years with German speakers, he can barely communicate in the language, but he knows this word. He stumbles over it and says it again, "It is all *Aktionismus.*" Then he sits back, pleased with himself. Linguist I might not be, but you get my point.

And in fact, for all the intense cooperation between U.S. and Swiss prosecutors, the charges that Nada financed terrorism have never been proven or explained publicly in a convincing way. In hindsight, Nada's Banque al-Taqwa was a disastrous investment for members of the Muslim Brotherhood but less likely a secret funding vehicle for terrorists. Perhaps it could be proved that some of the initial profits from the bank were given to terrorist organizations such as Hamas. Investors had given Nada wide latitude to donate their *zakat* — their tithe, one of the five pillars of Islam. Thus when money came in during the bank's early, profitable days, he was authorized to skim off the requisite 10 percent *zakat* and channel it to any charity he chose. It's conceivable some went to questionable groups close to the Brotherhood, but that hasn't been proven. None of his bank's transfers — and authorities had access to all of them because they were executed through mainstream Swiss banks — were dubious enough to allow prosecutors to even bring a case to trial, let alone get a conviction.

Not only were Nada and Himmat not tried, but the travails of the past years apparently rejuvenated them. Nada has relished the role of underdog, setting up a website to refute some of the more absurd allegations made against him. He has spent countless hours regaling journalists, academics, and prosecutors with tales of his Islamist exploits. In a series of long interviews on Al-Jazeera television, he even claimed to have been the Brotherhood's foreign minister. Himmat, true, had to resign as head of the Islamic Community of Germany, but like Nada he remains in his villa, essentially in retirement. Both are now over seventy.

Their fates highlight an interesting development: in some ways the 9/11 attacks were the best thing that happened to the Brotherhood. Yes, there was a crackdown and for a while the Brotherhood suffered. But more important, the attacks made most Westerners judge Islamists by one criterion: is the person a terrorist? If so, then the full weight of government power would be brought to bear, from torture and war to prosecution and jail. But if not, then the person was okay. He or she wasn't Al Qaeda. Such people weren't blowing things up. They were not only tolerated but valued. Far from problematic, their extremist and undemocratic views were a sign of credibility. They could talk to the "Muslim street." They became one of democracy's most highly valued commodities: a dialogue partner.

Hervé Terrel strides briskly into a café with oak and brass fixtures across from the Madeleine, a huge church in central Paris that looks like a Greek temple. It is early morning, and Terrel is on his way to work in the French government's interior ministry, where he helps formulate policy related to the country's Muslims. When I first met him in 2004, France was literally burning—Muslim ghettos were aflame with burning cars—but Terrel was unperturbed, absolutely certain that France had the right strategy: co-opting the Muslim Brotherhood.

With more than four million Muslims, France has one of Islam's largest populations in Europe. The immigrants have added a youthful element to an aging population and helped forge business and cultural ties to the Muslim world. But most are concentrated in ghettos like Amriou's, where they live cut off from French society, with poor prospects for education and jobs. The 9/11 terrorist attacks focused attention on these communities, where young Muslims were recruited to fight the West in Afghanistan. In 2005, tens of thousands rioted, burning cars night after night. Terrel is part of a group of high-level civil servants charged with coming up with a solution.

In 2003, French officials had already decided that Muslims needed a voice and set up the French Council of the Muslim Faith. The body was to be elected, but officials had a problem: who should vote? French citizens don't register their religious affiliation, so the country has no list of Muslims. The solution was for mosques to elect representatives. Bigger mosques would get more votes, based on the theory that they represented more Muslims. That formula helped one group in particular: the UOIF, the group in France closest to the Muslim Brotherhood.

The UOIF is an amalgam of several Islamist groups with roots in Said Ramadan's Islamic Center of Geneva. The group came to prominence in 1989 when two girls were ejected from school for wearing headscarves. The UOIF began to organize protests and quickly established itself as a force in the slums of major French cities. Until then, France's Muslim organizations were divided according to their members' countries of origin. The UOIF, by contrast, advocated an "Islam de France," although it saw no contradiction in paying for this with foreign money. The group receives extensive funding from Arab countries. Even today, UOIF officials say, one quarter of its annual budget of just under three million euros, or about $4 million, comes from donors abroad, especially Saudi Arabia, the United Arab Emirates, and Kuwait. That support means the UOIF mosques are large, claiming more votes in the council elections — far beyond the UOIF's actual strength. In 2003 elections, the UOIF won control of twelve of the twenty-five regional councils that represent the central council across France — it suddenly was thrust into a position of power.

The UOIF was affiliated with the Muslim Brotherhood, Terrel readily conceded with a cocked eyebrow, but he could handle them.

"If you say the UOIF is not the Muslim Brotherhood, it's a kind of naïveté. They are. But they also accept the rules here and want to play the game. That's why they're so seductive to people who don't really understand things."

I wondered if he fell into that category. Why then fix the voting rules to favor the big Saudi-funded Muslim Brotherhood mosques? Perhaps the interior ministry should have set up a voting system that tried to reach other Muslims — more secular ones who didn't go to mosque every day.

Terrel disagreed emphatically. "Favoring the Brotherhood was the point. It's not a problem to deal with them; on the contrary. In all of Europe, the only groups that have thought of how to find their place in society are Islamists." True, the Brotherhood does not represent all Muslims, but for Terrel they are attractive because "they have the intellectual level to talk with a government official" like him. In other words, they wear suits, have university degrees, and can formulate their demands in ways that a politician can understand. It reminded me of Amcomlib's decision to drop its support of the old Muslim leader Ibrahim Gacaoglu in favor of Said Ramadan. Ordinary people don't make good interlocutors. They don't have a political program that you can discuss. Ordinary people are messy.

The UOIF was also attractive because it helped fill a hole in social services that the state was unwilling to address. UOIF mosques offer after-school tutoring, day care, and activities for women. One outside supporter of this work was Dounia Bouzar, a prominent French Muslim social scientist, who argued in a book of 2001 that groups like the Brotherhood make valuable mediators between mainstream society and Muslim immigrants. Their services, she argued, help Muslims integrate. But after watching the situation develop over the next few years, Bouzar changed her views. Instead of integrating Muslims, the Brotherhoood's all-embracing form of Islam builds a cocoon around its people, allowing them little contact with mainstream society. Education is often stunted and chances

for professional success limited. "It's a vision of society that sepa-
rates people into two camps, Islamic and non-Islamic," said Bouzar.
"They have a need to Islamicize everything." By embracing groups
like the UOIF, Western politicians essentially went along with this
paradigm, tacitly accepting the Islamist tenet that Islam is the answer to every problem.

Bouzar and other Muslims began to realize that most difficulties
that Muslims face don't have to do with religion — and thus it didn't
make sense to put a religious group in charge of solving them. Muslims' problems were common among all poor immigrants: unemployment, poor education, street crime. There is nothing specifically Muslim about these issues. The argument that Islam is the
answer, however, was so seductive that soon Washington was formulating similar policies, echoing its actions from half a century
earlier.

In late 2005, the U.S. State Department decided that European Muslims needed America's help. Too many were living in parallel societies, cut off from the mainstream. Extremism and violence were
rampant; it was no coincidence that three of the four 9/11 hijacker
pilots had been radicalized in Europe or that Islamist terrorists had
killed hundreds in London and Madrid. What Europe needed, the
State Department figured, was help to set up an international network "to discuss alienation and extremism."

The idea was intriguing. The United States was the target of Islamic radicals, but its own communities had not produced the violence found in Europe. Experts had long debated the reasons for
this. Some cited the fact that often the Muslims who immigrated to
the United States either had jobs or planned to study. In Europe, by
contrast, Muslims had come to work in industrial jobs that didn't
exist anymore. They had working-class levels of education and
lacked the skills to find new employment, leaving many frustrated,
with too much time on their hands. Social services were thought to
be related to the problem. In the United States, unemployed Mus-

lims had few welfare benefits to help them out. If they wanted to survive, they had to work long hours. In Europe those who lacked employment could claim relatively generous welfare benefits and have time to indulge in extremist politics. Other explanations were batted around too: that Islamic violence was largely an Arab and Pakistani phenomenon; whereas a high percentage of Muslims in Europe had immigrated from these regions, those in the United States represented a broader array of homelands.

But no one made the single argument that informed the State Department's plan: that the United States had better Muslim leadership. A State Department–sponsored conference on November 15 and 16, 2005, called Muslim Communities Participating in Society: A Belgian-U.S. Dialogue, brought together sixty-five Belgian Muslims and U.S. tutors from the Islamic Society of North America. The U.S. diplomats thought so highly of ISNA that it seems to have been appointed as a co-organizer of the conference.

From a historical perspective, this was almost comical — a case of taking coal to Newcastle. ISNA, as seen in Chapter 14, was founded by people with extremely close ties to Nada and the Muslim Brotherhood leadership in Europe. The State Department was importing Muslim Brotherhood Islamists with roots in Europe to tell European Muslims how to organize and integrate. Even more interesting, some of those European Muslims invited to the conference were themselves part of the current Muslim Brotherhood network.

One participant was a Belgian convert named Michael Privot, who at the time was vice president of a Saudi–Muslim Brotherhood organization called the Forum of European Muslim Youth and Student Organizations. This body was founded with direct support from the Muslim Brotherhood's umbrella organization in Europe, the Federation of Islamic Organizations in Europe. Privot was also vice secretary of the Complex Éducatif et Culturel Islamique de Verviers, a center of Muslim Brotherhood activity in Brussels. It was also the home of one of Hamas's fund-raising groups, the Al-

Aqsa Foundation (a group banned in several European countries, including Germany and Holland, for supporting terrorism). The meeting offered a chance for Muslim Brotherhood activists like Privot to meet their U.S. counterparts. In addition, the State Department helped bring Belgian Muslims to the United States — to be trained as imams by ISNA and to participate in an ISNA summer program in Chicago. In short, it was a networking session for the Muslim Brotherhood — paid for by U.S. taxpayers.

State Department officials acknowledged that they had invited people accused of extremism but said they did not care about track records. Instead, all that mattered were the groups' or individuals' current statements. In testimony before the Senate Foreign Relations Committee, the U.S. ambassador to Belgium, Tom Korologos, said, "Some of the organizations whose members participated in the Conference have been accused of being extremist. It is possible that some individual members of those organizations have made statements that have been termed extremist. Our view, however, was to base our selection on the stated policies and specific actions of organizations and individuals today with regard to harmonious Muslim integration into American and European society." And then, with a rhetorical flourish, he concluded that "four or five more conferences like this can lead to a network of moderate Muslims."

In internal communication, however, Mr. Korologos's staff revealed a less altruistic goal. In one cable sent at the end of 2006, the U.S. embassy in Brussels conceded that "the embassy's engagement with Belgian Muslims is seen by some members of the majority community, and some Muslims also, as interference in Belgium's internal affairs." This was justified, the cable concluded, not to build a network of moderates, but rather to "increase our credibility with both Muslims and mainstream Belgians with the ultimate goal of creating a more positive image of the U.S., its policies, society, and values."

In 2007, a similar project took place in Germany. The U.S. consulate in Munich actively backed the creation of an Islamic academy in the town of Penzberg. The group behind the academy had close ties to Milli Görüs — essentially a Turkish version of the Muslim Brotherhood, which regularly appears on lists of extremist organizations in Germany. That is why the Bavarian state government, led by the conservative Christian Social Union, was opposed to the academy. The situation was complex — members of the group in Penzberg seemed to make a good-faith effort to distance themselves from extremism — but many German officials were not convinced and wanted to wait a while before accepting the group's newfound moderation. Thus the State Department's quick embrace of the group created a bizarre political constellation: the Bush administration, which had lambasted "old Europe" for being weak on fighting extremism, was actively undermining a conservative European government for being too tough on Islamists.

The embassy's actions formed part of a broader change in strategy — but one debated largely in secret. The strategy was, as a 2006 cable from the U.S. embassy in Berlin put it, a "policy of using American Muslims to reach out to other Muslims." This paralleled U.S. efforts in the 1950s to enlist Muslims in Munich for similar public relations purposes. Though it did smack of manipulating Islam, in many ways this activity is not controversial: why not send U.S. citizens to tell the story of the United States? The problem lay in who got chosen for this role. Just as in the 1950s and '60s, the United States opted for the Brotherhood.

The most public advocate of this new strategy was the prominent political scientist Robert S. Leiken of the Nixon Center think tank. In a widely read piece in *Foreign Affairs*, he and his colleague Steven Brooke made numerous sensible points. For example, they pointed out that the Brotherhood has often been treated as a monolith and that Western officials have ignored moderates in the movement. They also noted that terrorists have often held the Brotherhood in contempt for not embracing global jihad — thus, in the context of Middle Eastern politics, the Brotherhood is not the most extreme group. They also rightly said the United States should not be afraid of engaging the Brotherhood, or any group, if it furthers U.S. interests.

These are all valid observations, but the article misses a few key points. While it is correct, for example, that the Brotherhood does not embrace global jihad against the West, its support of jihad in Israel and Iraq means it explicitly endorses terrorism. The authors also do not seriously address the sheer volume of the group's anti-Semitic utterances over the years, up to the present. They acknowledge the existence of this problem, but more as a historical fact than a present and ongoing reality. To exemplify the Brotherhood's thinking today, the two political scientists cite one moderate sermon that they heard in London. It's worth considering that the authors were present in the mosque as the guest of the man giving the sermon; perhaps his words were tailored to please them? The authors make no effort to balance positive developments with recurring problems — for example, the continuing role of Youssef Qaradawi. They note only that the UOIF in France doesn't invite the imam to its conferences anymore, but fail to acknowledge his role in setting norms in Europe through his fatwa council, websites, and television broadcasts. Maybe most important, the article conflates the Brotherhood in the Middle East and the West. One can argue that Western countries should reach out to oppressed Brotherhood members in authoritarian Egypt. But this doesn't mean that one also has to endorse the Brotherhood's role among Western Muslims. What seems moderate in Egypt can be radical in Paris or Munich.

This endorsement of the Brotherhood began to spread beyond the State Department. The Department of Homeland Security continued to oppose the Brotherhood and made any sort of affiliation with the organization grounds for refusing a person entry into the United States. Thus Tariq Ramadan, Said Ramadan's son and a popular lecturer among young European Muslims, was refused admittance. Besides his familial affiliations, the younger Ramadan wrote a foreword for the first collection of fatwas issued by Qaradawi's fatwa council. The merits of the department's actions can be debated — Ramadan was hardly a terrorist, and if his views are objectionable, they should be debated, not silenced — but in any case it was largely a rearguard action. By the second half of the decade, even the CIA — reflecting its mindset of the 1950s — was backing the Brotherhood. In 2006 and 2008, the CIA issued reports on the organization. The former was more detailed, laying out a blueprint for dealing with the group. Called "Muslim Brotherhood: Pivotal Actor in European Political Islam," the report stated that "MB groups are likely to be pivotal to the future of political Islam in Europe . . . They also show impressive internal dynamism, organization, and media savvy." The report conceded that "European intelligence services consider the Brotherhood a security threat and critics — including more pluralistic Muslims — accuse it of hindering Muslim social integration." But the report nevertheless concluded that "MB-related groups offer an alternative to more violent Islamic movements."

The new Obama administration evinced similar support. During the presidential campaign, the Obama team appointed Mazen Asbahi as its Muslim outreach coordinator, although Asbahi had extensive contacts with Brotherhood organizations and was even head of the Muslim Student Association, which was founded by people with ties to the Munich mosque. This information was either disregarded or missed when Asbahi was vetted during the campaign. He resigned in 2008 only when the facts, dug up by an online newsletter focused on the Muslim Brotherhood, were published in a national newspaper.

In power, the Obama administration has continued its predecessor's endorsement of Islamists. In January 2009, for example, the State Department sponsored a visit of German Muslim leaders to one of the bastions of the Muslim Brotherhood in the United States, the International Institute of Islamic Thought — the organization set up after the epochal meeting in 1977 at Himmat's home base near Lake Lugano. The German visitors were key government officials in charge of integration or recruitment of minorities into the police. One of the briefers (or "one of those giving the briefing") was Jamal Barzinji—who as seen in Chapter 14 had worked for Nada in the 1970s and later was one of the triumvirate who set up a number of key Brotherhood-inspired structures in the United States.

Like many Brotherhood-related groups, IIIT faded from public view after the 9/11 attacks but has experienced a renaissance recently. IIIT had been closely associated with a raft of Islamist organizations in northern Virginia that were raided by federal agents because of their suspected ties to extremist Islam. As elsewhere, this action followed a familiar pattern. The groups in question, including IIIT, were primarily problematic for ideological reasons—for trying to push the Brotherhood's vision of an Islamicized society, which clearly cannot work in a pluralistic culture. But instead of being challenged on the field of ideas, where they could easily be shown to hold beliefs antithetical to democratic ideals, they were accused of supporting criminal activities and were raided. This had a double effect: it created the strange spectacle of the legal arm of the government trying desperately to prosecute these groups while, at the same time, the diplomatic arm held them up as models of integration. In addition, the failure to convict the Muslims was seen as an exoneration, almost a seal of approval.

Few people illustrate the West's fascination with and repulsion toward the Brotherhood better than Ibrahim el-Zayat, the young Muslim leader given the reins of the Islamic Community of Germany in 2002, when Ghaleb Himmat was forced out. Just thirty-three years old at the time, he became only the fourth head of the organization, after Said Ramadan, Faisal Yazdani, and, for nearly thirty years, Himmat. Zayat represented the new generation, in some ways the culmination of years of Islamist efforts to find a foothold in Europe and build something lasting.

Born in Europe to an Egyptian father and German mother, Zayat was perfectly at home in the West but had close ties to the old country. He spoke German and English fluently and held a master's degree in political science from a German university. He understood how political decisions are made in Germany — the complex interactions of think tanks, church, and political foundations where "opinion makers" meet and discuss ideas, which filter up through the political parties to become a consensus that is eventually implemented. It is not grassroots activism or organizing, but a system that gave power to elites, who are meant to cull out radical ideas and come up with sensible solutions. A consummate lobbyist, Zayat knew this. At times, he seemed to do nothing but go from one conference to another: to a Protestant church's political academy, a Catholic church's roundtable, a Social Democrats' intercultural dialogue, the European Parliament's subcommittee on minorities, and so on, always present, always cutting an impressive figure, usually dressed in a blue power suit with a pressed white shirt and richly patterned tie — a man who might be a junior executive at an investment bank.

But what sets him apart from other politically ambitious men of his age are his ties to Islamism. His father, an Egyptian, had settled in Marburg and became a leader in local Muslim affairs. Zayat assumed this mantle. He seemed to have either founded or been closely involved with every recently established Muslim Brotherhood–related group in Europe. These included the European Trust (board of directors with power of attorney), the Federation of Islamic Organizations in Europe (board of directors), the Muslim Student Union (past president), the European Mosque Construction and Support Community (power of attorney), the World Assembly of Muslim Youth (European representative), the Islamic Education Institute (member), the Society of Muslim Social Scientists (associate director), and the Forum of European Muslim Youth and Student Organizations (board of directors).

And that was only his pro bono work. He made his money through Islam too, as head of SLM Liegenschaftsmanagement

GmbH, a company that buys and sells real estate on behalf of mosques. One of his biggest clients is the Turkish Islamist group Milli Görüs. Given the large population of ethnic Turks in Germany, Milli Görüs has somewhat eclipsed the Muslim Brotherhood in terms of influence in that country, but Zayat has helped bridge this gap through his business and personal ties. He founded SLM at the age of twenty-nine, in 1997, along with another young Islamist, Oguz Ücüncü, the current head of Milli Görüs. Zayat is married to the daughter of Mehmet Erbakan (the former head of Milli Görüs) and the niece of the movement's founder, Necmettin Erbakan. Zayat's ties to global Islamism are so extensive that he has been featured in long profiles in major German media. In one sensationalistic work, he was described as the spider in the center of a web of terrorism. The book *The War in Our Cities* was so riddled with factual errors and shrill assertions that Zayat's lawyers had a field day forcing the book publisher to strike out passages or issue retractions. But its overall point was valid: Zayat is one of the most influential Islamists in Europe.

The question remains whether Zayat and others like him — from ISNA functionaries in Chicago to UOIF members in Paris — can be called members of the Muslim Brotherhood. Is it even fair to use that term when most of these people were born in the West, might not speak Arabic or Urdu, and support local laws and customs? In Zayat's case, the Egyptian government simply claims that he is a member of the Brotherhood, implying that it still has a functioning overseas network of people who take orders from Akef in Cairo and support the party back in Egypt. The Egyptian government tried him in absentia in a military court. But then again, Egypt's track record on human rights is so miserable and persecution of the Brotherhood so extensive that it's hard to trust anything its officials say on the matter. More intriguing, Ikhwanweb, the Brotherhood's official website, also claimed he was a member. Later, however, it issued a retraction and a denial from Zayat.

The question is to some degree pointless because the Brotherhood nowadays functions as two phenomena: One is narrowly defined as an Egyptian political party. The other — more relevant in the West in the twenty-first century — is an ideological universe that includes the works of Qaradawi and Qutb, Ramadan and von Denffer, and could be defined even more broadly as including nearly identical movements around the world, including Pakistan's Jamaat or Turkey's Milli Görüs. In this sense, it's hard to see how Zayat, with his extensive ties to all these groups, could be considered as functioning outside the Brotherhood. Although he tries to prevent this label from being attached to him, he seems to be losing the fight. In 2005, he unsuccessfully sued a German parliamentarian to prevent her from using the term in reference to him. The court affirmed her right to express her opinion that he "clearly is a functionary of the Muslim Brotherhood."

Personally, I avoided the term when talking to Zayat. Over the years, I had come to know him fairly well. I had interviewed him twice and we had participated in numerous conferences, including a series of closed-door roundtables sponsored by the Catholic Church, aimed at breaking down the barriers between Islamists and Germany's security services. At one of those meetings, I had seen him emotionally defend the Brotherhood as an important reform movement — undoubtedly true in the context of Egyptian politics. But I also could see why he rejected the label. He was born in Germany, his kids went to Montessori schools, and he had a sharp, if somewhat bitter, sense of humor. He didn't want to be pegged as a puppet of Akef's and of the other old men in the Brotherhood's Cairo headquarters.

Our final meeting took place in his office in Cologne. After taking over, Zayat had essentially moved the Islamic Community of Germany's operations to Cologne from Munich, although officially the group was still based in the Munich mosque. In a way, this reflected the group's history of strongman rule. When Himmat ran it, he was based in Switzerland. Now Zayat was running it from Cologne. The mosque remained in Munich, a pawn in larger struggles.

Zayat's office in Osterather Strasse is home to numerous other

Islamist-leaning organizations, including the Society of Muslim Social Scientists, the Muslim Student Association, a Muslim bookstore, a kindergarten for the Islamic Community of Germany, and
the national offices of the Islamrat, an umbrella group of Islamic organizations, most notably Milli Görüs. I arrived early and sat waiting for him in the bookstore. A clerk greeted me with a suspicious
look, a grunt, and a gesture toward a chair, but later he warmed up
when I asked if he could recommend an introduction to Islam. He
thrust into my hands a copy of von Denffer's *On Islamic Comport-
ment,* a collection of essays by well-known Islamist authors, including von Denffer's mentor, Khurshid Ahmad.

A few minutes later, Zayat came in, looking stockier and grayer
than he did when I had last seen him, but as professional as ever.
We headed out in his BMW 3-series sedan, a comfortably messy
older model with an old-fashioned car phone. As we zipped into
traffic, I was reminded of why I liked him.

"A lot of people say that Ian Johnson is a CIA agent because you
write so little."

"My boss says that too," I said.

"You should write more. Sloth is a sin."

We tore through traffic, exchanging more pleasantries and jokes
on the way to lunch.

We parked and stepped into a cafeteria-style Turkish restaurant.
Zayat immediately took command, ordering a tureen of soup and a
huge plate of sliced meat topped with croutons and doused in gar-
licky yogurt. At the cashier he whipped out his wallet and paid before I could react. "You're with an Arab now, you have no chance!"
he said, leading us to a table.

Zayat had been having a hard time. German officials want a dialogue with "Muslims" — in some ways a strange term that lumps
together completely different people, from first-generation Turks
who speak little German to Bosnian immigrants and local converts.
They know that Zayat and his allies in Milli Görüs represent many
Muslims, especially the more troubled youth, who pose the biggest

security threat. But Zayat's web of links has begun to be known in Germany, and he is not always welcome. The Federal Center for Political Education, for example, had listed him as an approved interlocutor on Muslim issues. That had carried a lot of weight because the center was set up after the war to promote democratic education in West German society, and its recommendations are generally seen as safe. But when commentators pointed out Zayat's links to the ideological world of the Brotherhood, the center quickly pulled his name off its website. Then he seemed to achieve a breakthrough when he participated in the German federal government's Islamkonferenz, a government effort to establish a formal dialogue with the Muslim community. But when Zayat's presence was made public, he was dropped. In 2009, police raided several mosques and prayer rooms linked to the Brotherhood, and some German newspapers said the head of the organization in Germany was Zayat, further tarnishing his reputation.

All this has helped push Zayat out of the front row of acceptable dialogue partners, but he continues to organize and keep the network functioning, allowing others to step forward. This background role is probably not what he wants, but it's something he and the Brotherhood have mastered over the years. A few years earlier, he had wired money to the Taibah International Aid Association, a Bosnian organization linked to fundamentalist groups. He concedes that he made the transfers, but says he was just doing this on behalf of Saudi donors. When I ask him why he was involved with the Saudis, his answer is disappointing: "To prevent worse from happening," one of the classic cop-out answers given by people who stay in bad groups too long.

"I don't deny that I'm in these groups," he says, getting a bit tense. "When I'm asked clearly, then I answer."

That's part of the problem, of course. Brotherhood figures and groups are always saying they have no ties with extremists, but only admit them when asked about specific connections. They never make clear statements, nor clean breaks with the past. The Islamic

Community of Germany has never owned up to its past, for example, or taken a real interest in its history. At its annual meeting in late 2008, the group celebrated its fiftieth anniversary, even though it wasn't legally established as the Mosque Construction Commission until 1960. It claims, on its website, that it was founded by the old soldiers (who had first met in 1958, hence the anniversary), but the group didn't mention that it threw the soldiers out. It has begun offering a Said Ramadan Prize for people who have helped the cause, but doesn't note that Ramadan was also kicked out. It acknowledges that a string of radicals have passed through its mosques, but says each one is an exception. The past is always being rewritten or excused away.

That doesn't prevent Zayat from winning friends. Some people are swayed by the group's claim that its rough edges represent authenticity. One of the best examples is Werner Schiffauer, a prominent German anthropologist who has written extensively about Islamists in Turkey and Germany. His approach is rigorously modern: informants are given pseudonyms, and their statements taken at face value. He does no investigative work and only checks stories against each other for internal logic — he never consults public records or tries to create a historical narrative. His research is also driven by a sense of guilt: that foreigners are victims and German society is oppressive. Thus he has become an advocate for groups like Milli Görüs; for example, he once served as a friendly witness on behalf of a group member. I remember seeing Schiffauer's ideological worlds collide when Zayat's Society of Muslim Social Scientists gave him an award at its annual meeting. When Schiffauer, speaking as a good leftist, said Muslims were victims of society, just like homosexuals, the room exploded in anger. One man had a violent fit of anger and had to be escorted from the room. Schiffauer ended up arguing with the man, stating that he didn't care what the man thought. In essence, the Muslim man was supposed to act as a proper subject of study, supplying partial proof of a theory that defined Muslims as victims.

Cultivating friends is important, Zayat says, but he wants me to understand something more important. With our meal long finished and teas drunk, he waves away all the groups he's joined and all the troubles he's had. There is an important lesson in this, and he wants to impart it to me. I hunch over the table and listen. It has to do with a group that wanted to build a mosque in Berlin, Inssan e.V. The group was founded by Muslims after the 9/11 attacks and needed money. Zayat arranged for the European Trust to donate several million euros to buy a piece of land for it in Berlin. When the purchase became public, a furor erupted over Zayat's involvement, and the local district government denied Inssan a building permit. So I asked Zayat if that was because his group was involved.

"No, you can't say that. If a plan to build a mosque is made public, everyone is against it. Mosques must always be built secretly."

Surely that can't be right, I said. I'd been to German cities and seen how local Muslims had built bridges to local communities and gotten wide support for their projects. It didn't always happen that way — racism was still a big problem — but it seemed to me that over the long term, transparency was the best bet. Wasn't the fact that Inssan's mosque project was undertaken by a small group of activists funded by the Brotherhood the real problem?

Zayat's answer was timeless, something that could have been uttered by von Mende, Dreher, or Ramadan: "No, it's not that. It's secrecy. If it's not public, you can build any mosque, regardless of who's behind it. You just have to keep it secret."

EPILOGUE
Inside the Mosque

I T IS A WEEKDAY in December, and the Islamic Center of Munich is almost empty. It is bright inside — the large windows and shiny tiles make it look warm — but the concrete walls do little to protect against the early winter weather. The heat is off and the mosque is cold.

Ahmad von Denffer wears a parka as he shuffles through the mosque. A burly fifty-five-year-old with a thick beard, he could be a Bavarian forest ranger, but for the knee-length robe that pokes out from the parka. Surgeon green, the robe is von Denffer's uniform, his announcement to the world that he hasn't just converted to Islam but identifies with one of its groups. In his case, it would be the Pakistani movement Jamaat-e-Islamiya.

Von Denffer's parents were born in Riga, the capital of Latvia, where von Mende's family originated. Founded in medieval times by German knights and merchants, the old Hanseatic seaport had a large German minority until Germany's twentieth-century meltdown, when the country lost not only vast territories but also its dominance in eastern Europe. When his parents were deported at the war's end, they settled in the Rhineland, and von Denffer was born there in 1949. He was a classic West German baby boomer. He grew up comfortably in the banking capital, Frankfurt, got a high school diploma, and then did his military service. It was there he discovered Islam: "I had too much time on my hands in the army. Back then we had to serve eighteen months and I read and read. I read about world religions. The one that made the most sense was Islam."

He began to practice it haphazardly and slowly gravitated to Munich. He started visiting the Islamic Center of Munich regularly in the late 1970s, just a few years after it had opened. This was the time when the Muslim Brotherhood was trying to make a comeback after years of oppression; it was actively organizing. Even though ordinary Turkish Muslims were shut out, the mosque had changed its bylaws to allow prominent Islamist organizers from around the world to join the governing council. That included the Jamaat-e-Islamiya leaders Khurshid Ahmad and Khurram Murad. Von Denffer says Murad played a big role in his life. Soon, von Denffer went to Jamaat's British center in Leicester to study and then to Pakistan for advanced training. It was the time of the jihad against the Soviet Union in Afghanistan, and Pakistan was a hotbed of political Islam.

For years, von Denffer was the young German convert among the mosque's senior Arab and Pakistani political activists. But with time, he began to take on an important role. He authored books in English and German that supported the classic positions of political Islam: special enclaves for Muslims, implementation of sharia in Western countries, and support for military jihad wherever Muslims might be in trouble. He became a leader of the mosque.

Von Denffer is interested in discussing the history of the mosque. Most of the time, all that outsiders want to know about are the links to terrorism or extremism. He has answered too many questions about Abouhalima and the first World Trade Center bombing, not to mention Salim and Al Qaeda. And then 9/11, the financial freeze on Himmat, and his resignation from all posts. More recently, German federal police raided the Islamic Center of Munich, looking for proof of money laundering and other financial misdeeds.

Von Denffer finds it much more interesting to talk about the

1950s. He knows of the ex-soldiers but says they left voluntarily, not that they were kicked out. Obliquely, he acknowledges the students' ambitious goal of a worldwide revival of Islam.

"They had different views," von Denffer says. "The refugees were locally oriented, the students were internationally oriented."

He also knows about Said Ramadan. And what he says about Ramadan is probably true, at least as seen from the perspective of a movement that ignores its own history. "If you were to ask people who come here to pray, only a very small number would know his name."

Said Ramadan might have been cut out of the Munich mosque and the revival of the Muslim Brotherhood, but he remained a semimythical figure in the world of political Islam, even after his retreat to Geneva. He remained in Switzerland, cultivating his image and popping up from time to time at the center of a controversy.

Right after he left in the mid-1960s, he was the focus of the *"affaire des Frères Musulmans."* Another attempt to kill Nasser had been uncovered, and the Egyptians claimed that Ramadan was at the center of it. Nasser's secret police provided hordes of documents, guns, and money to prove their point. But coming as it was from a dictatorship, the material was hard to judge — how much of it was real? The Swiss police vigorously debated Ramadan's status. At this point they came to a conclusion: "Said Ramadan is, among others, an information agent of the English and the Americans." In another report, a Swiss officer reminded the authorities that Ramadan had cooperated closely with Swiss federal police. He was allowed to stay.

Around this time, in 1965, he got a letter (which would become famous) from Malcolm X, who was seeking advice. Later, he went on a whistle-stop tour of the Muslim world, denouncing Nasser. Soviet newspapers alleged that he was a U.S. agent trying to undermine the United Arab Republic — a short-lived experiment at unifying Egypt and Syria under socialist leadership.

Like many Muslim Brothers, Ramadan was also fascinated by the

Islamic revolution in Iran, which took place in 1979. Although he was Sunni Muslim and the Iranians were Shia, he cultivated good ties with Tehran. In the early 1980s, that got him involved in one of his messiest controversies: the assassination of an Iranian diplomat in Washington. The diplomat had remained loyal to the shah, prompting a fanatical American convert, Dawud Salahuddin, to gun him down. Dressed as a delivery man, Salahuddin rang the diplomat's doorbell. Salahuddin had hidden a pistol in a package, and when the diplomat opened the door, Salahuddin opened fire. Salahuddin fled — to Geneva, where Ramadan was able to secure him safe passage to Tehran, where he remains today. Salahuddin says Ramadan was definitely not involved in the murder. He is keen to protect him from any charges. The two had met in the mid-1970s in Washington when Ramadan was giving a lecture. Salahuddin clearly still reveres him. But he essentially admits that Ramadan's role was accessory after the fact, sheltering him in Geneva and arranging his escape. "If he hadn't made a call, I wouldn't have come here," Salahuddin said in a telephone interview from Tehran.

Over the last fifteen years of his life, Ramadan slid into irrelevance. Islamism was on the rise, but Ramadan was often ill, and many assumed he had already died. His son Tariq, who is a famous Muslim activist in his own right, described his decline in a touching essay. He wrote that his father spent many years able to follow world events only from afar, prone to "long silences sunk in memory and thoughts and, often, in bitterness."

What of those shut out of the mosque? After von Mende died, the exile groups lost their main benefactor. But they didn't disband. Veli Kayum led the Turkestanis. Hayit continued to work for the West Germans and was the subject of attacks in the Soviet press. He also kept up his academic work, writing a volume on the Basmaci rebellion, the great uprising in Central Asia against communist rule that the novelist Ahmad Kamal claimed to have joined.

One wonders what would have happened if von Mende had lived longer. Would his people have regained control over the mosque?

It's possible but doubtful. For three years after von Mende's death, his deputy, Walter Schenk, ran the office. But it became increasingly anachronistic — a small group of hard-line cold warriors battling on as the world moved toward détente. When the office finally was closed in 1966, Schenk — who like von Mende had had strong Nazi ties — was unable to find significant work. He ended up drinking himself to death. Perhaps von Mende had followed a similar path, but instead of drink, he had worked and worried himself to death. It's hard to imagine that the Research Service Eastern Europe was positioned to play a role in Germany's new, Islamic future.

Some of von Mende's other creations continued. Namangani continued to run the Ecclesiastical Administration, the group that had given birth to the Mosque Construction Commission. He eventually retired and moved to Turkey, drawing a West German and then a united German pension. Until the end, he and Gacaoglu continued their sparring, like two wrestlers locked for eternity. Gacaoglu would occasionally write to Bavarian state or federal officials, accusing Namangani of all manner of incompetence. Namangani died in 2002. For all their differences, Namangani and Gacaoglu shared the same fate. To the end, neither was able to build a mosque for his followers. Both had to use small rooms at the back of factories, rented cheap. Neither man attended the Islamic Center of Munich. As for Garip Sultan, the young soldier who worked in the Ostministerium and then for Amcomlib, he returned to Munich after several years of covert propaganda work in the United States. When Amcomlib began focusing exclusively on radio broadcasting in the mid-1960s, he became head of the Tatar desk. He retired and still lives in Munich. He also avoided the mosque. And the Muslims at the grassroots? Some stayed with Namangani or Gacaoglu. Over time, they were outnumbered by the tens of thousands of Turkish migrants who came to work in Munich's booming economy. Some attended the mosque for big holidays; many faded away.

*   *   *

Von Denffer is back from the afternoon prayer. "The history of the mosque," he says, and muses. Yes, it was important, even internationally important. Now he says it is a local institution. History has moved on, even for it. After an hour of sitting, von Denffer is getting cold. It is midafternoon but the sun has almost set. The inside of the mosque is blanketed in a dull pink light, a winter sunset. The possibility of knowing what happened in Munich seems to recede. As if on cue, von Denffer says consolingly, "It was fifteen, twenty years after the war. It was a completely different time back then. The circumstances under which things happened here are hardly imaginable."

ACKNOWLEDGMENTS
SOURCES
NOTES

ACKNOWLEDGMENTS

This was by far the most complicated project I have worked on. It consumed three years of research and another year of writing, taking me to a dozen countries and even more archives. I say this only to point out that it wouldn't have been possible without the extraordinary help of many different people. Most readers can skip this section, but I feel it is absolutely necessary to thank . . .

Especially:

When I returned to Berlin in 2001, I had the good fortune of working with Almut Schoenfeld, a researcher and reporter in the *Wall Street Journal*'s Berlin bureau. Her contagious enthusiasm and genuine interest resulted in many incredible finds among the living and the dead. Without her work this book would not have been possible.

David Crawford, also of the *Journal*'s Berlin bureau, has been a friend and colleague for over twenty years. Together we covered the initial stories on Islamic terrorism in Germany. More important, David showed me that there was a bigger story to write.

Steve Merley, an outstanding investigative researcher, helped me with innumerable points regarding the Muslim Brotherhood. He is easily the best-informed person on the modern Saudi–Muslim Brotherhood nexus in the West. The last section of the book would not have been possible without his help.

In Europe:

Special thanks to Ahmet Şenyurt, a leading expert on contemporary Islam in Germany. Ahmet was a constant reminder that the problem has never been Islam; it is the religion's misuse by opportunists, politicians, and misguided idealists.

I was helped greatly by the expertise and camaraderie of Dr. Stefan Meining, a journalist with Bavarian Broadcasting. It was Stefan who first looked in the Bavarian state archives for clues to the history of the mosque. He also produced an hourlong documentary on the mosque for German public television.

I would also like to thank the following people, in alphabetical order:

- Malik Aoudia and Samir Benyounes for companionship and research help, especially at the fatwa council meeting in London and in Paris's *banlieues*
- Sylvain Besson, of the Swiss newspaper *Le Temps,* for pointing to files in the Swiss national archives
- Abby Collins, of Harvard University's "Berlin Dialogues," for sponsoring my talk in 2007 on the Munich mosque and for many stimulating conversations
- Johannes Kandel, of the Friedrich Ebert Stiftung in Berlin, for hosting discussions on Islam in Europe
- Gilles Kepel, at the Fondation Nationale des Sciences Politiques in Paris, for discussions on Islamism in Europe
- Kristina Klein, Nicole Menck, and Ruth Scherpf of the *Journal's* Berlin bureau
- Bertil Lintner (of Sweden, via Chiangmai) for helping identify Ahmad Kamal's work in Burma
- Dr. Juergen Micksch, of the Interkultureller Rat in Deutschland e.V., who allowed me to attend several discussions on Islamism
- Dr. Herbert Landolin Müller, at the Landesamt für Verfassungsschutz in Baden-Württenburg, an expert on the Muslim Brotherhood, who exemplifies the true meaning of intelligence work

- Gary Smith, of the American Academy in Berlin, for encouraging me to write a piece on Islamic law for the academy's *Berlin Journal* and who also organized many stimulating discussions on the topic that enriched my thinking
- Assistant Professor Riem Spielhaus, of Berlin's Humboldt University, for many patient conversations
- Professor Dr. Ursula Spuler-Stegemann, at Marburg University, an early and prophetic writer on Islamism in Germany
- Dr. Guido Steinberg, of the Stiftung Wissenschaft und Politik, for conversations on Islamism
- Michael Whine, of the Community Security Trust in London, for his inspiring evenhandedness
- Raimund Wolfert, a historian of Norway, for insights into von Mende's wife, Karo Espeseth

In Egypt:
- researcher extraordinaire Mandi Fahmy
- Gamal al-Banna, who shared ideas and insights into his brother, Hasan

In the archives:

Much of this book is based on archives and was possible only because many archivists went out of their way to track down files. I would especially like to thank, alphabetically:

- Salim Abdullah of the Islam-Archiv Deutschland in Soest
- Simon Braune of the Middle East Institute in Washington
- Dr. Caroline Gigl at the Bayerisches Hauptstaatsarchiv in Munich
- David Haight and Chalsea Millner of the Dwight D. Eisenhower Presidential Library in Abilene, Kansas
- Scott Koch, the CIA's information and privacy coordinator
- Dr. Ingo Loose and Ilona Kalb at Humboldt University's archive
- Mr. Knud Piening and Johannes Freiherr von Boeselager in the German Foreign Office's political archive in Berlin
- Anatol Shemelev of the Hoover Archive in Palo Alto, California
- Ruth Stalder of the Swiss Federal Archives

- John Taylor, Sammy Popat, Matthew Olsen, Paul Brown, and William Cunliffe at NARA in Washington
- Scott S. Taylor and Nicholas B. Scheetz of Georgetown University's Special Collection

Émigré families:

This book would also not have been possible without the friendly support of many individuals and families who opened their personal archives to me, even though it sometimes meant revisiting painful memories. I would like to thank, alphabetically:

- the late Dr. Baymirza Hayit
- the family of Ahmad Kamal, whose recollections helped illuminate their mysterious and mercurial patriarch
- the late Professor Dr. Gerhard Kegel for his personal file on Said Ramadan
- Professor Dr. Erling von Mende for making available part of his father's files
- Ehrenfried Schütte, a tireless campaigner on behalf of the victims of the Yalta agreement, who shared valuable reminiscences and documents on the Ostministerium
- Garip Sultan, who in the true spirit of Tatar hospitality invited me into his home numerous times
- Karin West, who made available priceless reminiscences and her tape recording of Bob Dreher's farewell party

In the United States:

Because I was based in Berlin during the initial phase of my research, I was aided by several American researchers. One, Chris Law, formerly a reporter with the National Security News Service in Washington and now an investigator with the Senate Committee on Finance, helped obtain FOIA information from the CIA and army intelligence, a feat for which I remain in awe. He also helped track down CIA agents from that period. Many thanks also to Chris's former colleagues at NSNS, David Armstrong and Joseph Trento, for valuable advice. In addition, Chris Conkey, a news assistant and later reporter in the *Journal*'s Washington bureau, helped get files from various archives.

I would also like to thank, alphabetically:

- Zeyno Baran, Eric Brown, Hillel Fradkin, and S. Enders Wimbush, of the Hudson Institute, for discussions on contemporary Islamism and for sponsoring my talk and paper in 2007 on the Munich mosque
- Daniel Benjamin, of the Center for Strategic and International Studies, for discussions on terrorism
- Professor Richard Breitman, of American University, for helping navigate archival releases through the Nazi War Crimes Disclosure Act
- Ron Bright, who helped crack parts of the Ahmad Kamal story. Ron, through FOIA, obtained Kamal's FBI papers; thanks to him for sharing that information, and to Ric Gillespie, executive director of the International Group for Historic Aircraft Recovery, which published Ron's paper.
- Jeffrey Burds, at Northeastern University, for his advice on covert operations in the early Cold War
- Stephen L. Crane, author of a little-known masterpiece on the Turkic Nazi soldiers, who shared his archive
- Jim Critchlow for a scrupulously honest book on Radio Liberty and for guidance as I tried to fathom the world of 1950s broadcasting and exile politics
- Bob Dreyfuss, who shared his files on Said Ramadan's trip to Princeton
- Jim Engell, of Harvard University's English department, for discussions on writing
- Jenny Fichmann, a freelance researcher in Palo Alto, for help in the Hoover archives
- Merle and Marshall Goldman, of Harvard University, for support and ideas
- Hope Harrison, at George Washington University, for many fruitful discussions and for sponsoring a talk that highlighted flaws in my original thesis
- Stephanie Ho and David Hathaway for hospitality and support
- Nancy Kobrin for discussions on psychology and terrorism
- Anita Kolaczkowska and family for discussions on Ahmad Kamal
- Mark Kramer, the writer and former head of the Nieman Foundation's narrative writing program, for editing work and discussions on

how to frame the book. Also thanks to members of Mark's narrative writing class, who were unstinting in their criticism.

- Professor Mark Kramer, head of Harvard University's Cold War Studies Program, for advice and discussions
- Andreas Krueger, then of the German embassy in Washington, for helping organize a talk I gave to the U.S. Congress on Islamism.
- Jonathan Laurence, of Boston College, for public and private debates about engaging the Muslim Brotherhood
- Robert Leiken, of the Nixon Center, for stimulating conversations on the Muslim Brotherhood
- Jim Mann, writer-in-residence at Johns Hopkins University–SAIS, for FOIA advice
- Tom McIntyre, of San Francisco, for discussions on writing as well as support and hospitality
- the Nieman Foundation for Journalism at Harvard and its director, Bob Giles, for sponsoring me during the 2006–2007 academic year. The stay there helped immeasurably in broadening the book.
- Kenneth Osgood, of Florida Atlantic University, for his expertise on covert propaganda
- Christian Ostermann, of the Wilson Center's Cold War International History Program, for advice and criticism
- Richard Pipes for recollections of Soviet-Islamic studies in the Cold War.
- Glenn R. Simpson, of the *Journal,* for sharing ideas and notes
- Gene and Gloria Sosin for their generous time and for Gloria's small gem of a book
- Scott T. Taylor and family for insights into Washington
- Roger Thurow, of the *Journal,* for companionship and reporting advice in Switzerland
- Tim Weiner, of the *New York Times,* for generously sharing material and advice

Readers, critics, and family:
I am grateful to a number of readers and editors who helped guide this project over several years, including Leslie T. Chang and Peter Hessler of Skinflint, Colorado; Doug Hunt of the University of Missouri; Lorne

Blumer of Toronto; James Scott of Charleston and Craig Welch of Seattle; Yaroslav Trofimov of the *Journal;* the *Journal's* editing staff, especially Mike Miller and Mike Allen, and above all former chief editor Paul Steiger, who in an era of declining news holes recognized the value of the initial story, gave me time to work on it, and found the space to run six thousand words.

Special thanks to Andrea Schulz and Tom Bouman at Houghton Mifflin Harcourt, whose insightful editing and support shaped the book; manuscript editor Susanna Brougham for a very close reading; and, as always, my agent, Chris Calhoun, of Sterling Lord Literistic, who made it all happen.

Finally I owe a great debt to family members: my father, Denis, who read and discussed this book from its inception; my sister Cathy and her family for support, especially with Longmorn on Darß; and Elke, for years of help and support.

SOURCES

Archives

PUBLIC

AA B40 Auswärtiges Amt, Berlin, Bestand 40, "Referat IIA3, Ost-West-Beziehungen" (Foreign Office, Berlin, Record Group 40, "Division IIA3, East-West Relations")

AAPA ZA Politisches Archiv des Auswärtiges Amt, Zwischenarchiv (Political Archive of the Foreign Office, Temporary Archive), Berlin Amstgericht München, Registerakten (Sonderband) VR 6256, Islamische Gemeinschaft in Deutschland e.V.

BA Bundesarchiv (Federal Archives), Koblenz

BA-MA Bundesarchiv-Militärarchiv (Federal Archives-Military Archives), Freiburg

BAR Schweizerisches Bundesarchiv (Swiss Federal Archives), Bern

BAR Ramadan BAR E 4320(C) 1994/120, Bd. 220, Dossier (4183:0) 420/36 Ramadan, Said, 1960–1988

BAR Touhami BAR E 4320-01(C) 1996/202, 34 Fiche Louahala, Touhami, 1956–1986

BayHStA Bayerisches Hauptstaatarchiv (Bavarian Central State Archives), Munich

BayHStA LaflüVerw Landesflüchtlingsverwaltung (State Refugee Administration), Record Groups 1894 and 1900

BStU Die Bundesbeauftragte für die Unterlagen des Staatssicherheitsdienstes der ehemaligen Deutschen Demokratisch Republik (Federal Commissioner for the Records of the State Security Service of the Former German Democratic Republic), Berlin

CIA Central Intelligence Agency, Freedom of Information Act release to author, "Subject: von Mende, Gerhard" and "Subject: Gacaoglu, Ibrahim"

Georgetown Georgetown University Special Collections: Diplomacy, International Affairs, Intelligence, Name file on "Kelley, Robert F." and "Lodeesen, Jon D."

GHWK Haus der Wannsee-Konferenz, Gedenk- und Bildungsstätte (House of the Wannsee Conference, Memorial and Educational Site)

Hoover Hoover Institution Library and Archives, Stanford University, Palo Alto, CA

Hoover Dallin Hoover "Alexander Dallin" collection

Hoover Henze Hoover "Paul B. Henze" collection
Hoover RFE/RL Hoover "Radio Free Europe/Radio Liberty Inc." collection
ICRC International Committee of the Red Cross, Geneva
Islam-Archiv Islam-Archiv Deutschland, Soest (Islam-Archive, Germany, Soest)
IZ Institut für Zeitgeschichte (Institute for Contemporary History), Munich
NA National Archives, Kew Gardens, UK
NAFO 141 NA Foreign Office (Egypt: Embassy and Consular Activities)
NARA National Archives and Records Administration, Washington, DC
NARA RG 59 NARA, General Records of the Department of State
NARA RG 263 NARA, Records of the Central Intelligence Agency, Directorate of Operations, records released under the Nazi and Japanese War Crimes Disclosure Acts, including separate name files for "Kedia, Michel," "von Mende, Gerhard," "al-Hussaini, Amin," and "Unglaube, Heinz"
NARA RG 319 NARA, Records of the Army Staff, Investigative Records Repository, unprocessed files for "Ibrahim Gacaoglu Personnel File Folder XE306651," "Gerhard von Mende Personal File Folder D007362," "Gerhard von Mende Personal File Folder XE007362"
NAWO 208 NA War Office (Military Intelligence, Middle East and Egypt)
UAHUB Universitätsarchiv, Humboldt Universität Berlin (University Archive, Humboldt University, Berlin)
WASt Deutsche Dienststelle für die Benachrichtigung der nächsten angehörigen von Gefallenen der ehemaligen deutschen Wehrmacht (German Authority for the notification of next of kin of members of the former German Wehrmacht who were killed in action), Berlin

Private

Dreher Dreher, Robert, papers relating to CIA service of Robert H. Dreher in Germany and Vietnam. In possession of the Oerkvitz family.
Hoffmann Papers and correspondence relating to works of Joachim Hoffmann. In possession of the Hoffmann family.
Mende Personal and work correspondence, 1945–1963, of Gerhard von Mende. In possession of the von Mende family.
Narzikul Papers relating to wartime service of Isakjan Narzikul. In possession of Stephen L. Crane.
Schütte Personal papers, Ostministerium files, and correspondence of Dr. Ehrenfried Schütte. In possession of Dr. Schütte.
Sultan Personal papers and letters of Garip Sultan. In possession of Mr. Sultan.
Ungermann Personal papers, British intelligence documents relating to Siegfried Ungermann. In possession of the Hoffmann family.
Unglaube Manuscript of autobiography of Heinz Unglaube. In possession of the author.

Interviews

Abdel Khalek, Mohamed Farid. 13 September 2004, Cairo.
Abdullah, Mohammad Salim. 14 December 2004, Soest, Germany.

Akef, Mahdi. 14 September 2004, Cairo.

Allam, Fouad. 15 September 2004, Cairo.

Allworth, Edward A. 7 January 2006, New York City.

Alshibaya, Nina. 16 August 2004, Munich.

Amriou, Mourad. 10 September, 1 November and 3 November 2004, Paris.

Banna, Gama al-. 13 September 2004, Cairo.

Bouzar, Dounia. 4 September 2004, Paris.

Critchlow, James. 3 February 2006, Cambridge, MA.

Denffer, Ahmad von. 9 December 2004, Munich.

Grimm, Muhammad Abdul Karim, 21 October 2004, Hamburg.

Hayit, Baymirza.† 25 October 2004, Cologne.

Helbawy, Kamal al-. 20 October 2005, London.

Himmat, Ghaleb. Telephone inteview, 1 June 2005, Campione d'Italia.

Kamal-Haller, Tura. 16 June 2006, Munich.

Kassajep, Margaret.† 17 August 2004, Munich.

Kegel, Dr. Gerhard.† 25 October 2004, Cologne.

Klump, Will. 17 January 2006, New York City.

Kolaczkowska, Anita. 12 April 2007, Palo Alto, CA.

Kuniholm, Bruce. Telephone interview, 18 April 2006, Durham, NC.

Lahaty, Mohamed. 2 September 2004, Paris.

Louahala, Touhami. 30 July 2006, Montélimar, France.

Mahgary, Mohamad Ali el-. 17 December 2004, Nuremberg, Germany.

Melbardis, Alexander. 6 September 2005, Pfaffing, Germany.

Mende, Dr. Erling von. 31 January 2005, Berlin.

Mogaddedi, Obeidullah. 1 February 2005, Springe, Germany.

Murphy, David E. 7 May 2006, Punta Gorda, FL.

Nada, Youssef. 2 June 2004, Campione d'Italia.

Nasar, Rusi. 10 May 2006, Falls Church, VA.

Oerkvitz, Chuck and Helen. 7 February 2006, Gwynedd, PA.

Patch, Isaac. Telephone interview, 23 May 2005, Franconia, NH.

Pipes, Richard. 25 October 2006, Cambridge, MA.

Rawi, Ahmed al-. 21 July 2004, Markfield, UK.

Rhoer, Edward van der. Email exchanges, 31 January and 1 February 2006, Washing-
    ton, DC.

Said, Refaat al-. 14 September 2004, Cairo.

Salahuddin, Dawud. Telephone interview, 28 February 2006, Tehran.

Schütte, Ehrenfried.† 27 January 2005, Munich.

Sosin, Gene and Gloria. 3 May 2006, White Plains, NY.

Stewart, Gaither "Jack." 1 October 2005, Rome.

Sultan, Garip. 27 January and 9 March 2005; 28 March and 31 May 2006, Munich.

Terrel, Hervé. 14 May 2004, Paris.

West, Karin. 27 March 2006, Munich.

Yazdani, Faisal. 28 January and 13 December 2005, Munich.

Zaidan, Amir. 18 March 2005, Berlin.

Zayat, Ibrahim el-. 19 April 2005, Cologne.

---

†deceased

Books and Articles

Abu-Rabi', Ibrahim M. *Intellectual Origins of Islamic Resurgence in the Modern Arab World.* Albany, NY: SUNY Press, 1996.

Ahmed-Ulla, Noreen S., Sam Roe, and Laurie Cohen. "A Rare Look at Secretive Brotherhood in America." *Chicago Tribune* (online edition), 19 September 2004.

Alexiev, Alex. *Soviet Nationalities in German Wartime Strategy, 1941–1945.* Santa Monica, CA: Rand Corporation, 1982.

Altalib, Hisham. *Training Guide for Islamic Workers,* Herndon, VA: International Institute of Islamic Thought, 1991.

Andrew, Christopher, and Vasili Mitrokhin. *The Mitrokhin Archive: The KGB in Europe and the West.* London: Allen Lane, 1999.

Armstrong, Karen. *Islam: A Short History.* New York: The Modern Library, 2002.

Awaisi, Abd al-Fattah Muhammad el-. *The Muslim Brothers and the Palestine Questions, 1928–1947.* London: I. B. Tauris Academic Studies, 1998.

Barbour, Nevill. Untitled review of Serge Bromberger, *Les rebelles algériens. International Affairs,* Vol. 35, No. 1 (January 1959): 113.

Battle, Joyce, ed. *U.S. Propaganda in the Middle East — The Early Cold War Version.* National Security Archive Electronic Briefing Book No. 78, 13 December 2002.

Bigart, Homer. "Coney Islander Assails Red Crimes at Bandung." *New York Herald Tribune,* 21 April 1954: 53.

Birn, Ruth Bettina. "Austrian Higher SS and Police Leaders and Their Participation in the Holocaust in the Balkans." *Holocaust and Genocide Studies,* Vol. 6, No. 4 (1991): 351–72.

Bostom, Andrew, ed. *The Legacy of Islamic Antisemitism: From Sacred Texts to Solemn History.* Amherst, NY: Prometheus Books, 1968.

Bräutigam, Otto. *So hat es sich zugetragen: Ein Leben als Soldat und Diplomat.* Würzburg, Germany: Holzner, 1968.

Breitman, Richard, *Architect of Genocide: Himmler and the Final Solution.* Waltham, MA: Brandeis University Press, 1992.

Breitman, Richard, et al. *U.S. Intelligence and the Nazis.* New York: Cambridge University Press, 2005.

Bromberger, Serge. *Les rebelles algériens.* Paris: Plon, 1958.

"Bundesweite Razzia bei Islamisten," *Süddeutsche Zeitung,* 11 March 2009: 5.

Burds, Jeffrey. "The Soviet War Against 'Fifth Columnists': The Case of Chechnya, 1942–44." *Journal of Contemporary History,* Vol. 42, No. 2 (Spring 2007): 267–314.

Caeiro, Alexandre. "Transnational 'Ulama,' European Fatwas, and Islamic Authority: A Case Study of the European Council for Fatwa and Research" in S. Allievi and M. van Bruinessen, eds., *Production and Dissemination of Islamic Knowledge in Western Europe.* London: Routledge, 2008.

Cakars, Maris, and Barton Osborn. "Operation Ohio: Mass Murder by U.S. Intelligence Agencies." *Win* (Brooklyn, NY), 18 September 1975: 5–19.

Caroe, Olaf. *Soviet Empire: The Turks of Central Asia and Stalinism.* 2nd ed. New York: St. Martin's Press, 1967.

Carruthers, Susan L. "Between Camps: Eastern Bloc 'Escapees' and Cold War Borderlands." *American Quarterly,* Vol. 57, No. 3, September 2005: 911–42.

Caute, David. *The Dancer Defects: The Struggle for Cultural Supremacy During the Cold War.* Oxford, UK: Oxford University Press, 2002.

Central Intelligence Agency Political Islam Strategic Analysis Program. "Muslim Brotherhood: Pivotal Actor in European Political Islam." Unpublished report, 10 May 2006.

———. "Muslim Brotherhood Rhetoric in Europe: Deception, Division, or Confusion?" Unpublished report, 29 January 2008.

Coll, Steve. *Ghost Wars: The Secret History of the CIA, Afghanistan, and bin Laden from the Soviet Invasion to September 10, 2001*. New York: Penguin Books, 2004.

Copeland, Miles. *The Game of Nations: The Amorality of Power Politics*. London: Weidenfeld and Nicholson, 1969.

Crane, Stephen L. *Survivor from An Unknown War: The Life of Isakjan Narzikul*. Upland, PA: Diane Publishing Co., 1999.

Critchlow, James. *Radio Hole-in-the-Head/Radio Liberty: An Insider's Story of Cold War Broadcasting*. Washington, DC: American University Press, 1995.

Cwiklinski, Sebastian. *Wolgatataren im Deutschland des Zweiten Weltkriegs: Deutsche Ostpolitik und tatarischer Nationalismus*. Berlin: Klaus Schwarz Verlag, 2002.

Czechowicz, Andrzej. *Sieben schwere Jahre*. Berlin: Militärverlag der DDR Berlin, 1977. [Originally published in Polish as *Siedem Trudnych Lat*. Warsaw: Wydawnictwo Ministerstwa Obrony Narodowej, 1974]

Dallin, Alexander. *German Rule in Russia: A Study in Occupation Politics*. 2nd ed. London: The MacMillan Press Ltd., 1981.

Dalton, William D. "Islamic Society of North America," in *Encyclopedia of Indianapolis*. Indianapolis: The Polis Center, 1995.

Dawood, N. J., trans. *The Koran*. London: Penguin, 1999.

Denffer, Ahmad von. *ABC der Zeitschrift al-Islam: Stichwortregister, 1958–1992*. München: Islamisches Zentrum München, 1993.

DGAP, "Geschichte des Hauses Rauchstrasse 17/18." Information Brochure from DGAP. http://www.dgap.org/dgap/ueberuns/geschichte_haus/.

Dorril, Stephen, *MI6: Fifty Years of Special Operations*. London: Fourth Estate, 2000.

Dreyfuss, Robert. *Devil's Game: How the United States Helped Unleash Fundamentalist Islam*. New York: Metropolitan Books, 2005.

Elpeleg, Zvi. *Grand Mufti: Haj Amin al-Hussaini*. London: Frank Cass & Co., 1993.

Espeseth, Karo. *Sår som ennu blør (Sores That Still Bleed)*. Oslo: Gyldendal Norsk Forlag, 1931.

———. *Livet Gikk Videre (Life Went On)*. Oslo: Gyldendal Norsk Forlag, 1983.

Feferman, Kiril. "Nazi Germany and the Mountain Jews: Was There a Policy?" *Holocaust and Genocide Studies*, Vol. 21, No. 1 (2007): 96–114.

Forrest, Fred. "Allies We Don't Need." *New Leader*, 3 September 1951: 19–20.

Frangenberg, Helmut. "Kleine Migrationsgeschichte der Türken nach Köln," in Franz Sommerfeld, ed., *Der Moscheestreit: Eine exemplarische Debatte über Einwanderung und Integration*. Köln: Kiepenheuer & Wisch, 2008.

Gaddis, John Lewis. *We Now Know: Rethinking Cold War History*. Oxford: Clarendon Press, 1997.

Gensicke, Klaus. *Der Mufti von Jerusalem, Amin el-Husseini, und die Nationalsozialisten*. Frankfurt am Main: Peter Lang, 1988.

Golan, Galia. *Soviet Policies in the Middle East from World War Two to Gorbachev*. Cambridge: Cambridge University Press, 1990.

Grose, Peter. *Operation Rollback: America's Secret War Behind the Iron Curtain.* Boston: Houghton Mifflin Company, 2000.

Hawari, Mohammad. "Sex and Sexual Education Under the Light of Islamic Shariah," in European Council for Fatwa and Research conference material for July 2004 meeting. A copy of this paper is available at www.iandjohnson.com.

Hayek, Lester "Target: CIA." *Studies in Intelligence,* Vol. 6, No. 1: 29–56. (Internal CIA publication, Approved for Release 2005103115: CIA-RDP78T03194A0001000 60001-8.)

———. *"Basmatchi": Nationaler Kampf Turkestans in den Jahren 1917 bis 1934.* Köln: Dreisam Verlag, 1992.

Hayit, Baymirza. *Turkestan im XX. Jahrhundert.* Darmstadt: C. W. Leske, 1956.

Heiber, Helmut, ed. *Hitlers Lagebesprechungen: Die Protokollfragmente seiner militärischen Konferenzen, 1942–1945.* Stuttgart: Deutsche Verlags-Anstalt, 1962.

Heine, Peter. "Die Mullah-Kurse der Waffen-SS," in Gerhard Höpp and Brigitte Reinwald, eds., *Fremdeinsätze: Afrikaner und Asiaten in europäischen Kriegen, 1914–1945.* Berlin: Studien/Zentrum Moderner Orient 13, 2000: 181–88.

Henker, Michael, ed. *Bayern nach dem Krieg: Photographien 1945–1950.* Augsburg: Haus der Bayerischen Geschichte, 1995.

Hentges, Gudrun. "Reeducation — Propaganda — Heimatdienst: Kontroversen um die Gründung der Bundeszentrale für Heimatdienst / politische Bildung," in Heinz-Werner Wollersheim, ed., *Jahrbuch der Theodor-Litt-Gesellschaft 2004.* Leipzig: Leipziger Universitätsverlag, 2005.

Herf, Jeffrey. *Nazi Propaganda for the Middle East.* New Haven: Yale University Press, 2009.

Hoffmann, Joachim. *Die Ostlegionen, 1941–1943.* Freiburg: Verlag Rombach, 1986.

Höpp, Gerhard. "Frontenwechsel: Muslimische Deserteure im Ersten und Zweiten Weltkrieg und in der Zwischenkriegszeit," in Gerhard Höpp and Brigitte Reinwald, eds., *Fremdeinsätze: Afrikaner und Asiaten in europäischen Kriegen, 1914–1945.* Studien 13. Berlin: Das arabische Buch, 2000.

Höpp, Gerhard, ed. *Mufti-Papiere: Briefe, Memoranden, Reden, und Aufrufe Amin al Husainis aus dem Exil, 1940–1945.* Berlin: Klaus Schwarz Verlag, 2004.

Höpp, Gerhard, Peter Wien, and René Wildangel, eds. *Blind für die Geschichte?: Arabische Begegnungen mit dem Nationalsozialismus.* Berlin: Klaus Schwarz Verlag, 2004.

Johnson, Ian. "The Beachhead: How a Mosque for Ex-Nazis Became Center of Radical Islam." *The Wall Street Journal,* 12 July 2005: A1.

———. "Conflicting Advice: Islamic Justice Finds a Foothold in Heart of Europe." *The Wall Street Journal,* 4 August 2005: A1.

———. "A Course in Islamology." *Berlin Journal,* Autumn 2005. Berlin: American Academy.

———. "How Islamic Group's Ties Reveal Europe's Challenge." *The Wall Street Journal,* 29 December 2005: A1.

———. "The Muslim Brotherhood in Europe." Testimony to House Human Rights Caucus, 9 February 2006. Published online at http://lantos.house.gov+C6/HoR/ CA12/Human+Rights+Caucus/Briefing+Testimonies/02-23 06+Testimony+o f+Ian+Johnson+Muslims+in+Europe.htm.

Johnson, Ian, and John Carreyrou. "Walled Off: As Muslims Call Europe Home, Dangerous Isolation Takes Root." *The Wall Street Journal*, 11 July 2005: A1.

Johnson, Ian, and Alfred Kueppers. "Missed Link." *The Wall Street Journal*, 19 October 2001: A1.

Kamal, Ahmad. *Full Fathom Five*. Lincoln, NE: toExcel, 2000. [Originally published by Doubleday, 1948]

——. *Land Without Laughter*. Lincoln, NE: toExcel, 2000. [Originally published by Charles Scribner's Sons, 1940]

——. *One-Dog Man*. Lincoln, NE: toExcel, 2000. [Originally published by Random House, 1950]

——. *The Sacred Journey*. Lincoln, NE: toExcel, 2000. [Originally published by Duell, Sloan and Pearce, 1961]

——. *The Seven Questions of Timur*. Unbound folio edition, undated. Bound book published at Santa Ana, CA.: Fine Arts Press, 1938.

Kamal, Ahmad, and Charles G. Booth. *The Excommunicated*. Lincoln, NE: toExcel, 2000. [Originally published by The Falcon Press, 1952]

Kepel, Gilles. *Les banlieues de l'Islam*. Paris: Éditions du Seuil, 1991.

——. *Jihad: The Trail of Political Islam*. Cambridge: Harvard University Press, 2002.

——. *The Prophet and Pharaoh: Muslim Extremism in Egypt*. London: Al Saqi Books, 1985.

——. *The War for Muslim Minds*. Cambridge: Harvard University Press, 2004.

Kirimal, Edige. *Der Nationale Kampf der Krimtataren*. Emsdetten (Westf.): Verlag Lechte, 1952.

Kozlov, Victor Ivanovich. *The Peoples of the Soviet Union (Second World)*. Trans. Pauline Tiffen. Bloomington: Indiana University Press, 1988.

Kračkovskij, Ignaz. *Der historische Roman in der neueren arabischen Literatur*. Trans. Gerhard von Mende. Leipzig: Oto Harrassowitz, 1930.

Küntzel, Matthias. *Djihad und Judenhaß. Über den neuen antijüdischen Krieg*. Freiburg: Ca Ira Verlag, 2003.

Leggewie, Claus, Angela Joost, and Stefan Rech. *Der Weg zur Moschee — eine Handreichung für die Praxis*. Bad Homburg v.d. Höhe: Herbert-Quandt-Stiftung, 2002.

Leiken, Robert S. "Europe's Mujahideen." Center for Immigration Studies newsletter, April 2005.

Leiken, Robert S., and Steven Brooke. "The Moderate Muslim Brotherhood." *Foreign Affairs*, Vol. 86, No. 2, 107–21.

Lia, Brynjar. *The Society of the Muslim Brothers in Egypt: The Rise of an Islamic Mass Movement, 1928–1942*. Reading, UK: Ithaca Press, 1998.

Loftus, John. *The Belarus Secret*. New York: Penguin, 1982.

Loose, Ingo. "Berliner Wissenschaftler im 'Osteinsatz' 1939–1945: Akademische Mobilität zwischen Berliner Universität und Reichsuniversität Posen," in Christoph Jahr with Rebecca Schaarschmidt, eds., *Die Berliner Universität in der NS-Zeit, Bd. 1: Strukturen und Personen*. Stuttgart: 2005.

MacDonogh, Giles. *After the Reich: The Brutal History of the Allied Occupation*. New York: Basic Books, 2007.

Mallmann, Klaus-Michael, and Martin Cüppers. *Halbmond und Hakenkreuz: Das*

"Dritte Reich," die Araber, und Palästina. Darmstadt: Wissenschaftliche Buchgesellschaft, 2006.

Mattar, Philip. *The Mufti of Jerusalem: Al-Hajj Amīn al-Husaynī.* New York: Columbia University Press, 1988.

Matthews, Weldon C. *Confronting an Empire, Constructing a Nation: Arab Nationalists and Popular Politics in Mandate Palestine.* London: I. B. Tauris, 1988.

Meining, Stefan. "Die Islamische Gemeinschaft in Deutschland: Vom Moschee-Bauverein zum politischen Islam." Unpublished essay, 2005.

Mende, Erling von. *Turkestan als historischer Faktor und politische Idee: Festschr. für Baymirza Hayit zu seinem 70. Geburtstag.* Köln: Studienverlag, 1988.

Mende, Gerhard von. *Bulletin des Presse und Informationsamtes der Bundesregierung,* No. 881/S. 736, 11 May 1955.

———. "Erfahrungen mit Ostfreiwilligen in der deutschen Wehrmacht während des Zweiten Weltkrieges." *Auslandsforschung 1,* 1952: 24–33.

———. "Kaukasuspolitik." Unpublished essay, c. 1951, from Schütte archives.

———. *Der Nationale Kampf der Rußlandtürken: Ein Beitrag zur nationalen Frage in der Sovetunion.* Berlin: Mitteilungen des Seminars für orientalische Sprachen. Beiband zum Jahrgang XXXIX, 1936.

———. *Nationalität und Ideologie.* Duisdorf bei Bonn: Selbstverlag der Studiengesellschaft für Zeitprobleme, 1962.

———. *Studien zur Kolonisation in der Sovetunion.* Breslau: Verlag Priebatsch's Buchhandlung, 1933.

———. *Die Völker der Sowjetunion.* Reichenau/Saale: Rudolf Schneider Verlag, 1939.

Merley, Steve. "The Muslim Brotherhood in Belgium." Published by the Hudson Institute, http://www.futureofmuslimworld.com/research/detail/the-muslim-brotherhood-in-the-united-states, 6 April 2009.

Mitchell, Richard P. *The Society of the Muslim Brothers.* Oxford: Oxford University Press, 1969 (1993 reprint).

Mühlen, Patrik von zur. *Zwischen Hakenkreuz und Sowjetstern: Der Nationalismus der sowjetischen Orientvölker im Zweiten Weltkrieg.* Düsseldorf: Droste Verlag, 1971.

Munoz, Antonio J. *Forgotten Legions: Obscure Combat Formations of the Waffen-SS.* Boulder, CO: Paladin Press, 1991.

Murphy, David E., Sergei A. Kondrashev, and George Bailey. *Battleground Berlin: CIA Versus KGB in the Cold War.* New Haven: Yale University Press, 1999.

Neupert, Jutta. "Vom Heimatvertriebenen zum Neubuurger. Flüchtlingspolitik und Selbsthilfe auf dem Weg zur Integration," in Wolfgang Benz, ed., *Neuanfang in Bayern.* München: C. H. Beck, 1988.

Nielsen, Jørgen. *Muslims in Western Europe.* Edinburgh: Edinburgh University Press, 2004.

Osgood, Kenneth. *Total Cold War: Eisenhower's Propaganda Battle at Home and Abroad.* Lawrence: University of Kansas Press, 2006.

Parker, Jason C. "Small Victory, Missed Chance: The Eisenhower Administration, the Bandung Conference, and the Turning of the Cold War," in Kathryn C. Statler and Andrew L. Johns, eds., *The Eisenhower Administration, the Third World, and the Globalization of the Cold War.* Boulder, CO: Rowman & Littlefield Publishers Inc., 2006.

Pätzold, Kurt, and Erika Schwarz. *Tagesordnung: Judenmord. Die Wannsee-Konferenz am 20. January 1942.* Berlin: Metropol-Verlag, 1992.

Pauly, Robert J., Jr. *Islam in Europe: Integration or Marginalization?* Aldershot, UK: Ashgate, 2004.

Phillips, David Atlee. *The Night Watch.* New York: Atheneum, 1977.

Picker, Harry, ed. *Hitlers Tischgespräche.* Bonn: Athenäum-Verlag, 1951.

Porath, Y. *The Emergence of the Palestinian-Arab National Movement, 1918–1929.* London: Frank Cass & Co., 1974.

Prados, John. *Presidents' Secret Wars: CIA and Pentagon Covert Operations from World War II Through the Persian Gulf.* Chicago: Ivan R. Dee, 1996.

Prinz, Friedrich, ed. *Trümmerzeit in München.* München: C. H. Beck, 1984.

Prinz, Friedrich, and Marita Krauss, eds. *Trümmerleben: Texte, Dokumente, Bilder aus den Münchener Nachkriegsjahren.* München: Deutscher Taschenbuch Verlag, 1985.

Ranelagh, John. *The Agency: The Rise and Decline of the CIA.* New York: Simon and Schuster, 1986.

Rees, Ellen. "Sores That Still Bleed: Germany, the Great War, and Violence Against Women in the Modernist Literary Imagination," in Hillary Collier Sy-Quia and Susanne Baackmann, eds., *Conquering Women: Women and War in the German Cultural Imagination.* Berkeley: University of California Press, 2000.

Reiss, Tom. *The Orientalist: Solving the Mystery of a Strange and Dangerous Life.* New York: Random House, 2005.

Rupierer, Hermann-Josef. *Der besetzte Verbündete: Die amerikanische Deutschlandpolitick, 1949–1955.* Opladen: Westdeutscher Verlag, 1991.

Schenk, Herrad. *Wie in einem uferlosen Strom: Das Leben meiner Eltern.* München: C. H. Beck, 2002.

Schlögel, Karl. "The Futility of One Professor's Life: Otto Hoetzsch and German Russian Studies," in *Sketches of Europe.* Trans. Ray Brandon. Berlin: Osteuropa, 2005.

Schmitt, Thomas. *Moscheen in Deutschland: Konflikte um ihre Errichtung und Nutzung.* Flensburg: Deutsche Akademie für Landeskunde, Selbstverlag, 2003.

Schulze, Reinhard. *Geschichte er islamischen Welt im 20. Jahrhundert.* München: C. H. Beck, 1994: C87.

———. *Islamischer Internationalismus im 20. Jahrhundert.* Leiden: Brill, 1990.

Schwanitz, Wolfgang G. "Die Berliner Djihadisierung des Islams." Konrad-Adenauer-Stiftung: KAS Auslands-informationen, October 2004.

Seidt, Hans-Ulrich. *Berlin Kabul Moskau: Oskar Ritter von Niedermayer und Deutschlands Geopolitik.* München: Universitas, 2002.

Selig, Wolfram. *Chronik der Stadt München, 1945–1948.* München: Stadtarchiv München, 1980.

Shafiq, Muhammad. *The Growth of Islamic Thought in North America: Focus on Ismáil Raji al Faruqi.* Brentwood, MA: Amana Publications, 1994.

Shlaim, Avi. *Collusion Across the Jordan: King Abdullah, the Zionist Movement, and the Partition of Palestine.* Oxford: Clarendon Press, 1988.

Shultz, Richard H., Jr. Unpublished interview with Robert H. Dreher.

Simpson, Christopher. *Blowback: The First Full Account of America's Recruitment of*

Nazis and Its Disastrous Effect on the Cold War, Our Domestic and Foreign Policy.
New York: Collier, 1989.

Simpson, Glenn R., and Amy Chozick. "Obama's Muslim-Outreach Adviser Resigns."
The Wall Street Journal, 6 August 2008. Accessed at http://online.wsj.com/article/
SB11797906741214995.html.

Smal-Stocky, Roman. "The Struggle of the Subjugated Nations in the Soviet Union for
Freedom: Sketch of the History of the Promethean Movement." *The Ukrainian
Quarterly,* Vol. 3, No. 4, 1947: 324–44.

Smith, Martin. *Burma: Insurgency and the Politics of Ethnicity.* London: Zed Books,
1991.

Sosin, Gene. *Sparks of Liberty: An Insider's Memoir of Radio Liberty.* University Park:
Pennsylvania State University Press, 1999.

Sosin, Gloria Donen. *Red-Letter Year.* White Plains, NY: Kalita Press, 2004.

Stöver, Bernd. *Die Befreiung vom Kommunismus: Amerikanische* Liberation Policy *im
Kalten Krieg, 1947–1991.* Köln: Böhlau Verlag, 2002.

Sultan, Garip. *Die Gründung der Wolga-Tatarischen Legion.* Unpublished manuscript,
1947.

Takeyh, Ray. *The Origins of the Eisenhower Doctrine: The US, Britain, and Nasser's
Egypt, 1953–57.* Oxford: Macmillan, 2000.

Thomas, Evan. *The Very Best Men: The Early Years of the CIA.* New York: Simon and
Schuster, 1995.

Thorwald, Jürgen. *Wenn Sie Verderben Wollen: Bericht des großen Verrats.* Stuttgart:
Steingrüben Verlag, 1952.

Tolstoy, Nikolai. *Victims of Yalta.* London: Hodder and Stoughton, 1977.

Trento, Joseph. *The Secret History of the CIA.* New York: Basic Books, 2005.

Tudda, Chris. *The Truth Is Our Weapon: The Rhetorical Diplomacy of Dwight D. Eisenhower and John Foster Dulles.* Baton Rouge: Louisiana State University Press,
2006.

Tumanov, Oleg. *Tumanov: Confessions of a KGB Agent.* Trans. David Floyd. Chicago:
edition q, inc., 1993.

Uehling, Greta Lynn. *Beyond Memory: The Crimean Tatars' Deportation and Return.*
New York: Palgrave MacMillan, 2004.

Wachs, Philipp-Christian. *Der Fall Theodor Oberländer (1905–1998): Ein Lehrstück
Deutscher Geschichte.* Frankfurt/Main: Campus, 2000.

Wright, Lawrence. *The Looming Tower: Al-Qaeda and the Road to 9/11.* New York: Alfred A. Knopf, 2006.

Yaqub, Salim. *Containing Arab Nationalism: The Eisenhower Doctrine and the Middle
East.* Chapel Hill: University of North Caroline Press, 2004.

Zaydi, Mshari al-. "History of the Jordanian Brotherhood, Part One." *Ashara Alawsat,*
27 December 2005.

Zeillhuber, Andreas. *"Unsere Verwaltung treibt einer Katastrophe zu . . ." Das Reichs-
ministerium für die besetzten Ostgebiete und die deutsche Besatzungsherrschaft in
der Sowjetunion 1941–1945.* München: Verlag Ernst Vögel, 2006.

NOTES

Prologue

xiii **A peculiar map of the world:** Published by the Islamic Foundation, which is headquartered in the English town of Markfield, this map is discussed in Chapter 14.

1 **"Leaf of Eastern tree";** This is the first stanza of "Gingko Biloba," from Goethe's *West-Eastern Divan*. The next two stanzas of the poem are found on the opening pages of the sections entitled "Cold Wars" and "Modern Wars."

1. The Eastern Front

3 **Garip Sultan:** He was born Garif Sultan, 28 September 1923. For an explanation of his name change, see pages 46–47. The words of the German officer are as he remembers them; they could not be independently verified. All actions and feelings are as he described them in interviews on 27 January 2005, 9 March 2005, 28 March 2006, and 31 May 2006, in Munich. See also Garip Sultan, *Die Gründung der Wolga-Tatarischen Legion*.

Sultan's military service is also confirmed by U.S. intelligence documents found in NARA RG 319, Garip Sultan Personal File Folder XE615072. According to this information, he went to officer training school in Frolow near Stalingrad, was commissioned as a second lieutenant, and served in the 272nd Infantry Division.

The Tatars had lost: The Tatars are traditionally described as descendants of the Golden Horde, but their history is more complicated. Anthropologists such as Greta Lynn Uehling (*Beyond Memory: The Crimean Tatars' Deportation and Re-*

turn, pp. 30–31) believe they also in part stemmed from the Sunni Muslim peoples indigenous to the region who had settled there well before the Mongolian invasion. The traditional history given in this chapter is a shorthand, in part because this is how the people in this book and their contemporaries thought of the Tatars — as people with a proud, even fierce history.

6 **The Red Army's colossal collapse:** Alexander Dallin (*German Rule in Russia: A Study in Occupation Politics*, p. 69) estimates that the Germans had taken up to four million Soviet prisoners by the end of 1941. Others, such as Alex Alexei (*Soviet Nationalities in German Wartime Strategy, 1941–1945*, p. 8), say three million. I have chosen the lower number.

8 **Kayum visited a Muslim prisoner-of-war camp:** The soldier's quotation on dying, Kayum's address to soldiers, and the report of the meeting with Hayit are taken from Stephen L. Crane, *Survivor from an Unknown War: The Life of Isakjan Narzikul*, pp. 77–95. The book is a memoir, and the citations are given as a young Uzbek soldier, Isakjan Narzikul, remembered them and related them to Crane. Narzikul died in 1989.

   Shot by Nazi liquidation squads: Richard Breitman, *Architect of Genocide: Himmler and the Final Solution*, pp. 180–81. See also Crane, p. 74, and Dallin, p. 418.

9 **"You are the foundation":** Regarding Hayit's address, see Crane, p. 94.

   The famous Chāh-I-Zindeh mosque: See Antonio J. Munoz, *Forgotten Legions: Obscure Combat Formations of the Waffen-SS*, p. 172, for a photo showing a soldier with this patch. Crane (p. 169) includes a photo of a plaque with the same mosque but the phrase slightly changed to *Allah biz Bilen*.

   Operation Tiger B: German federal archives in Koblenz, cited in Joachim Hoffmann, *Die Ostlegionen, 1941–1943*, p. 27.

   Formations of Cossacks: OKH/GenStdH/GenQu an Befh Hgeb Süd, Mitte, Nord, 6. 10. 1941 (BA-MA, RH 22/v. 198), cited in Hoffmann, p. 21.

10 **"I am a Muslim":** Sebastian Cwiklinski, *Wolgatataren im Deutschland des Zweiten Weltkriegs: Deutsche Ostpolitik und tatarischer Nationalismus*, p. 38. The person doing the survey was Ahmet Temir, who worked for von Mende (ibid., p. 36).

   Two Turkish generals: They were Ali Fuad Erden, a member of parliament and the former head of the Turkish General Staff Academy, and Hussein Erkilet, a prominent pan-Turkist.

   Troops were also lightly armed: Hoffmann, p. 173.

   Turks, Caucasians, and Cossacks: Dallin estimates 153,000 (p. 540); Hoffmann says 250,000 (p. 172). Patrik von zur Mühlen (*Zwischen Hakenkreuz und Sowjetstern: Der Nationalismus der sowjetischen Orientvölker im Zweiten Weltkrieg*, p. 72) estimates that approximately one million Soviet citizens served, of whom 300,000 were Muslims. Similar estimates are found in Hoffmann (p. 11) and Alexiev (p. 4).

   An exception was made for "Turkic peoples": Hoffmann, p. 24.

11 **"I consider only the Mohammedans":** The exact quotation in German reads as follows: "Für sicher halte ich nur die Mohammedaner. Alle anderen halte ich nicht für sicher. Das kann uns überall passieren, da muß man wahnsinnig vorsichtig sein. Ich halte das Aufstellen von Bataillonen dieser rein kaukasischen

Völker zunächst für sehr riskant, während ich keine Gefahr darin sehe, wenn man tatsächlich rein mohammedanische Einheiten aufstellt." Cited in Helmut Heiber, ed., *Hitlers Lagebesprechungen: Die Protokollfragmente seiner militärischen Konferenzen, 1942–1945,* p. 73.

11 **The Warsaw city uprising:** Narzikul wrote this, as recorded in Crane, p. 144. He implausibly argues that they spent their time helping partisans and saving women by taking them as lovers.

   The Tatar liaison office: This discussion of Unglaube's affinity for the Tatars is drawn from Unglaube's unpublished autobiography, in the author's possession.

12 **His destination: the Ostministerium:** Information on Sultan's encounter with Unglaube is based on my interviews with Sultan. This meeting between the two men is confirmed in Cwiklinski (p. 40). Unglaube's words are as Sultan remembers them.

2. The Turkologist

13 **The term Silk Road:** This term was also used in the Byzantine era, although credit for coining it is usually given to the geographer Ferdinand von Richthofen. The explorer Albert von LeCoq contributed many archaeological treasures to the Museum für Völkerkunde, as it is referred to in German.

14 **The first modern use of jihad:** Wolfgang G. Schwanitz, "Die Berliner Djihadisierung des Islams."

   Gerhard von Mende: Biographical details have been drawn from personnel files, including a handwritten autobiography archived at Humboldt University, Berlin (UAHUB M 138 Bd. 1, résumé of 16 November 1939) and interviews with Ehrenfried Schütte (27 January 2005, Munich), Erling von Mende (31 January 2005, Berlin), Baymirza Hayit (25 October 2004, Cologne), and Sultan (27 January and 9 March 2005, and 28 March and 31 May 2006, Munich).

15 **Determined to succeed:** Herrad Schenk, *Wie in einem uferlosen Strom: Das Leben meiner Eltern,* pp. 214, 221.

   The historian Otto Hoetzsch: Karl Schlögel, "The Futility of One Professor's Life: Otto Hoetzsch and German Russian Studies," *Sketches of Europe.*

16 **Marrying Karo Espeseth:** Espeseth, in *Livet Gikk Videre (Life Went On),* pp. 83–84, describes how she initially drove von Mende away through her erratic behavior.

   The postwar outburst of creativity: Ibid., p. 100.

   Sullying the young nation's honor: See Espeseth, *Sår som ennu blør (Sores That Still Bleed),* and Ellen Rees, "Sores That Still Bleed: Germany, the Great War, and Violence Against Women in the Modernist Literary Imagination," in *Conquering Women: Women and War in the German Cultural Imagination,* pp. 62–75.

17 **"Because of the strict political unity":** Gerhard von Mende, *Der Nationale Kampf der Rußlandtürken: Ein Beitrag zur nationalen Frage in der Sovetunion,* p. 184.

18 **He had joined the SA:** For von Mende's reasons for joining, then leaving the SA, see Espeseth, *Livet Gikk Videre,* pp. 99–100. Also, the von Mende résumé (undated "Lebenslauf") at UAHUB M 138 Bd. 3 Bl. 1.

19 **"There should, according to my view":** Quotations from the evaluation of 19 August 1937, in UAHUB M 138 Bd. 3 Bl. 1. Thanks to Ingo Loose for his interpretation of von Niedermayer's comments. Loose, "Berliner Wissenschaftler im 'Osteinsatz,' 1939–1945: Akademische Mobilität zwischen Berliner Universität und Reichsuniversität Posen," *Die Berliner Universität in der NS-Zeit, Bd. 1: Strukturen und Personen,* pp. 62–63.

Follow the party line: For von Niedermayer's Nazi leanings, see Hans-Ulrich Seidt, *Berlin Kabul Moskau: Oskar Ritter von Niedermayer und Deutschlands Geopolitik,* pp. 271ff.

His letters show: For example, letter of 2 May 1938, UAHUB M 138 Bd. 3 Bl. 1.

The Adolf-Hitler-Schule: Letter of 16 March 1938, UAHUB M 138 Bd. 3 Bl. 1.

Regular contact with Georg Leibbrandt: Letter of 7 October 1940, UAHUB M 138 Bd. 3 Bl. 1.

She didn't like the Nazis: Espeseth, *Livet Gikk Videre,* p. 124.

Published by the Anti-Komintern: Letter of 6 May 1938, in Humboldt Archive, cited in Cwiklinski, p. 14.

20 **About a Jewish colleague:** Letter of 28 June (probably 1940) about Dr. Friedrich Levi, UAHUB M 138 Bd. 3 Bl. 1.

The Peoples of the Soviet Union: Gerhard von Mende, *Die Völker der Sowjetunion* (Reichenau/Saale: Rudolf Schneider Verlag, 1939).

21 **Old contact in the Nazis' Foreign Office:** Cwiklinski, p. 14.

The coveted rank of full professor: Letter of 27 November 1941, UAHUB M 138 Bd. 3 Bl. 1. The letter was signed by Hitler, but it was standard for high-ranking civil servants to be appointed by the head of state.

3. The Nazi Prototype

23 **An old friend of Hitler's:** Rosenberg biographical notes taken from Dallin, pp. 24–26.

24 **"The strong separatist movement":** The quotation from Rosenberg is taken from *Der Zukunftsweg,* p. 93, cited in Dallin, p. 47.

An anti-Soviet movement called Prometheus: Roman Smal-Stocky, "The Struggle of the Subjugated Nations in the Soviet Union for Freedom: Sketch of the History of the Promethean Movement," *The Ukrainian Quarterly;* Stephen Dorril, *MI6: Fifty Years of Special Operations,* pp. 184ff. On efforts to deploy Prometheans in Manchuria, see Jeffrey Burds, "The Soviet War Against 'Fifth Columnists': The Case of Chechnya, 1942–44," *Journal of Contemporary History.*

25 **The death of Mustafa Chokay:** Chokay is the Anglicized version of Čoqayoğlu, also known in Russian as Chokaev. Another Anglicization is Chokai.

He had been helping: In the 1930s Kayum had written reports for Georg Leibbrandt of the NSDAP's Foreign Office. Cwiklinski, p. 14.

Von Mende's boss in the Ostministerium: Dallin, p. 266, and von zur Mühlen, p. 79. Dallin writes: "Von Mende became in effect the master of the Ostministerium's nationality policy, embarking on a drive for the recognition of separatist 'national committees,' primarily for the non-Slavic groups."

25 **Emerged from the shakeup unscathed:** Based on interviews with Turkestani leaders, such as Nasar, 10 May 2006, Washington, DC.
26 **Sultan arrived in Berlin:** Interviews with Sultan.
The results were sensational: Tatar recruitment statistics are from Hoffmann, p. 42.
Newspapers crucial to the effort: Ibid., pp. 128–29.
Overseen by the Wehrmacht's: Cwiklinski, p. 50.
27 *Idel'-Ural* **anti-Semitic statements.** *Idel'-Ural,* No. 18, 6 May 1944, p. 4, cited in Cwiklinski, p. 81.
The high percentage of "German" topics: Sultan, p. 26, cited in Cwiklinski, p. 82.
Musa Ğälil, a prominent poet: Biographical details can be found in Cwiklinski, pp. 70–73.
Sultan was considered for the top post: Von zur Mühlen, p. 99.
28 **Jews and other undesirables:** GHWK, documents T/299 and T/300, from "The trial of Adolf Eichmann: Record of proceedings in the District Court of Jerusalem."
   Another person who attended the conference and played a role in the Munich mosque was Otto Bräutigam, who would serve in the West German Foreign Office, rising to high rank and occasionally helping von Mende shepherd his projects related to the Muslims.
The Harvard historian Alexander Dallin: Dallin's characterization of von Mende appears on p. 558 of his book.
The Karainen were protected: Kiril Feferman, "Nazi Germany and the Mountain Jews: Was There a Policy?" *Holocaust and Genocide Studies.* Thanks to Richard Breitman for pointing out this paper.
29 **"I still think back with some horror":** Letter of 24 August 1951, von Mende papers.
Tossing him in the air: The general was Ernst Köstring. Dallin, p. 246.
30 **Parroted Nazi slogans:** *Milli Türkistān,* No. 15, p. 9, as cited in Dallin, p. 275.
Brutally denouncing the dissidents: Von zur Mühlen, p. 97, citing 26 January 1945 document from BA, NS 31/30.
Turkestani congress in Vienna: Dallin, p. 610.
Destroyed in an air raid: Espeseth, *Livet Gikk Videre,* p. 190.
31 **Fears that they were religious fanatics:** Georgetown, Kelley papers, box 5, folder 3, 5 February 1952, "Transmission Memorandum of Conversation with Professor Gerhard von Mende, German Turcologist," p. 7. Identifying agency markers have been removed, but judging from the content, this is likely a Department of State cable.
The Grand Mufti of Jerusalem: Hoover, Dallin collection, box 1, folder 16, letter of 19 November 1953, von Mende to Dallin.
32 **Set up mullah schools:** Hoffmann, p. 169.
"Recognize" the national committees: Dallin, p. 654.
Tatars set up a provisional government: Cwiklinski, pp. 55–56.
Head of the military department: German federal military archives, cited in Cwiklinski, p. 55.

4. Reviving the Ostministerium

35 **Munich was a ruined city:** James Critchlow, *Radio Hole-in-the-Head/Radio Liberty: An Insider's Story of Cold War Broadcasting,* pp. 2–4, and Gaither Stewart, *Govar Killian,* excerpted at http://southerncrossreview.org/29/stewart-excerpt .htm. Statistics on rubble and U.S. army help from Wolfram Selig, *Chronik der Stadt München, 1945–1948,* p. 43.

37 **"Center of subversion":** Critchlow, p. 87.
Ideal home for Radio Liberty: History of Radio Liberty, including the quotation on "democratic elements," from Georgetown, Kelley papers, box 5, folder 5, "Biographical Sketch of Robert F. Kelley."

38 **"I would look out the window":** Critchlow, p. 4.
"We sometimes ate": Ibid., pp. 2–3.
Young, idealistic people: Critchlow's biographical details taken from Critchlow, pp. 50–54.

40 **The NSC was to advise:** The NSC directive on covert operations was NSC 10/2. Cited in Kenneth Osgood, *Total Cold War: Eisenhower's Propaganda Battle at Home and Abroad,* p. 39.
"Don't be afraid of that term": Ibid., p. 46.

41 **Half the CIA budget:** The broader mandate and the budget estimates are from Osgood, pp. 96–97.
The U.S. Information Agency alone spent: Figures are from "Draft Report on the Roles of Attributed and Unattributed Information and the Division of Responsibility Between the USIA and CIA," 22 April 1960, DDEL Sprague Committee, box 20, PCIAA#2, declassified 2 October 2007, MORI DocID: 1473135.
Half a billion dollars per year: Osgood, p. 90. One fifth of that, $100 million, was spent by the USIA.
Radio Liberty's parent: For its roots in the Truman administration, see NSC policy planning staff memorandum "The inauguration of organized political warfare," 4 May 1948, document 269, http://www.state.gov/www/about_state/ history/intel/260_269.html.

43 **On covert propaganda missions:** Peter Grose, *Operation Rollback: America's Secret War Behind the Iron Curtain,* p. 129.
U.S. government involvement: Hoover, Radio Liberty General Vol. C, "Minutes of the Meeting of the Executive Committee [subsequently the Management Policy and Program Advisory Committees]," 28 April 1954.
In 1955 its budget: Hoover, Radio Liberty Corp. Minutes Vol. II, 1955–66, Fiscal year statements 1955, 1960, 1961, and 1963. Other years are missing.
In general, Amcomlib was spending about $350,000 each year on the institute and $125,000 each year on émigré groups — excluding the $4 million it spent on employees, most of whom were émigrés. In 1964, its budget got a hefty bump up to $10.5 million.
"A single stoker or sweeper": Critchlow, p. 15.

44 **"Think about the massive volume":** Ibid., p. 16.
Schub called it his "left hook": Interview with Gene and Gloria Sosin, 3 May 2006, White Plains, NY.

44 "I would demean the many devoted": Ibid.
   "The boys in the back room": Ibid.
45 "Could not help seeing the anomaly": Ibid., pp. 28–29.
   Awash with "displaced persons": BA B/106-8643, "Bericht des Bundesministeri-
   ums für Vertriebene, Vertriebene, Flüchtlinge, Kriegsgefangene, Heimatlose
   Ausländer 1949–1952," Bonn 1953: 11. Thanks to Stefan Meining for pointing out
   this document.
47 Vouched for Hayit and Kayum: Interview with Hayit; interview with Sultan, 27
   January 2005; Crane, p. 200.
   Other estimates are higher: Hayit's estimate from Baymirza Hayit, "Basmatchi":
   Nationaler Kampf Turkestans in den Jahren 1917 bis 1934, p. 403. Estimate for Kalmyks from von zur Mühlen, p. 227.
   Committed suicide the night before: Hayit, "Basmatchi," p. 403.
48 Alshibaya took the hint: Interview with his wife, Nina Alshibaya, 16 August
   2004, Munich; she tells the story as he related it to her. Note also spelling of the
   name. The German spelling is Alschibaya, Alschebaja, or Alschibaja. I am using
   the English spelling, as per U.S. intelligence documents.
   The Tolstoy Foundation: Besides doing work for the army's CIC, the foundation
   seems to have had close links to Frank Wisner, from the CIA's Directorate of
   Plans and the most influential covert operations official from World War II
   through the late 1950s.
      In 1953, Eisenhower's Psychological Strategy Board received requests to aid
   the Tolstoy Foundation, which apparently had run into financial difficulties. The
   board referred financial aid requests to Wisner. In a subsequent letter, a White
   House official said Wisner agreed the foundation deserved help and "should not
   be allowed to collapse." DDEL White House Central Files, Confidential File, box
   84, Tolstoy Foundation file, 22 October 1953, "Memorandum for: Mr. C. D. Jackson," and 9 October 1953, "Memorandum to Mr. Jackson."
   Alshibaya's wife worked for the foundation: Interview with Alshibaya.
   The goal was to recruit: For evidence on how Western intelligence agencies began to recruit Germans during the war, see Burds; also, Christopher Simpson,
   Blowback: The First Full Account of America's Recruitment of Nazis and Its Disastrous Effect on the Cold War, Our Domestic and Foreign Policy.
   Sultan was looking for work: Interview with Sultan, 27 January 2005.
49 Scottish League for European Freedom: British intelligence support discussed
   in Dorril, Chapter 14.
50 75 to 80 percent: Georgetown, Kelley papers, box 4, folder 3, memo of 18 November 1958, "Subject: Ministerial Director, Dr. Taubert."
   "For Americans of my generation": Critchlow, pp. 93–94.
51 "To provide the myth": Interview with Will Klump, 17 January 2006, New York
   City.
   U.S. efforts went nowhere: A chronology of the Coordinating Center's activities
   is found in Isaac Patch's memo of 20 November 1953, including a reference to salaries. The salaries were terminated when the negotiations broke down. Georgetown, Kelley papers, box 5, folder 3. Also, Patch memo, 24 November 1953, "Confidential Draft Memo — Political Events, March to November, 1953." The events
   are also described in detail in Grose, pp. 129–35.

52 **"Whether this analogy is justified"**: Georgetown, Kelley papers, box 4, folder 2, 5 February 1952, "Transmitting memorandum of conversation with Professor Gerhard von Mende, German Turcologist."

"An almost complete failure": DDEL, Jackson Committee, box 1, folder 1, 5 January 1953 memo, "Strictly Private."

"A tall, shrewd string bean": Critchlow, p. 18.

"The Muslims against the Slavs": This and other Patch quotations are from a telephone interview, 23 May 2005.

An old friend of U.S. intelligence: Ibid.

An agent code-named Ruppert: Details of the operation are taken from "Mission Rupert," undated, CIA MORI DocID 868611, and "Mission Ruppert: Survey of Mission and Summary of results obtained as of this Date," 31 May 1945, MORI DocID 20055. Both in Michel Kedia Name File, NARA RG 263, A1-86, box 22.

The code name "Ruppert" is sometimes spelled with one *p*. I use the spelling *Ruppert* throughout because the second document, which uses this form, is longer and appears to be more authoritative. Also, Kedia's first name is variously given as Mikhail, Michael, or Michel.

Thanks to Jeffrey Burds and Richard Breitman for pointing out these documents.

53 **The German army's Abwehr**: NARA RG 263, RC 2002/A/11/6, box 73, folder 2, document number MC-002250, 24 March 1961, "Subject: Mende, Gerhard von Dr., aka Metrevelli, George."

Made his way to Switzerland: Espeseth, *Livet Gikk Videre*, 227–37. Her account of von Mende's flight to Switzerland and his stay in the U.S. camp also fits the account in U.S. intelligence documents, which notes that the men were found in Höchst and taken to Karlsruhe.

But Red Cross files show: Red Cross archives, ACICR B, G23, "Visites particulières (G-K), 04.01.1940-31.10.1950, M. Kedia."

"I am sure that in spite of everything": NARA RG 263, RC 2002/A/11/6, box 73, folder 1, 17 July 1945, "Subject: Georgian Group."

54 **Von Mende wrote for days**: NARA RG 263, RC 2002/A/11/6, box 73, folder 1, 31 October 1945, "Subject: Gerhard von Mende."

A moody prima donna: NARA RG 263, RC 2002/A/11/6, box 73, folder 1, undated evaluation, probably summer 1945.

"A man of exceptional intelligence": NARA RG 263, RC 2002/A/11/6, box 73, folder 1, undated 1945 evaluation reprinted on 15 November 1946, "Subject: Gerhart [*sic*] von Mende."

Never admitted to membership: For example, NARA RG 263, RC 2002/A/11/6, box 73, folder 1, undated (presumably 1945) résumé lists all groups he joined but omits the SA.

55 **"My husband has a group"**: Letter of 3 November 1945, von Mende papers. This is one of the few letters written in English. I corrected Espeseth's spelling mistakes but left the syntax.

The famous British historian: The letter has "Toynbee?" handwritten across the top and mentions that the recipient works for the Royal Institute of International Affairs, with which Toynbee was affiliated. According to the letter, the two had met at a conference in Berlin before the war.

56 **Direct contact with the British:** Believed to be the case by family members, his
former employees, and U.S. intelligence. Based on interview with Erling von
Mende; Narzikul, p. 258; NARA RG 263, box 2, folder 3, Counterintelligence Re-
port No. 213 to AC of S, G-2, Headquarters, United States Forces European The-
ater, APO 757, March 1947, U.S. Army; also, U.S. military intelligence X-2, von
Mende Personal File Folder D007362, which states that he "represents British
intelligence."
"Major Morrison": Letter of 31 October 1945, von Mende papers.
Von Mende drove down to Munich: The operation involving von Mende and
Alshibaya is described in NARA RG 263, Counterintelligence Report No. 213.

57 **Alshibaya drove up to Hamburg:** Ibid.
"Capriform": NARA RG 263, RC 2002/A/11/6, box 73, folder 1, 11 February 1949,
"Subject: von Mende visit."
The Americans weren't interested: NARA RG 263, RC 2002/A/11/6, box 73,
folder 1, 15 August 1949, document untitled.

58 **"Persil certificates":** Von Mende papers. For example, on 26 February 1946, he
wrote one for Ernst Tormann, a former Ostministerium employee. The "Major
Morrison" letter was also an effort to rehabilitate a colleague. On 31 December
1946 he also wrote a letter vouching for Walter Zeitler of the Ostministerium.
"Without you I would be": Letter of 24 February 1957, Hayit to von Mende, von
Mende papers. (In German: "Ohne Sie wäre ich in Deutschland ein Insel in eine
Totenmeer.")

59 **Reviewed in academic journals:** *The American Historical Review,* Vol. 63, No. 3
(April 1958), p. 742.
Carried a two-part series: Fred Forest, 3 September 1951 and 10 September 1951.
Among the employees it named were "Veli Kayum 'Khan,' war-time Führer of
the Turkestanis, who was reared in Germany and was a Nazi favorite; Vladimir
Glazkov, the 'inventor' of the Cossack 'nation' and an agent of various intelligence services; and Fatali-Bey, an Azerbaijani officer and intimate associate of
the Grand Mufti of Jerusalem."
Glazkov also worked for von Mende, while Fatali-Bey — whose name was
usually written without the hyphen, Fatalibey — was with Amcomlib and would
later be assassinated.

60 **Von Mende immediately sent a letter:** Letter of 29 October 1951, von Mende to
Stetzko, von Mende papers.
Von Mende paid Kayum: AA ZA 105707, 1958 FDO Budget, 3 February 1958.
"Earlier services for Germany": AAPA ZA 105706 Band 48, 7 July 1961, "Betr.:
Veli Kajum-Chan." (German: "in Anerkennung seiner früheren Verdienste um
Deutschland" and "der Ausbau der Beziehungen zu seinen Landsleuten schliess-
lich auch der deutschen Sache zugute komme, weil er aus alter Verbundenheit zu
Deutschland es für seine Pflicht ansehe, aufklärend über deutsche Verhältnisse
zu wirken.")
A German, Walter Schenk: Thanks to Ray Brandon for pointing out Schenk's
Lemberg ties. On Schenk's sacrifice of his university education for the Nazi cause,
see Schenk, especially pp. 49ff.
Constantly changing his office's name: Von Mende tried out two other names
first: Institut für Orientforschung (Sultan interview, 27 January 2005) and Insti-

tut Turkestan (Zentral-Archiv MfS 6940/68, 14 November 1962, "An den Leiter der Abteilung X, Gen. Major Damm"). To complicate matters further, von Mende's office was also known as Büro für Heimatvertriebene Ausländer, a variation on the Büro für Heimatlose Ausländer. The difference is the word *Heimatvertriebene*, or "homeland expelled," instead of *Heimatlose*, or "homeland-less." NARA RG 263, box 1, NN3-263-02-008, 25 May 1955, "Memorandum of Conversation Professor G. von Mende Büro für Heimatvertriebene Ausländer," NARA RG 263, 760.00/5-2655.

61 **Moved around the countryside:** Letters of 5 April 1946, 29 May 1949, 20 March 1950, and 20 August 1950, von Mende papers.

Von Mende took a grand office: It was located at Cecilienallee 51–52. The architect was Heinrich Schell and the city development company Bürohaus-Gesellschaft mbH. Thanks to Dr. Jörg A. E. Heimeshoff of the Institut für Denkmalschutz und Denkmalpflege of the city of Düsseldorf for information on the building and to Dr. Robert Kaltenbrunner of the Bundesamt für Bauwesen und Raumordnung for background on the style and history.

220,000 stateless foreigners: In an article written two years later, von Mende estimated that 220,000 lived in West Germany. Given that the number was declining over time, at least 200,000 must have been in Germany at this time. *Bulletin des Presse und Informationsamtes der Bundesregierung*, No. 881/S. 736, 11 May 1955.

An extra five thousand marks: AAPA ZA 105705, notes based on 13 February 1957 meeting.

He eventually added money: Except for the Bavarian intelligence agency's contribution, the exact breakdown of the funding of von Mende's organization is not clear from the documents. The federal Office for Protection of the Constitution and the Foreign Office are often cited in correspondence and third-party evaluations as von Mende's main backers. NARA RG 263, RC 2002/A/11/6, box 73, folder 2, 28 February 1955, untitled von Mende card file.

62 **One such meeting took place:** AAPA ZA 105774 Band 36, 3 May 1954, "Vermerk Betr.: Besprechung with 'American Committee for Liberation from Bolshevism.'"

63 **Patch organized a big dinner:** The meeting with von Mende took place on 9 February 1955, as described in NARA RG 263, box 1, 762A.00/2-1555 AmConGen Munich, "Memorandum of Conversation."

Another meeting took place in May 1955, as per NARA RG 263, box 1, 760.00/5-2655, 26 May 1955, AmConGen Munich, "Conversation with a German Official Regarding Refugees."

5. The Key to the Third World

65 **Pilgrimage to Mecca:** The trip is recounted in *Time* magazine, 27 September 1954, and in the *New York Times*, 15 September 1954. Accessed through online archive; no page numbers. Also, interview with Rusi Nasar, 10 May 2006, Falls Church, VA.

66 **The real action took place elsewhere:** John Lewis Gaddis, *We Now Know: Rethinking Cold War History*, Chapter 6.

68 "The traditional Arab mind": DDEL NSC Registry Series, 1947–62, box 16, PSB
    Documents, Master Book of— Vol. III (8), 6 February 1953, "Psychological Strat-
    egy Program for the Middle East," annex B, p. 4.
    Natural barrier to communism: Ibid., p. 15.
69 The CIA received a report: NARA RG 263, RC 2002/A/11/6, box 73, folder 2,
    April 1951, "Subject: [illegible] exile groups from Soviet-dominated Moslem ar-
    eas."
    "The Religious Factor": DDEL PSB Central Files Series, box 9, PSB 1953 (3) file,
    21 July 1953, "Subject: The Religious Factor."
    The great Wesleyan Christian revival: DDEL OCB Secretariat Series, box 5,
    Moral Factor (4) file, 19 February 1953, "Conversation with Mr. Lockard, PSB."
    The U.S. Air Force: DDEL OCB Secretariat Series, box 5, Moral Factor (4) file, 4
    September 1953, "Your memo of August 31 — Mecca Pilgrimage."
    Sent to the National Security Council: DDEL, papers of Edward P. Lilly, box 55,
    3 March 1954, "Subject: The Religious Factor and OCB."
71 Became known as the Bandung Conference: DDEL OCB Central File Series,
    box 85, file 9 (International Affairs — Conferences and Boards, January
    1954–April 1955), 11 January 1955, "Terms of Reference for Working Group on
    Proposed Afro-Asian Conference."
    "The Afro-Asian Conference": DDEL OCB Central File Series, box 85, file 9, 21
    January 1955, "Subject: Exposing the Nature of the Afro-Asian Conference."
72 Distribute covert propaganda: DDEL OCB Central File Series, box 85, file 9, 7
    February 1955, "Subject: Afro-Asian Conference in April."
    "Some 'Machiavellian'" engineering: NARA RG 59, box 2668, folder 670.901/2-
    1055, 16 February 1955, memorandum from Mr. Dumont to Mr. Jones.
    Working for the newspaper: NARA RG 59, box 69, folder 670.901/4-1155, 18
    April 1955, from Jakarta to Secretary of State.
        A survey of the newspaper's coverage of Bandung shows that Nasar did not
    write for the newspaper. Along with Said Shamil (spelled "Schamyl" in the arti-
    cle), Nasar was, however, interviewed by the newspaper, and accused the Soviets
    of colonialism. Homer Bigart, "Coney Islander Assails Red Crimes at Bandung,"
    New York Herald Tribune.
    The Soviet newspaper Trud: NARA RG 59, box 2669, folder 670.901/4-1955, 20
    April 1955, from Moscow to Secretary of State.
73 The National Turkestani Unity Committee: NARA RG 59, box 2669, folder
    670.901/4-155, "To the Government Representatives of the Participating States of
    the Asia-Africa Conference."
    Nasar's role in the Muslim propaganda: Interview with Nasar. On his posi-
    tion as a community leader, see http://www.sunshineuzbekistan.org/wordpress/
    archives/241.
        In interviews, James Critchlow (3 February 2006, Cambridge, MA), Gaither
    "Jack" Stewart (1 October 2005, Rome), and Edward A. Allworth (7 January
    2006, New York City) said that Nasar was widely known in the 1950s to be work-
    ing for the CIA. In addition, Crane (Chapters 2, 3, and 4) describes a CIA agent
    whose anonymity was protected by the pseudonym "Safi Oraz." In correspon-
    dence, Crane said he believes Oraz was Nasar.

74 **Nasar might have looked down:** The private nature of Amcomlib is mentioned in the *Time* magazine article.
A "damn good man": Georgetown, Kelley papers, box 5, folder 5, 1 December 1959, "Memorandum for the Record."

75 **The April 29 cabinet meeting:** DDEL, Papers of the President, Cabinet Series, box 5, file "Cabinet Meeting of April 29, 1955," 2 May 1955, "The Cabinet, Record of Action," p. 3.
Analyses of the conference: At this crucial phase, Hayit was recruited by French intelligence. Hayit was contacted by a former lieutenant in the 782nd Turkestani Volunteers Battalion, who was now living in the French sector near Baden-Baden. He suggested that Hayit travel to Bandung for France, which would pick up all the costs. Hayit turned him down and dutifully reported the offer to von Mende. AAPA ZA 105783 Band 61, 30 March 1955, "Aktenvermerk."
Nasar had claimed to represent: AAPA ZA 105783 Band 61, letter of 1 June 1955, Hayit to "Sehr geehrter Herr Professor."
"Prof. von Mende said that": NARA RG 263, box 1, folder 760.00/5-2655, NN3-263-02-008, 25 May 1955, "Memorandum of Conversation Professor G. von Mende Büro für Heimatvertriebene Ausländer."

6. Learning Their Lesson

76 **"Homo barrackensis":** *Frankfurter Allgemeine Zeitung,* 1952. Cited in Friedrich Prinz and Marita Krauss, eds., *Trümmerleben. Texte, Dokumente, Bilder aus den Münchener Nachkriegsjahren,* p. 160.
The southern Munich suburb: BayHstA LaflüVerw 2199, 17 May 1960, Balagija to Stein.

77 **When Gacaoglu formed the group:** BayHStA MK 49638, 20 June 1953, "An das Bayer: Staatsministerium für Unterricht und Kultus."
Gacaoglu was handing out: BayHStA LaflüVerw 1900, letter of 23 May 1959, Kurbah Bayba to Oberländer.
Goods from the Tolstoy Foundation: Ibid.
Bairam, a major event: *Süddeutsche Zeitung,* 30 July 1955.
A Chechen who taught at the CIA school: This was Abdurakhman Artorkhanov. Interview with Sultan, 9 March 2005.

78 **Melbardis was impressed:** Interview with Alex Melbardis, 6 September 2005, Pfaffing, Germany.
Gacaoglu's payments were also confirmed in my interview with Will Klump, deputy head of émigré relations for Amcomlib during the latter half of the 1950s; he became head in 1962.

79 **B. Eric Kuniholm:** For Kuniholm's personal history, see Georgetown, Kelley papers, box 5, folder 5, "Confidential: Report of Mr. B. E. Kuniholm on His Trip to the Middle East." Also, telephone interview with his son Bruce Kuniholm, 18 April 2006.
Kuniholm as a "splittist": AAPA ZA 105774 Band 36, 20 October 1954, "Betr. Veränderungen und andere Vorgänge im American Committee for Liberation from Bolshevism (AMCOMLIB)."

79 **Dreher was Kuniholm's opposite:** Biographical details taken from CIA and Amcomlib applications and Dreher papers.

80 **Dreher was detained:** This is according to Dreher's own account in the newsletter of the Central Intelligence Retiree Association (CIRA), 9–15, date uncertain,
Dreher papers.
   The incident was front-page news: "Espionage Denied," *New York Times*, 16 August 1948, and subsequent coverage.

81 **"I had more direct, intimate contact":** Taken from "Manuscript on Russia," an
unpublished and unfinished book Dreher wrote after he left the USSR in 1948.
Dreher papers.
   Eight years in the gulag: An account of Dreher's reunion with the medical stu-
dent was published in *People* magazine, 31 October 1994.
   On his CIA application: Dreher papers.

82 **She bore him a daughter:** According to interviews with Chuck and Helen
Oerkvitz (7 February 2006, Gwynedd, PA), Klump, Karin West (27 March 2006,
Munich), and Melbardis.
   The salary was also generous: Hoover, Radio Liberty Corporate Minutes Vol. I,
1951–54, "Minutes of the Political and Management Committees Joint Meeting,
March 26, 1953."

83 **A "WASPish bank":** Interview with Sosin.
   Especially Kuniholm and Dreher: Ibid. Both men attended all board meetings.
Dreher stopped attending when he left for Munich.
   Dreher was firmly in the latter: Interview with David E. Murphy, 7 May 2006,
Punta Gorda, FL. Murphy said Dreher worked for the head of OPC's Munich
operations, Walpole Davis.

84 **"Pining to get back":** Peter Sichel, cited in Evan Thomas, *The Very Best Men: The
Early Years of the CIA*, p. 24. Thomas Schmitt, *Moscheen in Deutschland: Konflikte um ihre Errichtung und Nutzung*, p. 24.
   "Bunch of old washerwomen": Cited in John Ranelagh, *The Agency: The Rise
and Decline of the CIA*, p. 135.

85 **"It was prankster stuff":** The veteran was Tom Braden, cited in Ranelagh, p. 221.
   The night train to Ankara: For Kuniholm's trip to Turkey, Germany, riots, and
meetings with Muslim leaders, see "Confidential Report."

87 **One such key leader:** Interview with Melbardis; Kuniholm report. Participation
in Nazi-era émigré policies, von zur Mühlen, p. 71. Work with pan-Islamic
causes, Schulze, p. 232. Schulze transliterates his name as Samil. Other documents have Schamyl.
   Shamil provided information: NARA RG 263, A1-86, box 22, "Kedia, Michael,"
17 February 1954, "Subject: Ali Kahn Kantemir."

88 **Contacts with U.S. intelligence:** Ibid.

Another key person whom Kuniholm met was Edige Kirimal, an old Tatar
leader who had worked closely with Garip Sultan during the war. A couple of
weeks before Germany's capitulation, von Mende had signed an Ostministerium
paper giving Kirmal a fanciful title: president of the Crimean-Tatar National
Central Committee, a position that got him a travel permit out of Berlin and
down to safety in Munich. "His trip lies in the most pressing interest of the Reich

and is important for the defense of the Reich," von Mende said. Koblenz, T-454, 15/1207, 22 April 1945.

After the war, Kirimal relaunched his life as a quasi academic. He wrote a book on the Tatars' national struggle, and von Mende added an introduction. Judging from the location of the tiny publishing house, located near von Mende's office at the time in the Westphalian countryside, von Mende also helped him get it published.

Kuniholm was unimpressed. He described Kirimal as "on the make" and dismissed his ideas for starting a newspaper and moving the Munich émigrés to Istanbul. Kirimal also pitched the notion that Amcomlib could do more to support his old friend Gacaoglu's religious society. Kuniholm, "Confidential Report," p. 25.

Gacaoglu was next on Kuniholm's list: Kuniholm, "Confidential Report," p. 27.

Munich's Bayerischer Hof hotel: Based on photos and interview with Melbardis; also von Mende's description in AAPA ZA 105762, letter of 10 January 1957, von Mende to Wolfrum.

89 **Important Munich newspapers:** "Die Trinkgelder der roten Pilger in Mekka," *Münchener Merkur,* 13 August 1956, p. 3; "Sowjetunion und Islam," *Süddeutsche Zeitung,* 13 August 1956, p. 5. The *Merkur's* article was the long feature.

The Turkish article was published on 2 August 1956 in *Milliyet*. Translation in AAPA ZA 105783, "Sowjetpilger fahren nach Mekka und Machen Propaganda für die Sowjets."

Sultan and Zunnun had been interviewed: "Meeting with the Turkestanian Pilgrims," four pages, by Veli Zunnun, and "Report on the Pilgrimage to Mecca," twenty pages, by Garip Sultan, Sultan papers.

Von Mende's office also received a detailed report on the pilgrimage: AAPA ZA 105792, 4 November 1955. The four-page report's presumed author, Hayit, emphasized the Soviet pilgrims' efforts to discredit the main Turkestani émigré group, the National Turkestani Unity Committee (known by its German acronym, NTEK). Again, von Mende's disadvantage is highlighted in the late arrival of the report, compared to when reports reached Sultan and Zunnun.

Happy with Sultan's performance: Letter of 3 October 1956, Robert F. Kelley to Garip Sultan, Sultan papers.

90 **"The notion of a simple, old Arab":** Sultan report, p. 15.

Didn't look like a religious leader: Ibid., p. 14.

Amcomlib's "Special Projects" department: Interviews with Sultan.

7. "A Politically Smart Act": The Mosque Is Conceived

91 **A memo from Theodor Oberländer:** BayHStA LaflüVerw 1894, 6 August 1956, "Grundsätze für die Betreuung nichtdeutscher Flüchtlinge." Thanks to Stefan Meining for pointing out this document.

Home to thousands of émigrés: See list of refugee flows on the website of the UN High Commissioner for Refugees: http://www.unhcr.org/static/publ/sowr2000/toceng.htm.

92 **Oberländer was the chief:** For a more-or-less sympathetic account of Oberlän-

der's life, see Philipp-Christian Wachs, *Der Fall Theodor Oberländer (1905–1998): Ein Lehrstück Deutscher Geschichte.*

93 **One of the first Wehrmacht units:** Its name was Sonderverband Bergmann.

94 **Discussed how to evacuate:** Memo, United States Information Agency Confidential Issue Date: 17 August 1954; date declassified: 17 October 1996; reproduced in Declassified Documents Reference System. Gale Group, 2006, document number CK3100109821.

"They are not Nazis in the sense": NARA RG 263, RC 2002/A/11/6, box 73, folder 2, 17 January 1956, "SJ: Target: Gerhard von Mende, Amt für Heimatlose Ausländer," attachment A, "Important Persons with Whom von Mende Maintains Operational Relations."

"Their chief agent is": Ibid.

The State Department was also concerned about von Mende. See Declassified Documents Reference System, Document Number CK3100109821, United States Information Agency, 17 August 1954, "Germany and the FEC," p. 11.

Aid Society of Former Volunteer Units: "Hilfswerk der ehemaligen Freiwilligenverbände e.V.," Amtsgericht München VR Nr. 5469. The group was discussed by the CIA in NARA RG 263, RC 2002/A/11/6, box 73, folder 2, 7 January 1955, "Ref: Congen Dispatch No. 144, December 7, 1954."

95 **Von Mende did have close ties:** NARA RG 263, RC 2002/A/11/6, box 73, folder 2, 23 September 1955, "Subject: Talk with Professor von Mende."

"Quite a small connection file": NARA RG 263, RC 2002/A/11/6, box 73, folder 2, 23 November 1955, "SJ: Gerhard von Mende and His Buddies."

"Try to recruit him": NARA RG 263, RC 2002/A/11/6, box 73, folder 2, 17 January 1956, "SJ: Target: Gerhard von Mende, Amt für Heimatlose Ausländer."

Kayum had outed Rusi Nasar: NARA RG 263, RC 2002/A/11/6, box 73, folder 2, attachment A, "Important Persons with Whom von Mende Maintains Operational Relations."

96 **Seeking a map of his office:** NARA RG 263, RC 2002/A/11/6, box 73, folder 2, 14 March 1956, "Subject: Gerhard v. Mende."

Again proposing von Mende: NARA RG 263, RC 2002/A/11/6, box 73, folder 2, 11 January 1957, "Investigative Aid — Possible RIS Exploitation of ex-Agents of the German Intelligence Services."

Nurredin Namangani landed: Crane's narrator, Narzikul, calls him "Nuridin [Namangani] Qari," Crane, p. 83.

In most postwar German documents he is referred to as Nurredin Namangani, which is the name I use throughout. In some documents he is given the middle name Nakibhodscha. This is at least partially an honorific. *Hodscha,* or *hodja,* is Turkish for "an educated person" and Nakib could be a given name or refer to a Sunni sect in Turkey, the Nakshbendi. The name is used, for example, in BayHStA LaflüVerw 1900, 8 May 1957, Nentwig to Wolfrum, "Berufung einese religösen Oberhauptes für die mohammedanischen Flüchtlinge."

The variation in names can probably be explained by the fact that many Uzbeks were flexible with surnames and sometimes used a form of their hometown in place of it — in this case, for the city Namangan in Uzbekistan. It may also be that Namangani wanted to hide his identity after the war and dropped Qari in favor of Namangani.

Von Mende had invited Namangani: Letter of 1 August 1956, Kayum to von Mende, von Mende papers.

One of von Mende's men: Details of Namangani's career from BayHStA LaflüVerw 1900, letter of 5 November 1958, Namangani to Burmeister.

The only unclear details about Namangani's life concern his time in Turkey. In his CV he wrote that he went to Turkey from 1947 to 1950 to study. In BayHStA LaflüVerw 1900, 17 April 1957, Wolfrum to Nentwig, Wolfrum writes that Namangani went to Adana in Turkey in 1954, returning only at von Mende's beckoning in 1956. The dates can be reconciled — accounting for two stays in Turkey — but this is speculation.

Namangani retired to Adana and died in 2002, drawing a West German, then a German pension, per interview with Hayit.

His long service to Germany: BayHStA LaflüVerw 1900, 17 April 1957, Wolfrum to Nentwig.

97 **"The majority of the Mohammedans":** BayHStA LaflüVerw 2027, 14 July 1955, "Beihilfe für die Religiöse Gemeinschaft 'Islam.'"

"Create a favorable echo": AAPA ZA 105762, 10 January 1956, von Mende to Lüder, "Unterstützung der Mohammedanischen Religiösen Gesellschaft 'Islam.'"

Von Mende and Namagani: Interview with Erling von Mende. Also, the letter from Wolfrum to Nentwig states that they knew each other during the war.

98 **Strict and humorless:** Hayit, who was married to a Christian, recalled that Namangani criticized him for having a Christmas tree. Anecdote from Narzikul; also Crane, p. 83.

"Denunciations" in Munich: Letter of 1 August 1956, Veli Kayum to von Mende.

Oberländer himself was brought: See Wachs.

The Stasi was taking aim: BStU, MfS HA II/5B, Reg. Nr. 2293/60.

99 **Baymirza Hayit:** AAPA ZA 195783. The broadcast is translated as "Inhalt der Sendung Radio Taschkent vom 20.7.1956, 19 Uhr."

How to knock out Gacaoglu: AAPA ZA 105762, letter of 28 December 1956, Gacaoglu to "Sehr geehrter Herr Bundesminister."

"Because no German office": AAPA ZA 105762, letter of 10 January 1957, von Mende to Wolfrum, opposing Gacaoglu and Sultan.

100 **"The unwanted American influence":** BayHStA LaflüVerw 1900, 17 April 1957, "Einführung des Hauptimams Namangani als Oberhaupt der mohammedanischen Gemeinde heimatloser Ausländer in der Bundesrepublik."

"I find it unbearable": BayHStA LaflüVerw 1900, letter of 17 April 1957, Wolfrum to Nentwig, no subject.

"Mr. Kelley from the local office": BayHStA LaflüVerw 1900, 9 November 1957, "Seelsorgerische Betreuung der moh, Flüchtlinge."

In Munich's Löwenbräukeller: BayHStA LaflüVerw 1900, 9 March 1958, "Einladung" and "Protokoll."

101 **Created the Ecclesiastical Administration:** Amtsgericht München Registerakten, VR 5991, 7 May 1958, "Protokoll."

Namangani got 650 marks: Ibid. Namangani received 650 marks per month plus 150 marks for travel costs. His deputy, Ibrahim Salih Sabanovic, received 250 marks. Namangani also oversaw a small social fund of 250 marks per month to help Muslims with a variety of needs.

The conversion is based on tables found at http://www.history.ucsb.edu/faculty/marcuse/index.html. Thanks to Professor Harold Marcuse at University of California at Santa Barbara.

101 **Gacaoglu's response to the new:** BayHStA LaflüVerw 1900, letter of 3 April 1958, Gacaoglu to Oberländer.

A central place of worship: BayHStA LaflüVerw 1900, 27 November 1957, "Betreuung der mohammedanischen Flüchtlinge."

102 **Raschid wrote a letter:** BayHStA MK 49638, 18 February 1959.

103 **Namangani called a meeting:** BayHStA LaflüVerw 1900, 22 December 1958, "Protokoll Nr. 5."

8. Dr. Ramadan Arrives

104 **The visitor was Said Ramadan:** Interview with Gerhard Kegel, 25 October 2004, Cologne. The meeting happened on or shortly after 6 March 1956, when Kegel wrote a letter to an assistant or university official, following up on his meeting. Letter in Kegel papers.

Shy of his thirtieth birthday: Ramadan was born on 13 April 1926, making him twenty-nine at the time of the meeting.

105 **A time of profound crisis:** History of the Brotherhood drawn from Richard P. Mitchell, *The Society of the Muslim Brothers;* Brynjar Lia, *The Society of the Muslim Brothers in Egypt: The Rise of an Islamic Mass Movement, 1928–1942;* and Gilles Kepel, *The Prophet and Pharaoh: Muslim Extremism in Egypt.*

108 **Banna's works contained:** Lia, p. 28.

"Wasn't like other sheikhs": Interview with Farid Abdel Khalek, 13 September 2004, Cairo.

109 **New members were recruited:** Muslim Brotherhood organizing methods drawn from Mitchell, pp. 14–32.

The first split in the movement: Lia, pp. 66–67.

Money from Nazi agents: NAWO 208/502, 23 October 1939, "Note on Wilhelm Stellborgen," p. 2. First cited in Lia.

Having a military wing: Banna's thoughts on politics and religion drawn from Lia, pp. 199, 202.

110 **Attacked shops owned by Jews:** Ibid., p. 244.

"You and your idols": Quotation from *The Koran,* translated by N. J. Dawood, 21:96, p. 233.

Christians "are not like the Jews": Translation from Andrew Bostom, ed., *The Legacy of Islamic Antisemitism: From Sacred Texts to Solemn History,* p. 37.

Karen Armstrong, in *Islam: A Short History* (p. 21), takes the opposite view, stating flatly that anti-Semitism was unknown among Muslims until the Nazi period, but she provides no evidence to back up this claim.

111 **Why Islam is less accepting:** See Matthias Küntzel, *Djihad und Judenhaß: Über den neuen antijüdischen Krieg.*

Nazi propaganda added fuel: See Jeffrey Herf, *Nazi Propaganda for the Middle East*.

A haven for ex-Nazis: Küntzel, pp. 26, 50.

Could not accept all Nazi ideas: See Klaus-Michael Mallmann and Martin Cüppers. *Halbmond und Hakenkreuz: Das "Dritte Reich," die Araber, und Palästina*, p. 43, and Küntzel, p. 39.

112 Some biographers have glossed over: For example, Philip Mattar (*The Mufti of Jerusalem*) seems to purposely leave out most details of the Mufti's contacts with the Nazis. The best treatment by far of the Mufti's links with the National Socialists is Klaus Gensicke, *Der Mufti von Jerusalem, Amin el-Husseini, und die Nationalsozialisten*, but this book is written in German and untranslated. His main conclusions are found in Mallmann and Cüppers. See also Küntzel, especially his epilogue.

His career in the 1930s and '40s: Biographical details drawn from Mattar and Zvi Elpeleg, *Grand Mufti: Haj Amin al-Hussaini*. On Hussaini's anti-Semitism, see Gensicke, pp. 149–59. A number of the Mufti's speeches, such as his radio address of 8 January 1943, are collected in Höpp, *Mufti Papiere*, and demonstrate this.

He contacted the Nazis: German Foreign Office records, cited in Gensicke, p. 45.

113 The propagandist Johann von Leers: AAPA ZA 105783, 18 February 1960, "Verbindungen Amin Lahar aus Kairo nach Bundesrepublik."

"The Mufti told him": Interview with Khalek.

Banna turned to one: Taken from Ramadan's obituary on the website of the Islamic Center of Geneva, http://www.cige.org/historique.htm, and as recounted to Dawud Salahuddin. Telephone interview with Salahuddin, 28 February 2006.

114 "Physically he was enormously strong": Interview with Salahuddin.

Concerning his work in Palestine: On his playing a crucial role in the defense of Palestine, see the Islamic Center of Geneva's account of his life on its website. On establishing the Brotherhood's branch in Jordan, carrying a passport, and German and Swiss police records, see "History of the Jordanian Muslim Brotherhood, Part One," http://www.aawsat.com/english/news.asp?section=3&id=3204.

115 Ramadan went to Pakistan: Biographical sketch in NARA RG 59, Decimal Files, 1950–1954, 511.80/7-2753, United States Embassy, Egypt Dispatch from Jefferson Caffery to the Department of State, "Colloquium on Islamic Culture and Saeed Ramadhan," 27 July 1953.

"If the Brotherhood had ministries": Interview with Gamal el-Banna, 13 September 2004, Cairo.

Ramadan and the Grand Mufti: Reinhard Schulze, *Islamischer Internationalismus im 20. Jahrhundert*, pp. 110, 111, 210.

The "World Muslim Congress" is how Ramadan, in his official correspondence (see Kegel papers; for example, Ramadan CV), renders *mu'tamar al-alam al-islami*, the Karachi conference held in 1951 of which he was elected secretary, and *al-mu'tamar al-islami al-amm li-l-Quds*, the Jerusalem-based conference of which he was elected secretary general in 1956. To distinguish one from the other, I have added "Jerusalem" when referring to the latter. Neither of these should be confused with the current Saudi-controlled Muslim World League, or *rabitat al-alam al-islami,* which Ramadan helped found in Mecca on 18 May 1962. See Schulze, *Internationalismus.*

116 **"Source states that the Mufti":** NARA RG 263, ZZ-18, box 96, Amin El-Hussaini, Vol. 1, 11 March 1946, "Views of the Jerusalem Mufti."

"Hoped-for result": DDEL Central Files, Official File, box 737, file 144-B-4, "Islamic & Moslem Religion," 24 August 1953, "Memo to: C. D. Jackson, from: Abbott Washburn."

117 **"These individuals can exert":** DDEL Central Files, Official File, box 737, file 144-B-4, "Islamic & Moslem Religion," 8 September 1953, "Subject: Islamic leaders."

The president's appointment book: DDEL, President's Appointments, 23 September 1953, Vol. July–December 1953, Eisenhower, Dwight D.: Records as President, Daily Appointments, 1953–1961. Thanks to David Haight at the Eisenhower Presidential Library for pointing out this document.

"On the surface, the conference": NARA RG 59, Decimal Files, 1950–1954, 511.80/4-3053, 30 April 1953, "Colloquium on Islamic Culture" and attached briefing paper. Thanks to the National Security Archives for drawing attention to this document.

Private sponsors stepped in: NARA RG 59, Decimal Files, 1950–1954, 511.80/2-253, Princeton University, letter of 2 February 1953, Bayard Dodge to Richard H. Sanger [Colloquium on Islamic Culture].

Paying for two Princeton professors: NARA RG 59, Decimal Files, 1950–1954, 511.80/5-853, "Colloquium on Islamic Culture," letter of 8 May 1953, Helen M. Anderson to Richard H. Sanger.

118 **Sanitized version of his career:** NARA RG 59, Records of the Department of State, Decimal Files, 511.80/7-2753, United States Embassy, Egypt Dispatch from Jefferson Caffery to the Department of State, "Colloquium on Islamic Culture and Saeed Ramadhan," 27 July 1953.

The resulting photo op: Thanks to Robert Dreyfuss, who generously provided a copy of the official Princeton program, including photos.

"Ramadan was invited": CIA RDP83-00423R001300710001, "Comments on the Islamic Colloquium."

119 **U.S. officials in Rabat:** NARA RG 59, Records of the Department of State, Decimal Files, 880.413/2-856, 8 February 1956, "Press Conference in Rabat of Said Ramadan of Islamic Congress in Jerusalem" and accompanying memo from Gerald Little.

A tough anticommunist battle: Associated Press report, printed in *The Lincoln Star,* 28 September 1956, p. 3. The report calls the group the Jerusalem Moslem Conference.

Nasser cracked down: Mitchell, pp. 141, 142, 153.

Five months after Kegel: Letter of 14 August 1956, Kegel papers.

The forty-four-year-old scholar: Kegel was born 26 June 1912, according to the Deutsche Dienststelle, and died in February 2006. An account of his remarkable legal career can be found in German at www.uni-koeln.de/jur-fak/instipr/leitung/Nachruf_Krueger.doc.

120 **He wrote a telegram:** 13 November 1956, Kegel papers.

In June 1958, Ramadan wrote: 21 June 1958, Kegel papers.

He was off to the Hajj: 28 August 1958, Kegel papers.

During this Hajj the exiled: Interview with Fouad Allam, 15 September 2004, Cairo. Allam was the former head of Egyptian domestic security.

Swiss officials seemed unaware: BAR Ramadan, 3 March 1966, interrogation of Ramadan, "Abhörungsprotokoll."

121 "Intelligent if also fanatical": Interview with Kegel.

122 Braving a snowstorm: Interview with Faisal I. Yazdani, 13 December 2005, Munich.

Printed in German and Turkish: BayHStA LaflüVerw 1900, "Protokoll Nr. 5 Am 22.12.58 hate eine Sitzung des 'Dini Idare'" and attached invitation flyers. Also, interviews with Yazdani, 28 January and 13 December 2005, Munich.

123 Syrian student, Ghaleb Himmat: Telephone interview with Himmat, 1 June 2005. Himmat did not say if he had invited Ramadan.

"Himmat invited him to take over": Interview with Mogaddedi.

124 "The students were all well educated": Interview with Muhammad Abdul Karim Grimm, 21 October 2004, Hamburg.

Von Mende's tiny card file: AAPA ZA 105731, 23 March 1959, "Aktenvermerk, Betr.: Said Muhammed Ramadan, Genf."

9. Marriage of Convenience

125 "Received my Kodachromes": Letter of 6 August 1957, "Dear Folks," Dreher papers. Thanks to Helen and Chuck Oerkvitz, Dreher's sister and brother-in-law, for access to his personal papers.

"Not a one-woman man": Interview with West.

126 "Deep down inside I realize": Letter of 19 May 1953, Dreher to Helen and Chuck Oerkvitz, Dreher papers.

On his CIA application: Ibid. Dreher attended all board meetings until he left for Munich.

He spoke broken German: See Chapter 12 for description of his farewell speech, which he delivered in poor German.

Show off to bewildered émigrés: Interview with Klump.

127 Church leader Edward Elson: Letter of 31 July 1958, "White House Letter from Dwight D. Eisenhower to Edward L. R. Elson," document 133 in the online archive "Documentation on Early Cold War U.S. Propaganda Activities in the Middle East," published by the National Security Archive of George Washington University, Washington, DC: http://www.gwu.edu/~nsarchiv/NSAEBB/NSAEBB78/docs.htm.

"The 'holy war' aspect": 7 September 1957, Goodpaster "Memorandum of Conference with the President," retrieved from Declassified Documents Reference Service.

Ad Hoc Working Group on Islam: DDEL OCB Central Files Series, box 2, file January–May 1957, 5 February 1957, "Informal Memorandum of Meeting: Ad Hoc Working Group on Islam."

128 "Strengthen the reformist groups": This was in specific reference to NSC 5428, "U.S. Objectives and Policies with Respect to the Near East."

In May, the coordination board: DDEL OCB Secretariat Series, box 4, file "Islamic Organizations," 3 May 1957, "Inventory of U.S. Government and Private Organization Activity Regarding Islamic Organizations as an Aspect of Overseas Operations."

129 **"We all thought the Soviet":** Interview with Klump.

"Offensive" and "defensive": Letter of 7 November 1961, Dreher to Howland H. Sargeant, Amcomlib president, Dreher papers. In the letter, Dreher reviews tactics used in Munich.

130 **Dreher's boss, Walpole Davis:** Interview with Murphy.

Most émigrés were eager: See, for example, Burds.

Automatic payments: Interview with Klump.

Might have been unsavory: See, for example, *Win* magazine. An antiwar publication prominent during the Vietnam War, it had an amazingly accurate description of Operation Ohio, a U.S. intelligence program to back émigré groups that had killed opponents in displaced persons camps after the war. The magazine lists Dreher and other Amcomlib employees as having been aware that they were funding people involved in the postwar killings. The allegations are impossible to prove, but based on subsequently released information (see, for example, Loftus, *The Belarus Secret*), they are highly plausible.

Washington's fears seem overblown: NARA RG 59, Decimal File 670.901/1-2158, 21 January 1958, "AmEmbassy, Cairo to Department of State, Subject: Talks with Members of Dipomatic Corps Regarding Afro-Asian People's Solidarity Conference."

U.S. diplomats spent: See, for example, cable traffic, such as NARA RG 59, Decimal File 670.901/10-457, 4 October 1957, State Department circular on how to prepare for the conference.

Such as Said Shamil: NARA RG 59, Decimal File 670.901/5-2059, 23 May 1959, "Subject: Document on Soviet Colonialism Addressed to AA Solidarity Council."

Dreher was trying to make use: On the conference, see NARA RG 59, Decimal File 670.901/1-2558, 25 January 1958, "Soviet and Egyptian Statements at Asian-African Solidarity Conference."

On Nasar's role, see Georgetown, Kelley papers, box 5, folder 5, 1 December 1959, "Political Affairs Discussion with Kelley."

131 **"Rusi Nasar tried":** Interview with Allworth.

A Jordanian passport: A BND official wrote to von Mende making this claim. Letter of 19 May 1961, Maurer to von Mende, "Sehr verehrter Herr Professor!," von Mende papers.

Swiss intelligence claimed: BAR Ramadan, 29 June 1967, "Note pour Monsieur Gelzer."

Ahmet Magoma: Georgetown, Kelley papers, box 5, folder 5, "Confidential Report of Mr. B. E. Kuniholm on His Trip to the Middle East," pp. 27–28.

Von Mende was outraged: AAPA ZA 105731, 3 February 1959, "Aktennotiz Betr. Besuch von Shamil and Magoma."

No influence in the Muslim world: In fact, Ramadan was at this time a key Islamist figure, receiving visits from, for example, King Hussein of Jordan. BAR

Ramadan, Index entry C.11.88, 24 November 1958, "Erw. im Bewachungsbericht König HUSSEIN's von Jordanien, Dieser hat am 20.11.59 nachtmittags R. besucht."

132 **West Germany's Foreign Office:** AAPA ZA B12 Band 411, 2 February 1959, "Betr. Besuch von Vertretern des Nordkaukasischen Komitees in Deutschland."

One of von Mende's key men: AAPA ZA 105731, 29 June 1959, "Auszug aus einem Schreiben von Dr. Hayit vom 24.06.59."

His own covert operation: AAPA ZA 105707, 16 April 1959, "Ausnutzung der turkestanischen Exilgruppen für politsiche Aufklärungsarbeit."

133 **Namangani reported to his boss:** AAPA ZA 105731, 22 September 1959, "Reisebericht von Haupt-Imam Namangani." The men had arrived back in Germany in July and Namangani was paid one thousand marks on August 26.

A resounding success: Details in Schulze, *Internationalismus*, pp. 149–51.

134 **The institute's *Arabic Review*:** Hoover, Radio Liberty Collection, box 214, letter of 16 March 1960, Ramadan to Kantemir.

Decided to move his family: Letter of 10 April 1959, Ramadan to Kegel, Kegel papers.

The European congress: BayHStA LaflüVerw 1900, 30 April 1959, "Betreff: Errichtung einer Moschee in München durch."

Gacaoglu wrote a letter: The text, including the quotation "The mosque to be built, " from BayHStA LaflüVerw 1900, letter of 27 April 1959, Gacaoglu to Stain.

135 **Ramadan was the chairman:** Amtsgericht München, Registerakten, VR 6256, 29 March 1960, "Betreff: Moscheebau-Kommission e.V."

Bring back money: BayHStA LaFlüVerw 1900, 13 June 1960, "Betreff: Bau einer Moschee in München."

Their old intelligence contact: BayHStA LaFlüVerw 1900, 8 March 1960, "Betreff: Religiöse Betreuung der mohammedanischen Flüchtlinge; hier: Bau einer Moschee in München."

"Germany is a gate": AAPA ZA 105783, 8 March 1960, untitled rough draft of report from Hayit to von Mende.

136 **"One comes to the conviction":** AAPA ZA 105783, 14 April 1960, "Bemerkungen zu den Tätigkeit des Geistlichesamt."

The mufti of Turkestan: AAPA ZA 105707, 2 November 1960, "Betr. Abteilung für die Propaganda des Islams in der SU beim ZK der KP Iraqs."

Advised him to see Ramadan: Letter of 27 May 1961, von Mende to Ungermann, "Betr.: Kartothek Dr. Said RAMADAN," von Mende papers.

Von Mende reluctantly agreed: Ibid.

137 **Break into Ramadan's office:** Ibid., as well as 8 May 1961, Aktennotiz "Betr.: Said RAMADAN," and letter of 19 May 1961, Maurer to von Mende, "Sehr verehrter Herr Professor!," von Mende papers.

138 **The burglary was called off:** This is an assumption based on von Mende's seeming agreement that the files wouldn't be valuable and on a lack of further correspondence. It's not impossible, however, that the burglary went ahead, but that details were arranged over the phone; alternatively the written record may have been destroyed or lost.

138 **"It is astounding"**: AAPA ZA 105784, letter of 5 June 1961, to von Mende, "Sehr geehrter Professor!," von Mende papers.

10. The Novelist's Tale

139 **A charity called Jami'at al Islam**: Jami'at al Islam should not be confused with the famous Pakistani political group of a similar name, Jamaat-e-Islamiya.
Moving their operations: BayHStA LanflüVerw 2199, 9 January 1960, "Betreff: Aufnahme der Tätigkeit einer JAI-Zweigstelle in Deutschland."
"I hardly think it's possible": BayHStA LaflüVerw 1900, 20 February 1960, "Betr. Bau einer Moschee in München."

140 **"Jami'at al Islam was founded"**: Ibid., attached document, "Jami'at al Islam, Geschichte — Richtlinien — Programm," Wien, 1959.

141 **The U.S. Escapee Program**: See, for example, Susan L. Carruthers, "Between Camps: Eastern Bloc 'Escapees' and Cold War Borderlands," *American Quarterly*, p. 934.
Afoul of Catholic agencies: Interview with Touhami Louahala, 30 July 2006, Montélimar, France.
Office of Refugee and Migration Affairs: *Jami'at al Islam* newsletter, No. 2, 1960, p. 2.
Photographed in front of a shack: About Kamal's visit to the camp, BayHStA LaflüVerw 2199, letter of 17 May 1960, Balagija to Stain, with accompanying photos.
American Council of Voluntary Agencies: That the council did not vet Kamal's group is explicitly confirmed in a letter from the council to Bavarian officials. BayHStA LaflüVerw 2199, letter of 5 January 1962, "Strictly Confidential: Ms. Ella V. Laursen."
Field Marshal Ayub Khan: BayHStA LaflüVerw 2199, article in *Münchener Merkur*, 24 January 1961, page number unclear.
A large conference in Munich: BayHStA LaflüVerw 2199, *Münchener Merkur*, 6 June 1961.

142 **His Ecclesiastical Administration**: BayHStA LaflüVerw 2199, 27 February 1960 memo to members, "Lieber Bruder in Islam."
"The Bavarian capital has recently": BayHStA LaflüVerw 1900, "Synagoge neben Moschee," *Münchener Merkur*, 26 March 1961.
Citing Jami'at's move: *Münchener Merkur*, 24 June 1960, "Spenden aus Mekka für München," p. 14.
Kamal's public life: Kamal's biography can be found on the back cover of all his reprinted works, available through the publishing-on-demand company toExcel. The copyright was renewed in 2000 and the packaging prepared by his son, Turan, a classical guitarist who wanted to keep up his father's legacy, according to Kamal's daughter, Tura. Interview with Tura Kamal-Haller, 16 June 2006, Munich.

143 **Kamal's Federal Bureau of Investigation file**: FBI Ahmad Kamal FOIA, 8 May 1956, "Ahmad Kamal, also known as Cimarron Hathaway, Ahmad Kamal Hathaway, Ahmed Kamal," p. 1.

He listed his father as Qara Yusuf: Ibid., p. 6.

He had left Kamal's mother: Ibid., p. 1.

144 Arrested by Chinese authorities: West German intelligence believed this was true. AAPA ZA 105792, 25 July 1955, "Betr.: Lage in Indonesien."

145 "I'm crying for what wasn't": Interview with Kamal-Haller.

Write-up in the New York Times: "A Picaresque Tale of Adventure," 31 March 1940. The Times also reviewed Full Fathom Five and One-Dog Man.

146 Kamal told the Los Angeles Times: "Prison 'Koran' Tricked Japs," 11 November 1945, p. 7.

147 The Sacred Journey: Author's note, pp. xiii–xv, toExcel edition.

Kamal tried to describe: According to a small notice in Jami'at al Islam, No. 2, 1960. In the author's possession.

The Saturday Evening Post: 26 September 1953, p. 19.

To work for the U.S. government: FBI Kamal FOIA, 4 May 1956, "Re: New York Air-Tel to Los Angeles, 4/30/56," p. 2.

A debt of $1,877.40: Ibid.

The view of West German intelligence: AAPA ZA 105792, 25 July 1955, "Betr.: Lage in Indonesien."

148 His son took music lessons: Kamal's son is in fact an accomplished guitarist. See http://www.classicalguitar.nl/ShowPost.aspx?PostID=9649, for example. Recordings of his music circulate among aficionados.

149 Touhami Louahala grew up: Interview with Louahala. The suicide of Dubois was widely reported in Swiss and foreign newspapers.

In Jami'at publications, Louahala's name is spelled Tuhami Ibn Ahmad El Wahla. See Jami'at al Islam, No. 2, 1960, p. 5.

150 The much more famous Pakistani group: Serge Bromberger, Les rebelles algériens, p. 222.

"What is fact and what is fiction": Nevill Barbour, review of Les rebelles algériens, International Affairs (Royal Institute of International Affairs 1944–), p. 113.

151 "That was Mr. James Price": For Price's ties to Amcomlib, see Hoover RFE/RL, Corp. Records, box 350, folder 5, 1 September 1971, "Memorandum of Conversation (by phone) with James Price, Library of Congress."

Almost blown through the roof: NARA RG 59, Decimal File 862A.411/10-1760, 17 October 1960, cable from Munich, "No. 156, October 17."

152 Louahala says he had nothing: Interview with Louahala.

Jami'at pulled out of Jordan: NARA RG 59, Decimal File 885.46/8-1161, 11 August 1961, "Subject: Letter from Jami'at al Islam (JAI)."

Mahmoud K. Muftic: Letters of 30 March, 17 April, and 19 April 1961, von Mende papers.

153 The Germans trusted Balagija: For Balagija's wartime service, see WASt, Schriftverkehrsakte.

An audit of Jami'at's management: NARA RG 59, Decimal File 862A.411/4-242, 24 April 1962, "Subject: Jami'at al Islam audit."

Concerned officials in Munich: BayHStA LaflüVerw 2199, 7 November 1961, "Betr. Förderung von zwei Projekten des Jami'at al Islam."

Charges that Balagija had: BayHStA LaflüVerw 2199, 4 December 1961, "Betreff:

Zusammenarbeit mit der mohammedanischen Hilfsorganisation Jami'at al Islam."

153 **More loyal to the Germans:** Letters recounting meetings with Balagija, Sahkul, 27 December 1961 and 2 January 1962, von Mende papers.

154 **Jami'at was closing all offices:** BayHStA LaflüVerw 2199, 1 March 1962, "Jami'at al Islam beendet Fluechtlingsprogramme in Europa."

Council of Voluntary Agencies: BayHStA LaflüVerw 2199, copy of letter of 6 December 1961, "Strictly Confidential: Attn Mrs. Charlotte B. Owen, Executive Director."

The council was later subsumed by the U.S. Agency for International Development. Its archives are incomplete and do not contain this exchange.

"We've been spared a common worry": BayHStA LaflüVerw 2199, 7 March 1962, "Sehr geehrter Dr. Burmeister."

The Burmese opposition leader: Telephone interview with U Kyaw Win, 31 July 2007.

U Kyaw Win, a veteran Burmese opposition figure, was with U Nu when Kamal made the offer in 1969. Kamal later traveled widely in Burma and told U Kyaw Win that he was in regular contact with Burmese opposition leaders.

Plans for a grandiose mosque: BayHStA LaflüVerw 1900, 4 October 1961, "Betreff: Bau einer Moschee in München."

11. Winning the Mosque

155 **Kantemir was almost blind:** Von Mende's description is in AAPA ZA 105706, 7 July 1961, "Betr.: Alichan Kantemir — Nordkaukas, Komitee."

"Dear Professor Kegel": Letter of 16 July 1960, Kegel papers.

Finding his way to Turkey and Pakistan: Ramadan's travels detailed in letter of 18 September 1960, Kegel papers.

His fund-raising success: For Ramadan's activities during the Hajj and while raising Saudi money, Kassajep's concerns, and the quotation "Our task is to build a mosque," see BayHStA LaflüVerw 1900, 21 August 1960, "ProtoKoll Nr. 5."

156 **An old battalion commander:** WAst records.

Kassajep met with Bavarian officials: BayHStA LaflüVerw 1900, 6 February 1961, "Betreff: Moscheebau in München."

157 **Only 78,890 marks:** BayHStA LaflüVerw 1900, letter of 17 February 1961, Kassajep to Burmeister.

Kayum started the trouble: AAPA ZA 105783, 27 March 1961, "Aktenvermerk Betr.: Dr. Hayit/BND."

Less clear is whether Hayit really was a BND informant. In his letter to the BND, von Mende did not dispute this assertion or any of the facts. He only seemed angry that Kayum was aware of them. In addition, it certainly fits with previous French intelligence efforts to recruit Hayit (see notes for Chapter 5). Still, this evidence is only anecdotal. Clearly Hayit thought of himself as a scholar and produced a fairly sizable body of academic work. I asked Hayit if von Mende's offices were affiliated with intelligence services, and he answered, "Not to my knowledge." Because I had not completed my research at the time, I was not aware of these letters and could not ask Hayit directly about Kayum. Hayit has since died.

Salary was another concern: Letter of 23 February 1961, "Lieber Rolf," von Mende files.

A monthly salary of 450 marks: AAPA ZA 105706, 7 July 1961, "Betr.: Veli Kayum-Chan."

158 **Implying that Himmat had:** AAPA ZA 105707, 12 September 1960, "Arabische-Kommunistiche Ring im Ausland."

His own international ties: BayHStA LaflüVerw 1900, letter of 27 July 1961, Ramadan to Stain.

Ramadan repeated the figure: Ibid.

He wrote back offering: Ibid.

Namangani had had enough: BayHStA LaflüVerw 1900, letter of 7 November 1961, Namangani to Ramadan.

159 **Commission finally met:** BayHStA LaflüVerw 1900, 30 November 1961, "Betr.: Information über den Moscheebau in München."

160 **Jordan withdraws passport:** This happened no latter than 1965. Swiss records contain a letter from the Jordanian embassy saying Ramada's passport had been revoked. Swiss Ramadan file, 1 October 1965, "Notiz. Said Ramadan."

Enough votes to block Kantemir: Ibid., handwritten note. Decision confirmed in BayHStA LaflüVerw 1900, 11 January 1962, "Betreff: Bau einer Moschee in München."

161 **Council of Islamic Communities and Societies:** AAPA ZA 105784, 3 April 1962, "Betr.: Islamischer Rat Deutschlands." Partially also described in *Al-Islam,* No. 5, 1962, "Gelebter Islam — Bruderschaft und Einigkeit," p. 1, and "Rat Islamischer Gemeinden und Gemeinschaften," p. 7.

162 **The Muslim World League:** On Schmiede's participation on the trip to Mecca, ibid. Schmiede is still alive but refused to be interviewed.

On the conference as a whole, the most reliable description, including a list of key participants and an analysis of coalitions, is found in Schulze, *Internationalismus,* pp. 181–212.

Muslims in West Germany: For this, and the Saudi visit to West Germany, see AAPA ZA 105706, 6 July 1962, "Islamische Weltkongresse."

163 **His ally Mahmoud K. Muftic:** Letter of 29 May 1962, von Mende to Ungermann, von Mende papers.

The most dangerous time: BAR Ramadan, 26 October 1962, "Attentatsplans gegen Dr. Said Ramadan."

A concealable handgun: BAR Ramadan, 15 August 1962, interrogation of Gailan Ramiz.

One of its best Muslim agitators: Interview with Sultan, 28 March 2006.

Philadelphia's venerable International House: "Modern Forms of Colonialism," Sultan papers. The talk is also on the house's list of events for March 1961.

164 **"The report fulfilled its objective":** Paper, no date, To: Mr. I. Patch. From: G. Sultan. Subject: Report on "The Modern Forms of Colonialism," International House, Philadelphia.

Sultan went to Cairo: Copy of speech in Sultan papers.

165　**Mailed Ahmad a $200 check:** Letter of 5 April 1962, Sultan to Ahmad, "My dear Dr. Ahmad," Sultan papers.

　　　Committee for Self-Determination: Technically, Sultan shouldn't have done this. According to an agreement between Amcomlib and the National Committee for a Free Europe, Amcomlib was supposed to focus on Muslim parts of the world; but for whatever reason, Sultan claimed to be working for the other group. 2 October 1961, "Memorandum to: Director, Special Projects Division. From: Garip Sultan. Subject: Talk with Mr. Pavlovich of the Free Europe Committee," Sultan papers.

　　　Getting Sultan an invitation: For Ahmad's offer to help arrange the invitation, see letter of 22 March 1962, Ahmet to Sultan, "My dear Garip," Sultan papers.

　　　But he promised to lobby: Letter of 18 April 1961, Ahmad to Sultan, "My dear Garip Sultan," Sultan papers.

　　　Sultan then contacted Ramadan: Interviews with Sultan.

　　　The sole U.S. representative: Official list of delegates, Sultan papers.

　　　West Germany should go ahead: For von Mende's thoughts and suggestions about the mosque, see AAPA ZA 105735, 14 December 1961, "Betr.: Moscheebau-Kommission in München."

166　**West Germany's generosity:** BayHStA LaflüVerw 1900, 22 March 1962, "Betreff: Bau einer Moschee in München, Zu Ihrem Schreiben vom 11.3.1962."

　　　St. Paul's Church—where the whole idea: BayHStA LaflüVerw 1900, 10 September 1963, "Betreff: Religiöse Betreuung der mohammedanischen Flüchtlinge."

　　　The old SS imam finally: BayHStA LaflüVerw 1900, 19 March 1962, Namangani's one-page cover letter to Burmeister, "Sehr geehrter Herr Regierungsdirektor," and accompanying seven-page "Erklärung."

　　　Namangani's letter was cast in perfect bureaucratic German and likely was written by Margaret Kassajep, Hassan Kassajep's wife. She wrote much of the men's correspondence but could not remember the specifics of this letter. Interview with Margaret Kassajep, 17 August 2004, Munich.

167　**Some surviving students:** For example, the interview with Mogaddedi. He said Namangani was initially respected not for his training in Islam but because he was von Mende's man, and the students knew how influential von Mende was.

　　　Gacaoglu reminded the community: BayHStA LaflüVerw 1900, letter of 14 June 1963, Gacaoglu to Hergl, "Sehr geehrter Herr Regierungsdirektor!"

12. Losing Control

169　**A bit of doggerel:** Interview with West. Karin West also tape-recorded the speeches and toasts. The citations are taken from this recording. Thanks to Denis Johnson for making the poetry scan.

171　**Letter to Arthur Schlesinger Jr.:** NARA RG 59, Decimal File 885.413/1-1762, cover letter of 17 January 1962, Schlesinger to Talbot, including two-page letter of 24 November 1961, Ramadan to Schlesinger, as well as original and translation of Ramadan's article "Choice for the Middle East: Communism or Islam?," undated, from *La Tribune de Genève*.

172　**Lose contact with Ramadan:** Interview with Klump.

Deployed to Vietnam: I am indebted to Professor Richard H. Shultz Jr. of the Fletcher School at Tufts University for a copy of his interview with Dreher. Shultz wrote an analysis of MACVSOG based on interviews and access to CIA papers. Dreher says in the interview that he and his U.S. team had little idea of what the South Vietnamese were broadcasting or its value.

173 **In 1972 Dreher retired:** Taken from Dreher résumé, Dreher papers.

Von Mende wrote to Sultan: Letter of 6 September 1962, von Mende to Sultan, "Lieber Herr Sultan!," Sultan papers.

174 **"He was known as a Nazi":** Interview with Richard Pipes, 25 October 2006, Cambridge, MA.

In early 1963, the ex-soldiers: For changes in the mosque project, see Amtsgericht München, Registerakten (Sonderband) VR 6256, Islamische Gemeinschaft in Deutschland e.V. List of members "Ergänzung Nr. 1 zum Protokoll der Generalversammlung v. 3.2.1963." For the commission's name change, see "Ergänzung Nr. 2 zum Protokoll der Generalversamlung v. 3.2.1963."

Ali Kantemir: For von Mende's attempt to erase evidence of their relationship, see AAPA ZA 105730, 24 July 1963, "Betr.: Nachlass von Herrn Alichan Kantemir."

Von Mende's impotence: Letter of 23 October 1963, "Sehr verehrter Herr Professor!," von Mende papers.

175 **Infiltrated a Muslim student group:** The group was the Islamische Studentengemeinde in Köln. It received six thousand marks, and von Mende had planned another payment, this time of four thousand marks, but he died before he could arrange it. His successors recommended not paying the balance. AAPA ZA 105708, 24 December 1963, "Betr.: Übersicht der vorhandenen Mittel des Forschungdienstes Osteuropa."

The Stasi seemed to take: BStU, MfS HA II/5B, Reg. Nr. 2293/60, 16 January 1962.

Told him to tone down: AAPA ZA 105730, letter of 12 December 1963, von Mende to Hayit, "Lieber Baymirza!"

Ordered him to stop smoking: Interview with Erling von Mende.

A massive heart attack: AAPA ZA 105706, 13 January 1964, "Betr.: Beerdigungskosten für Herrn Professor von Mende."

176 **The foreign ministry agreed:** AAPA ZA 105706, 15 January 1964, "Betr.: Beerdigungskosten des am 16.12.1963 verstorbenen Leiters des Forschungsdienstes Osteuropa, Professor von Mende."

Siegfried Ungermann: AA B40 Band 51, 21 January 1964, "Lieber Herr Wickert!"

Decided to close the operation: AA B40 Band 51, 12 June 1964, "Betr.: Auflösung des Forschungsdienstes Osteuropa, Hier: Räumung der Parterrewohnung in der Cecilienallee 52."

Precipitated an ugly scene: Ibid.

Asked if she could use the name: AA B40 Band 52, letter of 2 June 1965, Unglaube to Dr. Lane, "Sehr geehrter Herr Dr. Lane!"

Officials worried that the mass: AA B40 Band 51, 9 October 1964, "Betr.: Sicherungsmaßnahmen des Büros in Düsseldorf."

177 **Von Mende's use of Muslims:** Alexei, *Soviet Nationalities in German Wartime Strategy, 1941–1945,* p. iii.

13. The Brotherhood Triumphant

181 **The sixth in all of West Germany:** By 1973, Berlin had two mosques, Hamburg one, Frankfurt one, and Aachen one. Of course, the country had numerous prayer rooms.

Something appealing but affordable: Interview with Yazdani, 28 January 2005.

182 **Ramadan was so influential:** From the memoirs of Yusuf al-Qaradawi, according to Mshari Al-Zaydi: "History of the Jordanian Muslim Brotherhood, Part One," *Asharq Alawsat*. Online English edition: http://www.aawsat.com/english/news.asp?section=3&id=3204.

The Muslim World League asked: Schulze, *Internationalismus,* pp. 247–48.

Held a diplomatic passport: BAR Ramadan, 23 September 1970, untitled interview with Ramadan.

Traveled on a Pakistani passport: Swiss police records show he began using a Pakistani passport no later than 1980. Swiss Ramadan file, 21 February 1980, "Rapport de Wanner — inspecteur."

183 **"Maybe some new members":** Interview with Kamal al-Helbawy, 20 October 2005, London.

"The [students] disgusted him": Interview with Mogaddedi. Mogaddedi also believed that Himmat tried to bring Attar to Munich.

184 **"He was in a few meetings":** Interview with Himmat.

"What the Arabs are like": Interview with Yazdani, 28 January 2005. This is Yazdani's recollection of Ramadan's words.

Yazdani stepped in to help: Interviews with Yazdani, 28 January and 13 December 2005.

Protests from these embassies: Memo from West German embassy in Baghdad: BayHStA MK 49638, 12 January 1965, "Betr.: Errichtung einer Moschee in München." The Muslim World League and the Turkish embassy in Bonn also complained about the tax status.

185 **The cornerstone was laid:** See, for example, "Der Muezzin ruft zum Moscheebau," *Süddeutsche Zeitung,* No. 241, 9 October 1967, p. 13.

186 **Yazdani, however, was not present:** Amtsgericht München, Registerakten (Sonderband) VR 6256, Islamische Gemeinschaft in Deutschland e.V., 3 November 1973, "Protokoll."

A whispering campaign: Apparently Ibrahim Gacaoglu and his wife were behind these allegations of corruption. The dispute is described from Yazdani's perspective in a letter of 21 July 1970 to the Bavarian social ministry. It seems that the charges went nowhere and, given Gacaoglu's weak credibility, it seems likely that they were not accurate. Copy of letter courtesy of Islam-Archiv Deutschland.

"I have to say that I'm happy": Interview with Yazdani, 28 January 2005.

Turkish guest workers: Amtsgericht München, Registerakten, registered letter of 1 October 1974, "Sehr geehrte Brüder in Islam."

187 **In 1975 the Turks tried:** Amtsgericht München, Registerakten (Sonderband) VR 6256, Islamische Gemeinschaft in Deutschland e.V., 18 January 1975, "Protokoll."

188 **Nada was his opposite:** Details of Nada's friendship with Himmat, arrest, and flight to Austria, Tripoli, and Switzerland from interview with Youssef Nada, 2

June 2004, Campione d'Italia. Quotation about torture in prison from interview of Nada on 16 November 2003 by Glenn Simpson of the *Wall Street Journal*. Thanks to Simpson for making his notes available.

190 **Ramadan was officially kicked out:** Amtsgericht München, Registerakten (Sonderband) VR 6256, Islamische Gemeinschaft in Deutschland e.V., 3 November 1973, "Protokoll."

14. Beyond Munich

192 **Brotherhood's "supreme guide":** Interview with Mahdi Akef, 14 September 2004, Cairo.

194 **"Neo–Muslim Brotherhood":** See Kepel, *The Prophet and Pharaoh*, especially Chapter 4.

    Islamic Cultural Centres and Bodies: See *Impact International*, issue of 25 May–7 June 1973, p. 3.

195 **The Swiss lakeside resort:** Muhammad Shafiq, *The Growth of Islamic Thought in North America: Focus on Ismaʾil Raji al Faruqi*, pp. 27–28. "Hosted by Mahmoud Abu Saʾud, it was attended by such well-known figures as Ismaʾil al Faruqi, Abdul Hamid AbuSulayman, Taha al ʾAlwani, Yusuf al-Qaradawi, Muhammad al Mubarak, Jamaluddin Atia, Abdul Halim M. Ahmad, al Mahdi Ben Abbud, Ahmad Totonji, Mahmud Rashdan, Khurshid Ahmad, Jamal Barzinji, Ahmad al Assal, Jaʾfar Shaikh Idris, and many others."

    Some reports state that the meeting was held in Nadaʾs own home. In June 2003, for example, Soliman Biheri, an Egyptian businessman, told U.S. customs agents that "he had heard of a famous Islamic conference in Lugano, Switzerland." Mr. Biheri said the conference took place in Nadaʾs home and that it "provided a 'blueprint' for much of the worldwide Islamic movements in the 1980s." Department of the Treasury, U.S. Customs Service Report of Investigation, case number dc02pu02dc0005. In an interview (2 June 2004), Nada denied that the meeting took place in his home.

    Met in Saudi Arabia: Shafiq, p. 28.

    Instructed to open the center: Ibid.

196 **Barzinji signed the papers:** Ibid.

    Barzinji was an officer: Liechtenstein corporate registration, Asat Trust, "Zeichnungerklaerung" of 30 January 1978, "Beschluss."

    Barzinji's work for Nada in Saudi Arabia from Glenn Simpson's interview of Nada on 16 November 2003.

    He worked for Nada's companies: Ibid. Altalib and Barzinji joined and left the company at the same time.

    Nada sponsored him: Amtsgericht München, Registerakten, 3 April 1978, "Protokoll," p. 4. It is not clear if Altalib joined.

    Totonji, Barzinji, and Altalib: All three went to Britain to study engineering.

    On Totonji, see his Ph.D. dissertation: "Displacement Efficiency in Alcohol Flooding in Relation to Ternary System Phase Behavior," Department of Petroleum and Natural Gas Engineering, Pennsylvania State University, 1970. Shelving location: aa 900000009624 Thesis 1970 Totonji, A.

On Altalib, see Hisham Altalib, *Training Guide for Islamic Workers.*

On Barzinji, see "Islamic Trust to Build Mosque," *Indianapolis Star,* 5 May 1977.

196 **Totonji and others helped found:** See http://web.archive.org/web/2003021714
3532/http://msa-natl.org/about/history.html.

Three of his children: Italian intelligence report, The Intelligence and Democratic Security Service SISDE Counterterrorism Division 96ter, 6396 -187-A, Re: "B.J.," Operation Rome, 6 April 1996. In author's possession. Nada confirmed that his children were born in the United States, saying he had "business interests there." Interview with Nada.

Nada apparently helped: Ibid. Also, John Mintz and Douglas Farah, "In Search of Friends Among the Foes," *Washington Post,* 11 September 2004, p. A01.

The forty-two-acre site: Plans announced by Barzinji in "Islamic Trust to Build Mosque." For size and cost of mosque, see "Proposed Islamic Center Near Plainfield OK'd," *Indianapolis Star,* 5 March 1978. As headquarters of groups, see William D. Dalton, "Islamic Society of North America," in *Encyclopedia of Indianapolis.*

It formed the headquarters: For a detailed history of these founders and the Brotherhood's growth, see Steve Merley, "The Muslim Brotherhood in Belgium."

It is interesting to note that Totonji and Barzinji's U.S. Muslim Student Association was a founding member of the Saudi-run International Islamic Federation of Student Organizations (IIFSO). Totonji became the group's general secretary (see http://domino.un.org/unispal.nsf/0/2aa9c8845de74ebb05256562005c28 13?OpenDocument) and was succeeded by Altalib (see *Training Guide for Islamic Workers*). Over time, IIFSO morphed into one of the world's most important Muslim groups, the World Assembly of Muslim Youth. Headquartered in Saudi Arabia, it aims to inculcate in young Muslims the ideology of the Saudi Muslim Brotherhood. As the IIFSO website explains, "It was out of the IIFSO's experience of success that the WAMY was born. WAMY was founded in 1972 in Riyadh, Saudi Arabia, at an international meeting of Islamic workers involved in youth activities and representatives of youth organizations. It was established to help youth organizations around the world implement their planned projects" (http://web.archive.org/web/19990202092801/www.iifso.org/hist.htm). Totonji and Barzinji were both key players in WAMY. Totonji served as deputy to the first secretary general (http://web.archive.org/web/20030314125221/http://www.wamy.org/english/conferences/speech6.htm), while Barzinji was listed as a board member, with an address in Saudi Arabia (http://www.usc.edu/dept/MSA/humanrelations/crisis_in_the_muslim_mind/author.html).

197 **Issam al-Attar, the charismatic head:** Amtsgericht München, Registerakten (Sonderband) VR 6256, Islamische Gemeinschaft in Deutschland e.V., 4 December 1982, "Protokoll."

198 **Its chief, Ahmed al-Rawi:** Interview with Ahmed al-Rawi, 21 July 2004, Markfield, UK. Rawi has since retired. See also Ian Johnson, "How Islamic Group's Ties Reveal Europe's Challenge," *Wall Street Journal,* p. A1. Rawi has subsequently left the FIOE.

199 **The "big circle":** Rawi identified the countries as Britain, Italy, France, Germany,

Spain, and Yugoslavia; two of the countries had two organizations. The federation was made up of organizations from those countries plus Austria, Greece, Italy, the Netherlands, Rumania, and Switzerland, as well as the single organization that represented the Scandinavian countries. Individuals were not allowed to register.

15. Defining the Debate

202 **"Many of you are going"**: Theodor Marquard, head of the German Liaison Office, cited in Helmut Frangenberg, "Kleine Migrationsgeschichte der Türken nach Köln" in *Der Moscheestreit: Eine exemplarische Debatte über Einwanderung und Integration,* p. 72.

   In all cases the "guest workers": For a general history of this immigration to West Germany, as well as Europe in general, see Robert J. Pauly Jr., *Islam in Europe: Integration or Marginalization?* and Jørgen Nielsen, *Muslims in Western Europe.*

203 **A sizable number of Muslims**: For estimates on the number of Muslims living in western Europe, see Robert S. Leiken, "Europe's Mujahideen," Center for Immigration Studies newsletter, April 2005, p. 5.

206 **On the edge of London**: I attended the meeting of the European Council for Fatwa and Research, 8–12 July 2004, and heard Hawari's talk. Later, I obtained a transcript and all the working papers. The citations are from the written version of the text.

207 **"We should seek to collapse morals"**: *Protocols of the Elders of Zion,* as cited by Hawari in "Sex and Sexual Education Under the Light of Islamic Shariah." Translation by Mandi Fahmy. The complete paper is available at www.iandjohnson .com.

208 **Available online and published**: For online sources, see www.ecfr.org or www .islamonline.org. For books, see two collections of fatwas available for download at http://www.e-cfr.org/en/index.php?cat_id=336. On the council's use of these in training, interview with Amir Zaidan, 18 March 2005, Berlin. See also Alexandre Caeiro, "Transnational 'Ulama,' European Fatwas, and Islamic Authority: A Case Study of the European Council for Fatwa and Research," in *Production and Dissemination of Islamic Knowledge in Western Europe.*

209 **The current head of the organization**: For Mahdi Akef's denial of the Holocaust, see the BBC interview at http://news.bbc.co.uk/2/hi/middle_east/4554986 .stm.

210 **Mourad Amriou slowly warmed**: Interviews with Mourad Amriou, 10 September, 1 November, and 3 November 2004, Paris.

212 **The charismatic preacher Hassan Iquioussen**: Interview with Amriou, 10 September 2004. Anti-Semitic tape, "Palestine, Histoire d'une injustice." Thanks to Cécilia Gabizon of *Le Figaro* for a copy of the tape.

213 **Office for Protection of the Constitution**: Communication with the office, 25 August 2005.

   Influenced by Khurshid Ahmad: For von Denffer's studies and early influences, interview with Ahmad von Denffer, 9 December 2004, Munich.

213 **He cofounded a charity:** Its name is Muslim Helfen e.V., founded on 5 April 1985 in Lützelbach, a small town near Frankfurt that is home to another organization, Haus des Islams, with personnel ties to the Munich mosque. See Verfassungs-schutzbericht Hessen vom 24.05.2007, S.38. Muslim Helfen's files were later moved to Munich. Amtsgericht Michelstadt, 13 AR 6078/97.

Channeled money to Afghanistan: Ahmad von Denffer, *ABC der Zeitschrift al-Islam: Stichwortregister 1958–1992*, 1988/5, p. 29, or 1989/2, p. 3.

214 **Expert on Islam alleged:** Mohammad Salim Abdullah of the Islam Archiv in Soest, cited in *Al-Islam*, 1990/7, pp. 3–4. The article implied that Abdullah wasn't a real Muslim.

A conference in Sudan: *Al-Islam*, 1992/5, p. 2.

The Orient-Institut in Hamburg: *Al-Islam*, 1997/2, p. 18.

Mahmoud Abouhalima: Denials that Abouhalima and Salim had significant links to the mosque are found in *Al-Islam*, 2001/6, pp. 16–18.

Mamdouh Mahmud Salim: See Ian Johnson and Alfred Kueppers, "Missed Link," *Wall Street Journal*.

215 **Washington declared Nada and Himmat:** http://www.ustreas.gov/press/releases/po3380.htm.

Lost its status as a charity: Communication with Bavarian officials. Islamic Community of Germany officials confirm that they lost the status but deny it had to do with bookkeeping. They also refused to say why they lost it. Interview with Ibrahim el-Zayat, 19 April 2005, Cologne.

Himmat resigned in early 2002: Registerakten, 13 January 2002, no title on document. Himmat gave the explanation about the frozen accounts in a telephone interview.

16. 1950s Redux

217 **Nada sits in regal splendor:** Description of his home based on interview with Nada.

218 **In hindsight, the charges of terrorism:** Some charged that Nada had worked with the Nazis, which is extremely unlikely, given that he was born in 1931. For his date of birth, see http://www.treas.gov/offices/enforcement/ofac/actions/2001cum.shtml.

Charges that Nada financed: See 31 May 2005 press release by Swiss prosecutor's office: "Ordonnance de suspension des recherches."

Nada has relished the role: See Nada's website, http://www.youssefnada.ch/.

219 **Hervé Terrel strides briskly:** This is the only pseudonym in this book. Terrel is a senior official in the French interior ministry. He publishes papers under the name Terrel. Interview with Hervé Terrel, 14 May 2004, Paris.

220 **The UOIF began to organize:** The most direct link is through the AEIF (Association of Islamic Students in France), a group founded by Muhammed C. K. Hamidullah, a cofounder of Ramadan's Geneva center. The AEIF was also close to Issam al-Attar, the former head of the Syrian Muslim Brotherhood who settled in the German city of Aachen. According to people familiar with the AEIF's history, such as Mohamed Lahaty (interview, 2 Sep-

tember 2004, Paris), the AEIF was primarily a locally focused group, while the UOIF had international contacts and funding. The AEIF exists in name but is inactive.

Suddenly was thrust into a position: In subsequent elections, the UOIF lost some of its council seats when other groups copied its strategy and mobilized more mosques. But the group remains very influential, holding the vice chairmanship of the central council.

221 **Dounia Bouzar:** Interview with Dounia Bouzar, 4 September 2004, Paris.

223 **A State Department–sponsored conference:** Described on the State Department's website: http://usinfo.state.gov/xarchives/display.html?p=washfile-e nglish&y=2006&m=April&x=20060407162418MVyelwarCo.9064295&t=live feeds/wf-latest.html.

Thought so highly of ISNA: The group claims it co-organized the event. See http://www.isna.net/index.php?id=35&backPID=1&tt_news=460.

Michael Privot: See http://www.enar-eu.org/en/info/staff.shtml.

Federation of Islamic Organizations: According to its own website, the youth organization was founded through the direct efforts of the Federation of Islamic Organizations in Europe: http://p9445.typo3server.info/20.0.html. The Federation of Islamic Organizations in Europe is the umbrella group for Muslim Brotherhood organizations in Europe; see Chapter 14.

224 **The State Department helped:** See http://usinfo.state.gov/xarchives/display .html?p=washfile-english&y=2006&m=April&x=20060407162418MVyelwarCo .9064295&t=livefeeds/wf-latest.html.

U.S. ambassador to Belgium: See http://foreign.senate.gov/testimony/2006/ KorologosTestimony060405.pdf.

"Belgium's internal affairs": Unclassified cable sent 12 December 2006, "From: Amembassy Brussels, Subject: Muslim engagement strategy 2006–2007 for Belgium." Reviewed by author.

An Islamic academy: U.S. government involvement was widely reported in the German media and on the website of the U.S. consulate, for example, http:// munich.usconsulate.gov/speeches-nelson-09252007.html.

225 **"Using American Muslims to reach out":** Cable of 17 February 2006, "Amembassy Berlin" to "Ruehc/Secstate Washdc," "Assistant Secretary Fried's meetings in Germany."

The prominent political scientist: Robert S. Leiken and Steven Brooke, "The Moderate Muslim Brotherhood, " *Foreign Affairs.*

227 **The CIA issued reports:** "Muslim Brotherhood: Pivotal Actor in European Political Islam," 10 May 2006, and "Muslim Brotherhood Rhetoric in Europe: Deception, Division, or Confusion?," 29 January 2008. Reviewed by the author.

Called "Muslim Brotherhood": CIA Political Islam Strategic Analysis Program, "Muslim Brotherhood Rhetoric in Europe: Deception, Division or Confusion?" 29 January 2008. Quote from CIA Political Islam Strategic Analysis Program, "Muslim Brotherhood: Pivotal Actor in European Political Islam," p. 2. Documents in the author's possession.

Mazen Asbahi: For details, see www.globalmbreport.com, or Glenn R. Simpson and Amy Chozick, "Obama's Muslim-Outreach Adviser Resigns," *Wall Street Journal.*

227 **International Institute of Islamic Thought:** "German Muslim Delegation Visits IIIT," http://www.iiit.org/NewsEvents/News/tabid/62/articleType/ArticleView/ articleId/117/German-Muslim-Delegation-Visits-IIIT.aspx.
     Head of SLM: Details from Cologne corporate records office, UR. Nr. 1154/1997.

230 **It issued a retraction:** "Correction: Ibrahim el-Zayat is not a member of the MB," 20 February 2007, http://www.ikhwanweb.com/Article.asp?ID=752 &SectionID=121.

231 **It's hard to see how Zayat:** Oberlandesgericht München, case number 18 U 5181/05.

233 **German federal government's Islamkonferenz:** "Trojanisches Pferd," *Frankfurter Allgemeine Zeitung,* 8 May 2007, accessed online at http://www.faz.net/s/ RubCF3AEB154CE64960822FA5429A182360/Doc~E1EA28B0BA6D54481ACE 6C941FB9A167D~ATpl~Ecommon~Scontent.html.
     Tarnishing his reputation: "Bundesweite Razzia bei Islamisten," *Süddeutsche Zeitung,* 11 March 2009, p. 5.
     Wired money to the Taibah: BAO-USA report "Underground Banking" by the Federal Police Agency (BKA), UA ZVE /ST 44.

234 **Served as a friendly witness:** See Oberverwaltungsgericht Rheinland-Pfalz, & A 10953/04.OVG. He wrote a report on behalf of a member of Milli Görüs.
     The room exploded in anger: Society of Muslim Social Scientists Annual Meeting, 17 January 2004. Witnessed by author.

Epilogue: Inside the Mosque

236 **Ahmad von Denffer:** Biographical notes from interview with von Denffer.

237 **Khurram Murad:** For biographical details, see, for example, http://www.young muslims.ca/biographies/display.asp?ID=11.

238 **The *"affaire des Frères Musulmans"*:** BAR Ramadan, 12 October 1965, "Said Ramadan." For public discussion, see "Des 'Frères musulmans' accusés de complot contre Nasser," *La Tribune de Genève,* 11 February 1966, p. 19.
     "Said Ramadan is, among others": Quote from BAR Ramadan, 29 June 1967, "Note pour Monsieur Gelzer."
     Cooperated closely with Swiss federal police: BAR Ramadan, 17 August 1966, "Notice pour Monsieur Probst."
     He got a letter: See http://www.messageonline.org/malcolmx/cover6.htm.
     Soviet newspapers alleged: *Aziya i Afrika Segodnya,* No. 8, August 1966. Translated in CIA Foreign Documents Division, SP-1256, 27 September 1966, CIA declassified files, approved for release: CIA-RDP75-00001 R000300580002-0.

239 **American convert, Dawud Salahuddin:** Interview with Salahuddin.
     A touching essay: *Islam, the West, and the Challenges of Modernity,* p. vii.
     Kayum led the Turkestanis: See BayHStA LaflüVerw 1900, 5 October 1967, "Vormerkung."

Attacks in the Soviet press: *Izvestia*, 29 September 1968. Along with a nine-page rebuttal by Hayit. Narzikul personal papers, courtesy of Crane.

240   His deputy, Walter Schenk: Schenk, pp. 341ff.

He and Gacaoglu continued: BayStA LaflüVerw 1909, 7 July 1969, "Betreff: Religionsgemeinschaft Islam e.V."

INDEX